Transformation
of the Species

Conversations with P'taah, Part II

by Jani King, PhD

▼ Other P'taah Books
by Jani King

Act of Faith

The Gift

P'taah Videotapes

Divinity within Humanity

Transcendence

P'taah Guided Meditation CD

Meeting with Your Soul

▼ Acknowledgements

Profound gratitude to The Investors without whom there would be no books.

My thanks to Allan and Sylvia Rose for their continued loving suppport.

Thanks and gratitude to my dear friend Chris Fine and to Kathleen McGlynn for such painstaking proof reading.

Love and thanks also to Kim Gallagher for the delicious cover art and for the excellent work of both Toni Mertin for the cover design and Jennifer L. Carter for the book design.

And dearest Mickey, thank you, thank you for your dedication and hard work.

Jani King
September, 2001
Queensland, Australia

Transformation of the Species

Conversations with P'taah, Part II
by Jani King, PhD

Light Source Publishing
Post Office Box 1251
Joshua Tree, CA 92252, U.S.A.

ISBN 0-9707595-0-9 (trade paper)
(Previously published by Triad Publishers, ISBN 0-646-13606-2)

Cover artwork © 2001 by Kim Gallagher
Cover design by Toni Merton, TM Designs
Interior design by Jennifer L. Carter

This edition of Transformation of
The Species is dedicated to the memory of
Susan Aalto, dear friend, artist and poet.

Susan, you live in my heart and indeed in
the heart of everyone who had the privilege
of knowing and loving you.

▼ Introduction

These conversations are the result of a series of weekly meetings between P'taah and a group of people, some old friends and some newcomers. They met in a home high in the tropical rainforest in the beautiful town of Kuranda, Queensland, Australia.

The first group of meetings, from August through November, is covered in the book, Act of Faith. Transformation of the Species covers the later group of meetings, from December through April.

Many of the people who participated in these sessions experienced miraculous changes as they applied P'taah's little recipes to their day-to-day lives. We hope you, too, will find your life filled with more love and more joy as a result of his timeless message.

Namaste.

▼ Contents

▼ Interview with Jani King

Q: Jani, how did you and P'taah meet?

Jani: In 1947 I lived in New Zealand – I was born there. I lived in a very remote area in the middle of 350 square miles of pine forest. Bear in mind that it was just after the war and there was no transport so it was very, very isolated.

At the time I was a very little girl and I went wandering from our house into the forest. I remember very clearly going into the forest and then something occurred but I had no idea what it was. Sometime later when I came back to the house, it seemed much later in the day.

Extraordinarily enough, nobody had realized that I had gone. For those of you who are the mothers of little girls, if they are gone for just an hour, you start to become very worried. Yet nobody seemed to have noticed that I had gone, in spite of the fact that it had been for many hours.

Then sometime during 1988 I had picked up a book by Whitley Streiber called *Communion*. When I saw the book on a friend's coffee table, I experienced the most extraordinary feeling of being drawn to it.

I asked my friend what the book was about and he answered, "Some stuff about a guy being abducted by aliens." The cover of the book showed this triangular face with huge eyes and for some reason I reacted with goose bumps and I felt very emotional without having any idea what caused it. I held the book in my hands and had to force myself to put that book down.

The next day I locked up the house, disconnected the phone, and sat down and read the book from cover to cover. It seemed so familiar to me, except for the fact that Whitley Streiber was terrified when he came to understand what his ordeal was. I did not have that feeling at all.

During this time a channeled energy named St. Germain came to Australia. A couple of days after that I spoke to St. Germain. I do not know why I said it, but I asked, "Could you tell me about the experience I had as a child in 1947 that I do not remember?"

St. Germain said, "You were taken aboard a craft. There was a medical procedure performed to put in place certain knowledge and memory that will come to the surface in the next Now moment of your time." He went on to describe what this abduction was about. I sat there going, "Oh, yeah, yeah, yeah" with my eyes rolling in my head. Yet it seemed when he had finished and I had assimilated what he had said, it was not a surprise to me.

I also asked him about a visit I had from another being, and I am not talking about an apparition, but about physical reality. It was in 1961 and it was P'taah who came in a physical body – I do not know how many physical bodies he has. We had a communication that was quite, quite extraordinary. That is the only time in my conscious, waking knowledge that I have met P'taah.

I had hypno-regression about the early experience in 1947 and now I do have conscious memory of what occurred then. The experience in 1961 in a way was so extraordinary, it has left me still with a residue of grief. (Jani is deeply moved and pauses for a moment to regain her composure.) And this is because, really, I am still waiting...

I have to say to you that my experience with P'taah from day to day is very different from yours. For you it is almost—I cannot explain it—you have a different experience than I have. I can talk to P'taah in my head. He talks to me, but it is much more ephemeral than your one-to-one experience with him.

Q: Have you asked P'taah about this feeling of grief and what did he say?

Jani: Well, I guess he says the same thing to me as he says to you about grief, that it is all transmutable. In a way I have dealt with it because for a long time I was really waiting—I mean waiting day-to-day. Now I am not and it is okay if I never come face-to-face with him again. But there is still this thing in my heart, you know.

Q: Jani, where do you go when P'taah comes in?

Jani: I have no idea. Sometimes it is sort of as if I am about here (Jani points to the right and back of her head)—not very far away. Sometimes I have a sense of what has been going on. I have a recall of some things that he has said, yet I do not have any recall of what anybody else has said. Sometimes I think I do, but when I listen to the tape, I find that I only knew a small portion of what actually occurred. The answer really is that I have no idea.

Sometimes, and I don't know whether it's got anything to do with what P'taah says or what he is doing in the sessions, but I really don't want to come back. It can be a very emotional thing and again, when I listen to the tape later, I can't find anything that I would really get emotional about. All I knew was that I really would have preferred not to be here.

Q: Jani, the first time you left your body, how did you let yourself go?

Jani: I didn't. It was involuntary.

Q: How do you mean? Do you mean he just came and pushed you out?

Jani: No, no. I mean I didn't really understand what was happening. The first time it happened, it was not as if I had gone anywhere. It was that I heard this voice that sounded as if it was coming out of a cave, coming out of my mouth. I was quite taken aback, but I understood very quickly what was going on.

The other thing is that P'taah does pop in. I know he is there, and it is never ever without my permission, so to speak, that he comes in.

When it is a session like this, I actually go through a little exercise, which is what I do when I sit here with my eyes closed. I go mumble, mumble, mumble, then I leave and he comes in. But sometimes it can be as quick as a blink of an eye, which can be hysterical and can cause quite a furor, particularly when people are in the group who have no idea of what is actually happening. One minute I am there and the next minute there is someone else talking to them. A bit disconcerting.

It happens mostly, that involuntary stuff—I say involuntary because I do not go through all the mumbo-jumbo to get out—if I'm very relaxed and am having a good time, especially if I've had a couple of glasses of wine and feel really laid back. The next minute, whacko, here he comes, usually because he wants a glass of wine, too. Let there be no mistake about that! (*Gales of laughter.*)

Q: Jani, when you said P'taah appeared in physical form, do you mean as a man or woman or something different…something we wouldn't be familiar with?

Jani: Something different. It was a light body, but a physical body. Not as dense as ours. A humanoid form. He had very beautiful, very large eyes. That was the most incredible thing. I can't really tell you too much about it because what was happening was like being programmed, like a computer receiving all sorts of data.

But the other thing concerned my heart. I was being inundated with this most incredible love, unlike anything else I had ever experienced. Since then I have experienced the same feeling with Saint Germain—channeled through Azena Ramanda—and also while swimming with whales in the wild.

Q: Does P'taah communicate with you about what you, as an individual, should be doing for your own expansion?

Jani: He puts little gem-like jewels in my ear, and a great kick up the bum, when I am not doing what could be done for my greatest spiritual benefit.

Q: Do the sessions with P'taah tax you physically?

Jani: It depends. If I am feeling really on top and full of energy, I feel very energized after a session and that energy lasts for hours. If I am tired and not feeling very bright before a session, I feel energized when I come back, but when that wears off, I am exhausted.

Q: When people have personal sessions with P'taah, does he know all about that person—their beliefs and past and all of that stuff?

Jani: Someone who had a personal session once said that he knows what color undies you are wearing. (Gales of laughter.) Very personal!

Q: Every so often in the session, we hear about scales. What is that about?

Jani: It's a joke. After a very heavy emotional three-day workshop in Melbourne, P'taah was talking to the participants. The feeling among the people was very highly charged, a real high. P'taah told them that if he was in his own body, he would give them a light-show to reflect to everybody there how exquisitely beautiful they were and what beautiful lights they were radiating.

When he said this, the electric lights in the room flickered on and off a few times. Someone asked him, "What do you look like?" P'taah answered, "Oh, I am very beautiful." The facilitator of the workshop muttered out of the corner of his mouth to P'taah, "Yeah, if you don't mind green scales." Everyone shrieked with laughter, and P'taah turned to this friend and answered, "Ah, but beloved, you cannot see the scales for the light." So that has sort of become a standing joke with P'taah.

Q: Have you asked to go there, to the Pleiades?

Jani: Apparently, I have been. P'taah says there have been many times over the last 30 years when we have been together, when I have been off-world, have been to the Pleiades. I have to tell you, I have no conscious memory of it, although I have memory of being on a craft, apart from when I was a child. I cannot tell you much about it, though. It doesn't really make sense within the logical way we perceive things.

I keep saying that I really would like to remember these other experiences I'm supposed to have had, but he keeps saying that when the time is right, I shall have full memory of everything. He says the time is coming soon, although what 'soon' means as far as they are concerned, God knows. I try not to hang out for it, you know?

It is a bit difficult sometimes. Sometimes something sparks me off and I get this intense yearning. But most of the time I am pretty *au fait* with it. I cruise along with it and think that when the time is right, it's right. I trust P'taah and my own soul integrity in the knowing that whatever and however it all happens, it will be for my own highest good.

I have doubts and low times and wonder what the hell I am here for, the same as everybody else. But you know, when you come right down to it, I love him and there's nothing else I'd rather be doing than living right here and now. I guess I'd have to say that I am one helluva a happy person most of the time.

▼ First Session
December 4

P'taah: Dear ones, good evening. Indeed it is a joy to be here with you always. So, we ask forth for query.

Q: Would you speak to us about cyclic harmony?

P'taah: Cyclic harmony—that which all of humanity is yearning to experience. So it is through eons and eons of time before the remembrance of your species—prehistoric—your planet has gone through cyclic changes, as has humanity. That is the true meaning of the word prehistoric, that which is history before your recorded history.

Humanity was once united in full knowingness with the All-That-Is, choosing to experience separation merely to re-experience the joy of non-separation. So it is that it comes in cycles, and your Earth also, in its own wondrous timing of change.

Now, dear ones, the whole Earth is quickening. The heart of humanity is quickening in anticipation of the culmination of this epoch, this era of your history, to come into harmony, into non-separation. In this timing, as the change of consciousness, the expansion, is brought forth in these last years, so will the fear also be brought forth—the polarity of harmony—at last to be embraced into the light.

It is very important for you all to understand that in this timing, the world as you know it will fall into greater and greater chaos. It is not to be judged. It is not truly calamitous. It is merely an indication of how your consciousness is expanding—the Christus arising, indeed.

The failure of your institutions and the Earth changes have already begun but will accelerate. These changes are to be viewed as an occasion for great joyous celebration.

Dear ones, when you fear what appears to be occurring on your plane, it is to take one step back for the overview. To know that what you consider to be physical death is not annihilation, it is an illusion. There is no death. The shedding of the physical embodiment is indeed merely the soul's desire to experience in another form.

You know, there are those of humanity who are totally obsessed with physical immortality. We would say if they were to have it, they would be most unhappy because they are not yet in alignment, not comfortable in their bodies. They would still be creating wondrous drama and chaos within themselves.

As you can embrace the idea of death, it is to know, in truth, it is merely a transition. The lack of fear transmits itself to the physical body at the cellular level, and as the cells resonate to the joy and non-stress of the idea of death, so you may re-create and re-create the cells. Do you understand? It is the dichotomy.

When you no longer fear death, you may continue the physical embodiment as long as you wish. When you are aligned, it is not only that *all* of the universes ring with joy, it is also your physical body. So it is that we have ascension, indeed. A puff of smoke and off you go, taking the physical body with you. Wondrous. But you see, it is a matter of choice.

Dear ones, it is to remember that there is always, always, choice. As you choose to perceive yourself as a light filament, reflection of Divinity, so you cast the light filament forth, through your bodies, across the plane.

You know, there are many groups of people such as you all over your planet. And we will not speak of those *within* your planet who are casting forth the light filaments of joy to create a peaceful, wondrous, and joyous transition into the harmony to come.

The coming into the harmony is also called Goddess arising within the breast of all. Woman is to embrace the attributes within genetic memory of enslavement. Man is to embrace the fear of woman, the fear of the power of woman. To know that what he fears within woman is that which he fears within self. It is for woman to understand that it is all right to be strong, all right to recognize her own power.

So you see, coming into this harmony is to be found within the harmony of self, through the embracement of those aspects within self which have formerly been unembraceable. To love what you judged to be unlovable, and so it shall be because you have sent forth the desire. In this fashion you will understand your own power to manifest exactly what you want.

As you are all so desirous of coming into the understanding of non-separation within each and every breast, so you have chosen. It is that you have chosen the broad spectrum game-plan and that is why you have incarnated at this time. You merely get into a muddle now and again in your moment-by-moment life where you would sometimes seem to lose the plot.

That is all right because in this time you will certainly experience what you have been afraid to experience before. The fear will be called forth, and the situations will come forth with amazing rapidity until you have learned the lesson.

Q: So we have to embrace everything that we are afraid of?

P'taah: Indeed. Whatever it is, you will find that if you will step into the fear, that it is truly an opportunity. And you know, if you do not 'make it' on the first go, it is all right. Don't you worry. The soul will certainly bring it forth in one situation or another!

Q: P'taah, when you referred to prehistory and the projection of Divinity into separation to rediscover itself and to rediscover joy, the question arises. Why evolution in the first place when the origin is of Divinity which needs nothing, perfection seeking the absence of itself in order to rediscover itself?

P'taah: It is also to know that for something to contemplate itself, truly it needs to be separate from Self.

Q: There is a contradiction there.

P'taah: Indeed, it is a contradiction. It is always the dichotomy. It is infinity experiencing itself in all dimensions. We have mentioned to you before that it is very difficult for us to convey to you infinity, the All-That-Is, with these boxes of understanding called words.

You see, in non-separation you are both polarities at once. Do you understand? In a broad sense, you may say in the desire to experience one or another, there must be separation. There is also the desire to experience this plane of reality of this space-time continuum. It is all polarity. That is how your reality exists.

Q: Polarity, and the more common word is tension.

P'taah: Indeed. That is your scientific designation.

Q: So, in our phenomenal universe, the underlying tension is gravity and levity, activity and non-activity?

P'taah: Indeed. You know that even in the non-activity there is activity. That is the dichotomy because it is the void from whence springs all creation.

Q: And that is our origin?

P'taah: Indeed.

Q: P'taah, some of our religious teachings call the use of
psychedelics an illegal shortcut to consciousness. Could
you say something about this, please?

P'taah: We have certainly observed many uses of those
enhancements to consciousness, not only with
psychedelics. In the ancient days of your time, it was
called sacred. The use of natural hallucinogenic substances was utilized in a fashion to expand consciousness,
but within a certain framework.

This was particularly the case with cultures of the
Southern American continent. The consciousness of humanity would take wings and fly as they saw within their
mind under the influences of these substances. Also it
was with discipline and training, with much preparation,
leading to what to expect. Beliefs structured around what
is called a mythological world to create a different reality.
It was valid indeed.

Now, use of such substances at this time is certainly valid,
else it would not be. It is not a shortcut to enlightenment.
Indeed, it may create cellular damage, and in the non-
understanding of what is to be created, fear comes into play.

There has been much experimentation within certain
governments to this end of how psychedelics may be used
as a weapon to destroy the mind of humanity. Indeed,
widespread usage initially was promoted by governments
upon your planet.

We would suggest, we would recommend, that this is
not to be used, because truly, while it opens the conscious
mind to the possibilities of other realities, when you are
able to reach this stage without the use of outside substances, what is gained within the consciousness has
more value, so to speak.

I will tell you, beloved, there is no shortcut to enlightenment, and this you know. I understand in your asking that you truly are not asking for yourself. You are very much in the understanding that the only way for en-*light*enment is the embracement of all the fear and judgment. Moment-by-moment there is always the choice and whatever the choice is, it is valid. It is also Divine, else it would not be in existence.

Q: You said before that every wish we think of can become reality. Problems arise when one does not know exactly what to do and one has to make choices. I find it difficult to make choices, but is it not so that whatever we do is actually right?

P'taah: But always. We have been saying this very thing. There is no such thing as a wrong decision. We do not speak about the choice of what to do in your day-to-day life. In this instance we are speaking of choice of perception. You may choose to view any situation as affecting your emotional state through the eyes of fear or the eyes of love. That is the choice we are speaking of. Whatever the choice is, it certainly is valid.

Q: You mean basically as a decision forever, or is it a decision of every five minutes?

P'taah: Dear one, there is only the moment. There is no such thing as future. You do not have 'future.' Your future is built on every Now moment.

That which you regard to be your future in linear time really has no existence. You build what you understand to be future by how you create every moment. If you create your moments in the fullness of joy and love, then that is what your next Now moment shall be. And if you choose to create this moment in fear and judgment, then that is exactly what your next Now moment shall be. Do you understand? It is like building a castle.

Q: P'taah, how do people cope with total rejection?

P'taah: Dear one, it does not matter how the rejection is expressed with humanity. All, all of you know what it is to be invalidated because that is what you have built your life on. Whether it is called outright rejection or whether it is what we would call little drops of invalidation along the way, the result is the same.

You see, whatever story line it is—whether it is a child without a mother or father, or children born into a country torn by war, or a child suffering from malnutrition and abuse of the physical body—it does not matter what the story is, the feeling is the same. You may say, "This poor dear one has had such a terrible life and this one is so favored to have a loving family and abundance of wealth," etc., etc., but you see, it is the state of humanity.

Whatever the situation, all of you have grown with some sort of invalidation or another to create pain. It does not matter how great you judge the pain to be. Pain is pain is pain. It engenders the same feeling. We have explained how this may be changed. It is called transmutation.

So, we shall take a break. We would ask that you be silent for two minutes to create the transition and we will be in delight to speak with you again very soon.

(After the break)

Q: P'taah, sometimes I have people who ask me to help them with healing. I understand that I cannot help them, that I need healing myself first of all. Should I disappoint these people when they put their trust in me, when they ask for help? So far I have never refused them. I say I do what I can do within my capabilities and limitations. Would you suggest that I disappoint these people?

P'taah: Dear one, you know it comes down to this. What is it that makes your heart sing in every moment? When one would come forth desiring help, it is as you would feel at that moment, not out of duty, not out of obligation or responsibility to somebody else. The ultimate responsibility is for that who you be. So it is wondrous to give assistance if that is what is in your heart. You may certainly, with love in your heart, beloved, give forth assistance.

It is also to know that the healing of self is of utmost importance, but it is not to disregard everybody else because as you know in your heart, beloved, there is no separation.

Q: Regarding these cyclic changes, prior to this 50,000 year cycle was there third density on this planet?

P'taah: You could say that from the beginning of this planet, there has been third density reality, although there have been beings on this planet who were of much lighter density. Many of these beings have gone forth into other realms and some have chosen to stay within this density and thus become dense in Self. Always it has been of third density within this space-time continuum.

Q: Could you explain about density? I only know from reading the transcripts about third density, so could you explain the first, second, and fourth density to me?

P'taah: That which is called first density is the reality of what you perceive to be inanimate, like mineral, called rock, called your Earth itself. That which you perceive to be of non-consciousness.

Then of second density is what you would call flora and fauna. We are in this instance speaking of your conscious reality. There is nothing which does not have conscious reality, even that which you regard to be rock, earth, mineral. Every atom and molecule has its own, what is called aware-ized energy.

Third density you can say is humanity and that which is cetacean, that is whale and dolphin.

Fourth density is what you are going to be, what you will be transforming yourselves into. Now, it is really a frequency. Everything is made up of a frequency, and what you term to be highest in frequency of this density is called light. However, that which is beyond the frequency of light is called fourth density. In truth, it is only a designation and really is not of such importance.

There are many entities who will be asking, "What about sixth and seventh, etc." As you cannot even comprehend fourth density, it is pointless to ask what density it is. In fact, by asking you are showing that there is no comprehension.

So that which you are about to be traveling into, the transition, is merely a higher vibratory frequency. You will become lighter. Not that you will cease physical embodiment, but that the physical embodiment will be of lighter frequency. You will be able to perceive the light frequency of everything, of every particle. All right, beloved?

Q: Good evening, P'taah. I have been involved in natural birthing for years and have been very interested in water birthing. Is this a better way to bring children into the world? Is it a gentler way to help healing?

P'taah: It is indeed and it is of dolphin consciousness. As it has been said before, very often those who have created themselves to be birthed in water are those who are of dolphin consciousness, of dolphin energy, who have decided to create for themselves another form of being in physicality. There certainly is no difference in the soul energy. Indeed it is most harmonious.

Q: So it is really better than a dry birth?

P'taah: Dear one, that is really a judgment. All is valid. What we are saying is, it is indeed most harmonious to be birthed in water.

Q: With the dolphins?

P'taah: That is even more wondrous, beloved. Indeed there are those on your planet who have instigated that your children are birthed with dolphins and it is truly wonderful.

Q: Greetings, P'taah. Are you really saying that the soul energy of dolphins is the same as that of human beings?

P'taah: Indeed. You are of the same Source.

Q: Wow! *(Chuckles from the audience.)*

P'taah: Indeed, wow! And that which is whale is the oversoul of dolphin. That which is whale is truly grand. It has never lost contact with the star people. They are the historians of your planet, grand and wondrous beings in physical embodiment, multidimensional to be sure, and in full knowingness of their multidimensionality.

Whale and dolphin have great love of humanity and many would ask, "How could they still love humanity?" But you see, beloved ones, it is they who are indeed in understanding of unconditional love. They have much knowledge to impart to you and you may tap into the knowledge of Cetacea. You may indeed partake of that wisdom and knowing, the joy and spontaneity.

Q: How do human beings dare kill these creatures? That really makes me angry.

P'taah: But you see, humankind are still killing each other. Why would they worry about killing that which they deem to be merely animal, hmm?

It is not to judge, dear one, because it is all co-creation and that which be the whale and dolphin have indeed given themselves forth to bring about greater understanding and love of humanity.

It is a grand lesson and it is co-creation. The whale and dolphin do understand that there is truly no such thing as death. As humanity is coming into such love and reverence of whale and dolphin, it is a grand reflection of what may be love and reverence for Self and the understanding that there is no separation. So it changes.

Q: P'taah, how do the Yeti and the Big Foot fit into the picture?

P'taah: Well you know, it is as if they were remnants. Many other of the species when the Yeti and Big Foot were created upon the plane have taken themselves off to other realms. These ones, so beauteous and so shy, are in fear of humanity because in your prehistory they have been hunted down. So they exist in the remotest regions of your planet.

Of course, they have a different understanding of your planet and they are very in tune with that. It is a grand consciousness, but not as it is with humanity in your understanding and not so much with the knowledge as with the whale and dolphins who are in knowing of all things upon the plane. So it is a little pocket of humanity, but altered. Or perhaps we should say, in truth, not altered.

Q: Do we have the equivalent of the Big Foot in Australia?

P'taah: Not as such, beloved, nor yet in what is Africa.

Q: P'taah, there is controversial information given out about the consciousness of ape-type creatures being mixed with human consciousness in history. Can you explain that, please?

P'taah: Are you speaking of the missing link?

Q: I don't know. Is that what I am asking?

P'taah: Well, there has been a theory of your scientists put forth that man is descended from primate creatures.

Q: It is not the conventional scientific theory, but the material of certain channeled entities says that there has been some manipulation, genetic manipulation, in history with creatures who were not human.

P'taah: There has been great genetic manipulation.

Q: With humans?

P'taah: Indeed. It is in your time of prehistory.

Q: There are people who are fearing that we are the result of that. Are there people who are caught up in the fear that they are more of animal consciousness than of Divine consciousness?

P'taah: But of course, beloved, everything is Divine.

Q: So there is nothing to worry about, can you confirm that? I just want to hear you say it.

P'taah: As we have said before, there is much humbug put forth which creates great fear. There has certainly been genetic manipulation of humanity as you understand it now. You are all star-seeded. All of humanity as you understand it are star-seeded.

There indeed has been, not only on this planet, but on all of the planets, playing around with the genetics. The result is you on this planet and the result is wondrous, is it not? So why fear? You know nothing can harm you. What you are is a reflection of the All-That-Is and there is nothing in existence that is not. So, why would one fear, hmm?

Q: You speak of Divine consciousness. I work a lot with animals and this may be a judgment, but I very often think that what we call dumb animals are less cluttered with rubbish and may be just a bit more divine than we are.

P'taah: It is not that they are more divine, but they are certainly not cluttered, as you say, and certainly they are in knowing. You see, they are living in the Now moment in the integrity of their own soul-beingness. That, of course, is Divine.

Q: P'taah, you were speaking about star children. There are some people who have been regressed and found themselves on another planet. Is that possible?

P'taah: Indeed.

Q: Could you elaborate on that?

P'taah: There are many people who have journeyed forth from this world to other planets and who have been taken on craft to what is called mothership to experience another reality, another time frame within the soul-level desire. They bring forth certain experiences to be of assistance, although we are in understanding that humanity cannot imagine how they may be of assistance to the star people who are certainly technologically far in advance.

You see, dear ones, it truly is that the star people are your brothers and sisters. There has never been a time when there has been no interaction between the people of your planet and the people of other planets. In spite of the desire of most of you to experience conscious communication with the star people, there is much fear engendered. For that and many reasons, these communications are usually erased from conscious memory.

Soon these memories will be reignited and the humanity of this planet will take its place with the humanities of other star systems in a great federation. You know, you are all eagerly awaited indeed.

(A little boy addresses P'taah)

Q: P'taah, how do you change?

P'taah: How do we change? Because we desire to, and so may you merely by thinking about it and wanting it. Do you know that you can change the whole world merely by thinking about it. Indeed it is so.

Q: Two questions. First, what happened to the dinosaurs? Second, what is the power of a child?

P'taah: It is virtually without limit, dear one. Now first let us take what is called dinosaur. We have spoken before about creatures of your planet that you deem to be extinct, to be gone forever. But you see, nothing is gone, truly. It is only gone from your own perception, from your own awareness.

The dinosaur and many creatures of this time are still in existence in another time frame in your terms, and also upon other worlds. There is not a creature which has ever existed upon your planet which has gone forever. What you term to be extinct is merely extinct in this time frame.

Now, the power of children. There is a tendency in humanity to regard children and babes as helpless because they are very small in physicality. However it is for you to understand that, however you regard the child, in terms of soul energy, they are the same age as you.

For small children, their link with their own beingness is not as separated as yours. They are in tune with their own being. They are not so much in understanding of separation. They are not so much subject, as yet, to the conditioning of what is possible and what is not. They do not understand that they are not supposed to be able to do quite extraordinary things, that they are not supposed to be able to perceive what is not normally seen with the adult human eye and heard with the adult human ear. Very often a child does not know what limitation means, that is how powerful it is.

In this timing the children who are creating themselves upon this plane in many respects are bringing with them power which has not been manifested before. So it is that they may afford adult humans great learning. They have a knowing intact which adult humans have lost.

Also there are many of the star people and energies who have not normally desired to have the density of physicality who are sending forth a fragment of soul energy to be incarnated at this time of the transition of Earth.

So, indeed, it is to know that although children may appear to be helpless, they are not.

Q: Should we create another form of education for children in this area? And can you talk of the mechanics of the dinosaurs leaving the Earth.

P'taah: In terms of education, it is as you may choose it. Education as you understand it at this time—the form of education—will certainly be changing in the years to come. If you desire that your children have a different education, so be it. Do as you please. It is your choice.

We are not really in understanding of what you would wish us to say about the dinosaurs and other so-called extinct species, beloved. How did they translate? Some were taken from the planet in craft to live in other places and others simply transported themselves into another time frame which was more suitable according to the density of their physicality.

Q: P'taah, it sounds like we are up for a good and really great time with regard to the changes. Should we prepare ourselves for those changes, like putting food in our stores or something?

P'taah: It is not necessary. Now, much fear about survival has been created so everybody has been rushing about to store their food and live away from the danger, hmm? But you see, dear one, if you are not in fear of what is to come and you know that you live in a perfectly safe universe, it is merely to be in the moment in joy. To know that you will, of course, be safe, that you will survive. It is your reality. *You* create it.

Q: The reality I create consciously or subconsciously? How can I influence my subconscious?

P'taah: It is the knowing in your heart that there is no separation between that which you understand to be conscious and subconscious. The more you think to yourself that there is separation in these terms, the more it shall be. It is to know that as you can allow that energy to come forth, that which is called Goddess, intuition, then indeed what you are creating is non-separation.

If you are living in an area, for instance, which may be subject to a very sudden Earth change and you are in joy and not in fear, then on that day, beloved, you will be away visiting your mother. You see, it is you who create the reality in synchronicity.

Q: P'taah, are there life forms on the other planets in our solar system?

P'taah: Indeed.

Q: Can you tell us about them?

P'taah: It is not necessary.

Q: Oh, why not?

P'taah: It is certainly that your scientists have found indications of the existence of life on other planets. However, as it is that there are people living in your Inner Earth, it is of a different time frame. So, when the timing is right, humanity may have full communication with the people not only in this solar system, but in the other solar systems as well, and indeed in other galaxies undreamed of by your technologies at this time.

There are many, many planets, stars, earths whose life beings are sentient beings as are you. Humanoid. Some are not at all of the same physical form as humanity and some are indeed of humanoid form, but of very different structure, physiologically. Although you could say there would be two arms, two legs, and head, the internal structure is very different and very often not of a gender as you understand it.

Q: Water is a very important element on our planet. Is it important to star people, too?

P'taah: Let us not worry about the star people—we know you are in great fascination about them—but let us talk about your relationship with water.

Within water is a crystalline structure which is as you are, the resonance of conducting energy. Water has a very healing influence, not only upon your body, but also on your energy field. Water is called sacred, as all elements are sacred, as are you.

You may use water as a nurturing element for you, particularly your ocean. In the ocean are the energies of whale and dolphin conducted through the crystalline structure of the water which is a great magnifier. You may put forth a desire for magnification of the cellular structure of the brain within the water.

Once upon a time humanity was able to transform the oxygen within the water into usable oxygen to breathe under water. That structure is still in place in your bodies but not any longer of use to you. It is that you have forgotten. Many of you, and those of you who are in the resonance of dolphin consciousness, will have memory of what it was like to live beneath the sea.

Q: P'taah, in relation to non-separation, do you mean that in reality there is no such thing as different souls, but just one conglomerate?

P'taah: Ultimately, exactly.

Q: So every time you say there is no separation, you mean there is no single soul? Not one there, one there, one there?

P'taah: So indeed it is. But there is what you may term fragment of oversoul, and oversoul of oversoul, and you may say indeed that the soul energy may be divided into families of resonance. However, beloved, as we talk of this, it is already creating separation in your mind. This is why we say to you that there is no separation.

We are speaking of the totality because you think that you end where your skin ends in your physical reality. Also there is your sense of separation of the persona of you and everybody else. There is the feeling of separation in the alone-ness, the loneliness, the isolation that you all do feel. Do you understand? All of this creates more and more separation.

So what we are saying is this. You do not truly understand that you are indeed part of the All-That-Is. That the energy which keeps you going, that creates the life force within you, is Divine energy and that Divine energy permeates everything. *Every thing*. Every atom and molecule. In this fashion you are totally connected to every thing, but we would give it to you that you are connected with every human, closer than you can imagine.

If you can think of this unity of beingness with all, all of humanity, and know that everything and everybody outside of yourself is a reflection of who you are, then in this fashion you may understand how you judge yourself and keep yourself separate.

Q: Is it that we can never really understand this principle as long as we see separate people or can we fully understand that and still be a part of the separateness?

P'taah: We are in understanding that it is very perplexing, but it is not only you who find it perplexing. Even those who do have an intellectual understanding of what we are saying still do not know, in truth, what it is to be in a state of non-separation, at least for more than several instances at a time.

There are some, indeed, who have had wondrous and grand knowing of non-separation, of Oneness with All-That-Is, but it has been moments only. It is in the remembrance of that emotion, of that feeling of knowing one's own Divinity and non-separation, in the feeling of it, that they may recreate the light.

Now, what we are speaking of is not an intellectual understanding. We say the words to you and truly these words are only a sop for your intellect because it is so simple. You will not allow the simplicity so we must give forth the words, but as we have said before, we are not only speaking to your ears.

So indeed, beloved, use that imagination of yours and you may imagine there is you and there is a string of golden light which connects you to every other human. Then you may imagine the string of light connecting you to every tree and every blade of grass. Then you may imagine the string coming from the crown of your head to go forth into the stars, to connect you with every being that lives upon every planet of the universes. Do you understand what I am saying?

It is in this fashion that you create the non-separation. You may use your imagination to create the picture in your mind that it may resonate in your heart. When you

may be still with another and look into the eyes of somebody else, even if it is one who you judge to be an enemy,
you will know that you are looking at yourself.

Q: P'taah, when I was about 13 and not conscious of
what God was, I tried to work out what God was. I
imagined our cells to be like people, but not really people,
busily doing things and being fully conscious of what they
are doing within us. If this is so, why could we not also be
like those cells rushing around, doing things, but within a
greater body?

P'taah: But you are, beloved. You see, what you are is
called a macro-microcosm, a macromolecule of the
multiverses, and so it goes on into infinity. That is exactly
what you are, indeed. It is a very interesting concept.

Q: Just a technical question. The microcosm is according
to the macrocosm, right? Is the microcosm again another
macrocosm and so on into infinity?

P'taah: Is it not wondrous? So you see, beloved, there is
no separation whichever way you look at it, and what you
are is God indeed.

Q: It could be me in the outside world and it could be me
ten times in the inside world.

P'taah: Indeed, but it is not as you would regard yourself
to be as persona, as such. That which you regard yourself
to be as persona is merely a facet of what you really are.

You see, you are not your persona. You are not your
body. You are not your mind. You are more than all of it.
That is what really is the 'cat among the pigeons' when
you are trying to put everything into a logical box. Because
as you name it, beloved, you are already in limitation.

There is no limitation. You are truly beyond limit. As
you try to bring all of these things into your little boxes of

intellectual understanding, you are already placing upon it a box for your heart.

Now, it is always great fun to play with concepts, to stretch your mind, and that is all right, indeed. But it is to know, dear ones, that as you may clutter up your minds with trivia, it is called escape from who you are, and you will do anything to escape feeling. You will do anything not to have to look, truly, at who you are without judgment. You will do anything not to be vulnerable.

So when you set off in your mind, it is all right, but just remember in truth you are multi-dimensional, powerful, wondrous beings. *You* are creating your reality and you may do it from love which has nothing to do with your mind, or you may do it from fear which has everything to do with your mind. So it is a moment-by-moment choice of however it is you perceive your reality.

Well now, dear ones, sufficient unto the time of this night. We are very happy that you have brought forth the children this night. Magical beings, indeed.

Q: *(A little boy)* I enjoyed it!

P'taah: Did you, beloved? Well, I will tell you this. I enjoyed very much, too, to see you. You are very wonderful, indeed. Good night, beloved one. You will have wonderful dreams.

So, dear ones, it is to go forth in joy, knowing you are really as the dolphin, lots of laughter and much fun. To know, indeed, that who you are is God/Goddess bringing forth this experience of reality to truly understand who you are. I love you indeed.

And so, dear ones, until the next wondrous meeting. Indeed, you are so beautiful.

▼ Second Session December 11

P'taah: Good evening.

(P'taah walks among the audience and looks at every face, taking his time. Then he glances at a little Christmas tree, beautifully decorated and lit up with colored lights.)

P'taah: Very beautiful indeed. Do you know, sometimes humans look just like this. Beautiful packages and lots of lights.

Well, dear ones, let us begin. Query, indeed.

Q: As it is a time of celebration, and seeing that Christmas is based on the teachings of Jesus, on Christ-consciousness, could you expand on that?

P'taah: Beloved, you have pre-empted us. You know, this timing, called birthday celebration of the Christus, is particularly poignant because since the days of Jesus there have been celebrations of the birthday of one man. Of course, it is more than that. It is an idea-construct of what was put forth by this energy.

But you know, beloved ones, in these 2000 years, the consciousness of humanity has indeed grown and expanded, particularly in these last few years of your time.

Now, in this time of December, this Christmas—the mass of Christus—it is to bring forth a celebration, in truth, of the coming forth of Christ-consciousness for the whole planet, for the whole of humanity. So you are celebrating expansion. Those of you here and now in this room, and all of your brothers and sisters of like mind elsewhere on the planet, you truly do have something to celebrate. Christ-consciousness in expansion.

Christ, the crystal consciousness, that which is the most exciting era coming to hand that you have chosen to witness, will indeed ring hosanna galactically. The celebration of an event in your culture which is recorded in your history so picturesquely was, in truth, ordinary. A mother giving birth to a babe in a place of simplicity. Then, indeed, there were also hosannas.

From this there has grown a mythology and your idea of Jesus now is an idea-construct. What most of the people of your culture understand about Jesus really has not very much to do with what was the man called Yeshwa Ben Joseph.

But you see, it is immaterial at this time. What is important is that you understand that what has been created in this idea is an entity of its own. The idea-construct has become an entity. It is real. It does not matter whether or not you intellectually disregard the whole story, whether or not you accept it, for all of the millions of people upon your planet who really have no emotional attachment to the story, the idea-construct is nevertheless a reality. Such is the power of thought, beloved ones.

So in this time to come, it is to put forth jubilation and celebration of great dance because you have much wondrousness to celebrate and it is yours. You are creating a new world. What you are celebrating, in truth, is the coming forth of the Christus of every one of you. The light of the Christus, it is the Divine light of a crystal, igniting within you all.

In this fashion you will come to understand who you are. You will come to understand the grandeur of you, the multidimensional wonder of humanity, of your reality, of your universes. You will come into synchronization with the Goddess, your Earth. It is indeed cause for celebration.

Q: P'taah, did Buddhism build a similar idea around Buddha as Christianity built around Jesus?

P'taah: Indeed. And you know, the idea-construct of the Buddha has come, in its own way, into an expansion. As the people of your culture have taken the idea of the Christus and expanded on it, so the people who are culturally attuned to the Buddha have taken their picture of the Christus and expanded upon it. The Christians have taken the Buddha and expanded upon it.

So although it appears very much that each sect, each religion, is catalogued and limited in its own entirety, what is occurring at this time is that all of the religions are coming to be recognized for the core of truth that is within them all to be embraced. The outside story line, the mythology, the fairy story, can be put in its rightful place.

Q: P'taah, I have always been led to believe that I have guides. Can you expand on that?

P'taah: Beloved, we do not really talk about guides, although in these times—particularly when we are doing a discussion of one to another[1]—there are many who ask about guides.

Now you see, in a way the idea of guides is limited because what you are imagining then is a spirit of humanoid form standing behind you and giving you a little prod in the bum to tell you which way to go. That is what you ultimately think when thinking of guides for that is what you know.

And so it is with guardian angels. There are many who are in love with guardian angels. It is wondrous, of course. But you see, beloved, what we are doing in this time is really to create the expansion so that you know that there is no separation and that you may be in touch with the God/ Goddess within you, that you may know that there is nothing and nobody that you do not have access to within your heart.

---

[1] Personal session

We would suggest that, in a way, all of you have guides, but it is not really as you imagine it to be. We are not desiring to limit your perception of how it may be. Do you understand? If I speak to you of guides, you are immediately in separation and limitation.

It is to know that your universe is peopled by beings and energies without physicality and you may regard many of these energies to be of light form, without physical form at all. It is very often part of your own soul energy, in fact really it is always part of your own soul energy.

So we are very desirous that you become more expanded in your conscious thinking to be more aware of your intellectualization. You see, all of you want to put everything in little boxes, whether they are the little boxes of technology and part of the puzzle therein or whether it is curiosity and entertainment.

That is perfectly valid and we are certainly not saying you should not think of it. We are just here to remind you that who you are is called expansion.

Q: What reality or what influence do our dreams have on our lives?

P'taah: Well, dear one, you know when you are in your dreamtime, it is this life that is the dream and the dream is the reality. Very broadly speaking, this life is probably the grander illusion.

It is also for you to understand that in your very busy life, called other dimensions of reality, called dreams, your conscious rational mind will paint you all sorts of pictures. Very often what you are dealing with are concepts and lives on dimensions of reality that you cannot have any conception of in this life, so the rational mind creates a picture for you so that you may grasp symbolically the meaning of it.

There has been much discussion of the symbolism of dreams. I will tell you this, you all have your own symbols.

There has been much talk about archetypal symbols, however we would say this about your dreams—have fun with them.

It is very beneficial for you to write down what you may remember of your dreams for no less than 21 of your nights. As you make notes of your dreams, a pattern will emerge which will make sense to you, that will give you the story. It is so that you will bring forth many fears to deal with. You go traveling. You meet with friends. You meet with friends from other lives, other probable realities, other parts of your soul energy. Sometimes you are playing in the causal plane, other times you are going to realms far beyond. As we have said, it is to remember that really, seen from out there, this here is the dream.

Q: P'taah, I really enjoy spending a lot of time in the dream realm and I seem to have difficulty when I come back into the physical reality. I feel that I should be doing something, although I really like the time I spend in other parts of my consciousness. I know you say that we should be and not do, but there is a conflict and it is difficult.

P'taah: There is also the should and should not, hmm?

Q: Yes, there is old programming coming in the mind.

P'taah: That is all right, beloved. Enjoy it for what it is and when you find yourself should-ing and should not-ing, simply allow. It is all right. You will become easier and easier.

And you know, to dream is wondrous. Whether it is the dream you have when you are asleep or the dream you have when you are awake, it is wondrous. It is all right.

Certainly you may choose to be balanced about it, but there are no shoulds or should nots. There is no right or wrong. There simply is and however it is, is all right if you will allow it to be. What you call your daydreams and your imagination, dear ones, it is sweet and it is beautiful. Go for it, indeed.

Q: A few weeks ago a crystal disappeared from our place, from what is a sacred place for me. I still cannot understand what happened. I am still not at peace with it.

P'taah: But you know, beloved, exactly what it is, truly. You have had a discussion with our woman[2] about it.

Q: But it did not bring peace.

P'taah: That is because you are not in allowance of it. You are still angry. That is all right, but you see, beloved, you created it that you may find the pearl of wisdom or the crystal within, that you may find the sacred place within.

You know, when you create your rites and rituals and you have your power tool, it is wonderful. But we will remind you, the most powerful power tool is what you have within you. There is no place on this planet more sacred than another, and we will tell you this—that which is most sacred is within you. It is you.

So you have created a wondrous way to teach yourself, beloved. You are the sacred one, and you are the power tool. All else is play, indeed.

It is also to think of what has become of your crystal. Who has it now, dear one?

Q: Do you know?

P'taah: And who has another lesson to learn? So it is truly not important except in your own allowance. You may go to that place from whence your crystal was gone and you may create a little ceremony. The ceremony is for you to honor your own sacred beingness. Indeed? Very good, dear one.

---

[2] Jani

Q: Good evening, P'taah. I read one of the Seth books and Seth said that one of his soul fragments was a dog that he was not taking too much notice of. Given that we have a cat with kittens at the moment...

P'taah: Not fair, hmm? No justice, having a little fragment and taking no notice of it?

Q: Yes, and P'taah, there is also the terror that I, too, am a fragment of this oversoul that I am part of and maybe the oversoul is ignoring me occasionally. That hurts.

P'taah: Well now, you see, beloved, what you all do tend to forget is that in your grandeur, in your oversoul-ness, you may choose to experience consciousness on any level you desire, whether it be to experience what it is to be second density—that is flora and fauna—or what it is like to be a fragment of a crystal.

(At this moment one of the host's dogs barges through the room. P'taah comments) Now I wonder who this might be? *(Much laughter. The host puts on a stern face and calls the dog to his side. P'taah continues.)* Dear one, do not be too firm. It might be your grandmother. *(Shrieks of laughter.)*

Q: I was not too fond of her in any case. *(The audience roars with laughter.)*

P'taah: Now we know why you kick the dog. *(Hysteria from the audience who knows P'taah is teasing. Then P'taah continues his answer.)* So you may experience your consciousness, however it is. You may desire to understand what it is to be a tree or a crystal, or to be part of a flowing river, or what you understand to be a passage of time.

We have said to you before, to experience what it is to be a crystal for millions of years is really a blink of an eye. It means nothing in those terms. Of course this experience is with what you may term to be a fragment of soul energy and so it is that the fragment has its own sovereignty.

Now, dear one, your fear that you may be overlooked by your oversoul is the terror that there may not be someone up there looking after you. It is only because you do not trust who you are. You do not understand your own integrity of being.

When you are truly in understanding that you are creating your reality absolutely, moment by moment, when you understand truly that who you are has a wondrous integrity whether or not you know it, then it is so.

You also have free dominion and sovereignty, whether or not you choose to exercise it. There is on any level a certain knowing, and so when that wondrous entity was speaking forth, in a way it was a little joke. You know very often there are lessons which come in the form of a joke to make you think. Do you understand?

Q: Not entirely.

P'taah: That is all right, dear one. You will read the words.

Q: I mentioned the cat and the kittens. I do want them to go to good homes and I do not want them to stay with us. I want us to create a good home for the kittens to go to.

P'taah: Dear one, you have already done it, but it is also to understand that that is what you desire and they are creating their own reality. You are doing what is called your part in it, and wondrous it is.

Q: P'taah, as a parent, when one brings up children, one is supposed to teach one's children certain manners and certain considerations. For instance, some people may have loud music without consideration of neighbors. When one sees a child or friend being inconsiderate or selfish, how far are we allowed to teach or bring things to their attention? What do you think?

P'taah: Well, dear one, first we would say that what is called selfishness and lack of consideration is a judgment, and that which you judge of others is indeed a reflection of who you are. Now, you may speak forth as you desire, but you know, it has nothing to do with you.

It is certainly to bring up children to live in this world and we know that humanity is desirous to bring forth children to live with grace in your world. So it is to say that it is wondrous to be in compassion for all people, to have thought for people, and that is to be kind. To be kind, but within the integrity of self.

Now, if it is a friend and he is behaving in a manner considered by you as not with grace, then indeed, beloved, it is you who has created it, too, for a reflection on how it is in your judgment of other people. Do you understand?

You may speak to your friend and say, "Perhaps it would make life easier if you contemplated another way." That would be to speak from the compassion and kindness of your heart. It is to know that every judgment you have about your friends is really a reflection of who you are.

Q: The limits of physics dictate we cannot create energy, we can only change its state. Are we actually creating energy?

P'taah: Beloved, it is called changement.

Q: We are not creating energy at all?

P'taah: Not as such, dear one. In a fashion the energy is already there and you are choosing which way you will manifest it. So it is a choice of the moment, and how you perceive action or reaction, that you change the energy from neutral to however it is that you choose.

Q: But is the actual creation of energy caused by the Source?

P'taah: The Source is energy, beloved. That is it. And the Source is love. That is it. Do you understand? What you are doing really is just playing with intellectual ideas.

Q: I wondered if the statement 'let there be light' actually indicated the creation of energy in the universe.

P'taah: Light is considered by humanity as the highest energy. It is not. It is the highest perceivable energy of this density and that is why people use light as a measurement. But that was before your physicists discovered that which is millions of times faster than the speed of light which is at this time hypothetical. At this time, for instance, humanity is not able to travel in hyperspace, although of course you do because pure thought is beyond space and time. And you do travel in hyperspace in this instant.

(A lady is intrigued by the way P'taah holds his hands, which leaves the forefinger and little finger stretched out and the middle and ring finger folded in...)

Q: Why do you hold your hand in that particular manner?

P'taah: Because it is comfortable, dear one. It truly has no significance apart from that. It is called a habit. At one time in a gathering, there were some who were convinced it was an evil sign, the sign of the devil. *(The audience chuckles.)* It is not, I can assure you.

Q: I thought it might have to do with frequencies.

P'taah: Indeed it is because of this, that it is comfortable. It has to do with the direction of energy. It has nothing to do with that which you call devil.

Q: P'taah, could you just explain simply to me how time is speeded up?

P'taah: That which you understand to be time is a perception. The days that run away with you, hmm? And of course, when you are very much in resistance of something you have to do, it will last for eons of time. So you see, in a way it is your own perception. But we have to say that you may change it, and so you may. The first step is to know you can.

Q: P'taah, I understood all that. I just really wanted to know the technicality of how time is...

P'taah: Compressed?

Q: Yes.

P'taah: Well you know, we cannot really explain it in this fashion because it is that which is perceived to be. It is also called quickening of energy and that is one of the reasons that you find you are living in compressed time at this moment.

But when you change what you are doing, which we know that you do not want to do although you feel you should live more in the world at the moment, you will find again that time will change for you. But in this fashion it is really how you perceive it to be—where you are at the moment. At this moment, this will suffice.

Q: P'taah, coming back to the Christ. What do we actually meet when we meet with the spirit of Christ?

P'taah: Dear one, it is who you are. It is the Christ-consciousness within you. It is called expanded awareness, expanded consciousness. It is called non-separation. That is all it is. It is really quite simple. It is only terminology that we are using so that you may come into an understanding.

When we say Christ-consciousness, it is in your understanding that it be of Divinity. But that, of course, is who you are. In truth, Christ-consciousness is the recognition of your own Divinity, of your coming into the expanded consciousness of self.

Q: How is it when the star people come on the Earth? Will they be seen by people or do they move about unseen by humans?

P'taah: Dear one, it entails many scenarios. There are star people who come in craft and these people have been seen by many, many humans. We would say that the star people are masters of disguise and so there are craft disguised and often people look and do not see.

As for the star people themselves, you know they come in a variety of fashions, in their own bodies and in this form as we are at this time[3]. Others choose to be birthed. Many fashions, not just one.

Q: Do we sometimes meet them when we sleep and are out of body?

P'taah: But, dear one, of course. Indeed you do, and so it is. They are your brothers, and in your dreamtime you are traveling forth in consciousness to have grand communion with the star people. It is wondrous.

Now, we shall call for a break at this time. We shall be returning very soon. Very well, dear ones.

(After the break, a very young lady addresses P'taah...)

Q: Good evening, P'taah. Referring to the perception of inconsideration being a reflection of oneself, now that one knows it is a reflection of oneself and one still wants something done about it, what is there to do?

---

[3] channeled entities

P'taah: What do you think it might be, dear one?

Q: I don't know.

P'taah: What about, embrace the judgment?

Q: Embrace the judgment that it is a reflection of oneself?

P'taah: Indeed it is to identify that it is you. But it is also to embrace the judgment about somebody else.

Now you see, when it is inconsideration toward oneself, why do you think you have created it? Because, beloved, it is certainly a mirror. So it is to look at the judgment, to know that what you judge as negative about somebody else is a reflection of who you are. That is the thorny bit, the embracing of what is considered as unembraceable.

When it is inconsideration by somebody else, well indeed it is none of your business. It is social consciousness and we know about social consciousness. Indeed it is nonsense. Whatever it is that you judge to be negative is only there to show you who you are.

Q: So as soon as I realize that I have this judgment, but I can see inside me also that we are all one, it will change?

P'taah: But of course, as soon as you have no judgment about who it is you are. You see, beloved, when you are looking outside of yourself and you say this person is such and such, then think about how often it is that you say things about other people, things which are really sarcastic, judgmental, detrimental.

Really it is to look at that aspect within yourself that you truly do not want to look at, that you truly judge about yourself. But you know, it is all right. It is valid, and so the judgment is valid.

And as we say this, you say, "How is it aligned?" It is to be aligned by the understanding within the heart that whatever it is, it is called Divine aspect else it would not be. When you can embrace the aspect within self, then indeed it will change the perspective for everything about you. It is very simple. Do you understand? It is automatic. The embracement, the allowance, creates the change.

You know, there is also this. There is great fear when people are reading and hearing for the first time about the non-necessity for law, the non-necessity for the regard of social consciousness in this understanding. People will say, "But there will be anarchy, lawlessness, chaos, etc.," but we would say to you, dear ones, what is it that you have now?

Q: P'taah, I wanted to ask you something else as well. Why is it that fear-induced manifestations manifest faster than those which are manifested of desire?

P'taah: But, dear one, it is not so. It is only your perspective. It only shows you the measure of how much fear there is. At this time, as consciousness is expanding—the rising of the Goddess, the rising of the Christus—your knowledge of how it is rising is, in a way, in reflection of the rising of the Anti-Christ because you see, dear ones, you are all fear-based.

You are not so used to regarding the beauty and the joy, the light, the love, and the wondrousness of who you are. As you are not used to regarding this of who you are, so you are not used to regarding this in your outside world.

Your media, your communication systems, are in great delight of reporting whatever is of disaster. In this fashion, it is worldwide. It is global communication within minutes. In your personal day-to-day life, you are used to focusing on disasters and problems and in this time of quickening and great changement, you are creating faster and faster what is fear-based.

As you resolve one issue, another presents itself for the embracement because it is the quickening of time. It is the cyclic time of change.

So just when you think you have it all together and you are congratulating yourselves on how wondrous it is this day, then whammo, something else comes along for the embracement. For you to understand also that however it is, it is a Divine aspect. However it is. It is called dichotomy. It is always the opposite.

We would ask you to remember dichotomy, beloveds. As you are congratulating yourselves on how enlightened you are, suddenly you realize that truly you know nothing at all. As you can understand that you are truly on a wondrous, adventurous journey into exploration, acknowledgement, and love of self and of every aspect, so indeed you are allowing the space for the blossoming.

(A lady mentions it being exhausting and P'taah replies...) Indeed, beloved. You see, when you become very exhausted you say, "I give up. I surrender."

So it is that you are surrendering to who you truly are. Not to struggle. Not to do. To give up and relax into the light of who you are.

Q: At both sessions tonight, you were piped in by a frog[4]. Now, whether he is your assistant or not, it is part of our consciousness and we were asked to be still as you came in, yet this thing insisted on piping you in. Would you like to comment on that?

P'taah: It is wondrous, and do you know, it is very interesting because the sound of nature is always wondrous to our ears, even that which is called the detestable toad.

Creatures are very aware of energy. They respond. The frog and toad will tell you indeed about the change of your weather patterns.

Those of you who know the signs of nature will be able to understand what is occurring on the planet. Your biologists call this observed phenomena. Plants also behave

---

[4]   On both occasions this evening, a frog pierced the stillness of the tropical night very loudly with his repetitious call.

according to what they are feeling. That is how you may read what is occurring on your planet, with your beloved flowers and plants and with all the creatures. They are responding to the energy field of a gathering as this. It is very beauteous. So you may read the story, as well as the story about you, if you will take the time for observation.

The transition of consciousness between our woman and that which be I, well indeed it is that sometimes our woman will effect the transition in a very noisy area. In a gathering such as this where it is very still in essence, noise and sound within this gathering become very magnified, but if there were noise outside of this immediate gathering, it would not be so severe for her.

Q: Just to take that down another step and getting into biodynamics, I was to understand that the soil bacteria have the ability to change elements in the soil, elements that are not there to start with. Is this so?

P'taah: It is so. Where it is that you are desirous to help promote growth and for the soil to be fertile, it is that you may sing the soil. There are very elaborate tools that are being used to change the soil, but in truth it is you who are the power tools. You may sing the land and thusly you may create the change.

When you come together as a group to create the sounding, then that energy becomes magnified. All of you have a tone of your being. That toning you may hear when you become very still within self.

There are some of you who use a tone, the *om*, to create stillness. Now you may do this, creating a sound in your mind and it is a note. You need not voice the sound out loud—we are speaking for your own playing.

As you create the note in your mind, so the note becomes broader, it becomes higher and lower. Eventually it covers all the spectrum that you can imagine. So it starts off as if it would be a note in a symphony orchestra with one instrument and then with all the other instruments coming forth to make music.

In this instance, it is merely that you are expanding the sound. The sound can be likened unto a personal signature. You may send it forth into the universe. It is your own sound. It is what our woman calls for herself 'singing her song to the universe.'

The sound has also color and the color starts off with one note to be one color. As it becomes broader and higher and lower, then it becomes the entire spectrum of color. So it is that it reaches forth into multiverses.

It is in this fashion that you may come into contact with your own thread of Divinity that runs into the multiverses, the multi-dimensional Self of you. This way you may also sing the earth and create change in this fashion, elemental change. So it is a new game for you to play.

Q: Earlier a lady asked about experiencing God. Is it possible for a person who sings or plays a musical instrument or paints a picture to come into something that is very difficult to explain, to come to a point where there is nothing else but that? Is that experiencing God?

P'taah: Dear one, you know there is another name for God and it is called Oneness. It is called non-separation. It is called totality of beingness.

You know that is why we, in truth, do not use very often the word God as such because in the vocabulary of humanity, the word God is likened unto a person, a personal being.

That is all right because it *is*. But it is also limitation. It is also separation. So when you are thinking of God, then emotionally it is as you have imagined it in your childhood as an old man in the clouds. So it is that when we say God/Goddess or the All-That-Is, then what we are speaking of is the non-separation, the Oneness, the feeling of unity, of joy, of ecstasy.

But of course, beloved, when one becomes totally im-
mersed in the Now of whatever it is—whether it is paint-
ing a picture, singing a beautiful song, or whether it is
playing an instrument, whether it is feeding the child or
swimming in the ocean, whatever it is—when you are in
the Oneness and Beingness and totally in that moment,
then there is nothing else in existence but God, Oneness,
non-separation. That is indeed how it is.

Q: I have not been brought up with the word God so I
would like to know if Spirit is the same thing?

P'taah: As what?

Q: As what people term God.

P'taah: And what do people term God to be.

Q: Oneness, I presume.

P'taah: You see, when you say, "Is Spirit the same thing,"
then you are already compartmentalizing, thus creating
the separation.

Q: I do not know what God is. All I know is feelings I get.

P'taah: Indeed. That is wonderful.

Q: So is God and Spirit the same thing?

P'taah: You see, beloved, everybody has a different idea.
Do you understand? Everybody has a different idea of how
it is and each one has his own label. We said before, there
is persona, consciousness, subconsciousness, spirit, soul—
a thousand names for that which is the glory of you. Then
there is God, Grand Spirit, Source, All-That-Is, etc., and
it is all a name. And truly there is no separation between
any of them.

(Another lady, a newcomer...)

Q: The part I do not understand is what is actually separation. There is a yearning...it is painful.

P'taah: That is exactly what it is, beloved. It is the yearning. It is the pain and anguish. It is the fear. The separation is everything which is not of light, which is not of love. That is separation.

Q: So it is returning to the Beloved, making everything conscious?

P'taah: It is called being whole. It is called coming home. It is called super-consciousness. It is called transition into fourth density.

Q: P'taah, how do you see us? Are you able to discern immediately what our soul ray is? Could you discuss these things a little, please?

P'taah: The answer is yes. *(The audience chuckles.)*

Q: Can you then tell me what soul ray I am on?

P'taah: Dear one, what difference does it make to you?

Q: It helps me to check historic feelings that I have for...

P'taah: No, dear one, I will tell you what it does to you. It creates another way of separation because you are all the same, every one of you. We hear humanity talking about this density and that ray, etc., but you see what you are doing, truly, is just creating more and more separation by your desire for delineation.

Q: It is just as there are people with certain bodies fit for athletics, they shall capitalize on that gift and those with intellectual gifts shall capitalize on those. If we have an under-standing of these things, then we know the direction...

P'taah: Dear one, for you wanting to be in understanding of your ray, I will tell you this. When you come into the embracement of who you are, then you will know. It is not that we come here to tell everybody in these terms, which in truth mean nothing to humanity. It is truly not as you say, that you will understand what you may be fit for because that again is really imposing a limitation upon self.

You are used to this way of thinking about who you are. You see, it is for each and every one of you to come into the non-striving. It is that you come into the not-using of the intellect to know who you are. It is, indeed, that you come into the heart-knowing of who you are.

In this fashion it is very good for men, male gender, to throw away the labeling, for you see, women mostly do not have to do it because they are more in tune with heart-knowing. That is what men dislike very much. Men say that women are not so clever.

So it is that men should throw away labels. We under-stand that this is very difficult for men—to simply not worry about the where, the how, and how this one fits into that and the level of this and the level of that—just simply to be.

Now, shall we give you a little test, dear one? For one week of your time, we want you to listen to how often you make the delineation in your day-to-day thinking. You do not have to do it out loud.

When you find yourself making delineations, intellec-tualizations, make a note on paper that you may come into the knowing of the heart. In so doing, you may come into the embracement of the unembraceable. All right? And on our next meeting, we shall chat about it, if you desire to do so.

That is not only for this one. The technologists may also play this game and then you may face up. Very well.

You know it is not only the men. Let us not let the women off scot-free. Women are all patting each other on the back, saying how wonderful it is to be woman and not man and how wondrous it is to be the Goddess, and indeed, beloveds, it is.

However, it is what you have known for eons as masculine energy within female gender because it has been survival for you. So you indeed know masculine energy, called God-risen. But now it is about Goddess-risen and it is the non-doing. It is all called balance.

So, beloved women, in this week to follow, you may take note of how often you follow intuition, that you follow it indeed and not dismiss it. Write down on your paper how it is and then you may come forth in our next meeting and say how it has been and what you have discovered about who you are.

Q: P'taah, during the last session I had asked you if we have the equivalent of the Big Foot or Yeti here in Australia. You hesitated and then said, "Not as such," so you must have been thinking of something. What was it?

P'taah: Well, we will say this to you—there are beings of this continent, but not really the same as what is called Yeti. However, dear one, it is that these beings are really from what is considered to be another time dimension.

You know, very often humanity moves in and out of other dimensions of time. Very often when we are speaking of the Inner Earth and the people of this planet who are no longer in your understanding, it is possible that humanity may come into a time warp. They have glimpses of other beings who are not related to this time-space continuum of this Earth as you understand it in this time.

This has happened on your continent where people have seen beings likened unto Big Foot or Yeti. But they are not really as it is understood on the continent of the

Americas or in the Himalayas. Now do you wish to query further at this time, beloved?

Q: Is it like a time overlap?

P'taah: Indeed. That is what it is truly. Many of humanity understand dimensional doorways as having a physical location only, but this is not so.

Very well, dear one. At another time we will speak more fully about this and it is for the continent of Africa also.

And so, sufficient unto the time of this evening. Enough food for thought. So we are in anticipation of our next gathering. So be it, beloved ones. I love you dearly. Good evening.

▼ Third Session December 18

P'taah: Good evening, dear ones.

(As usual, P'taah walks around the audience, looking especially at the faces of the newcomers.)

P'taah: So, how are you all? *(Addressing a woman in a cast who broke her arm since the last session...)* And so, beloved woman, you are finding yourself more in harmony now, hmm? The great trauma has passed?

Q: I hope so. I feel much better.

P'taah: But of course. And so you have taught yourself a grand lesson. Next time it need not be so dramatic.

So, dear ones, without further delay we shall leap into questions, and indeed if there are none, we shall simply say, "Good evening" and be in much congratulations that you are perfect in your own knowing.

Q: Greetings, P'taah. If an undesirable situation arises and we do embrace it and do accept it and value it as any other situation...

P'taah: ...then it is no longer undesirable.

Q: Well—but I wish the situation to change.

P'taah: That's different. If you truly embrace the situation, then you are no longer in desire of a different outcome and so it is no longer undesirable.

Now, if it is that you looked at the situation and you still find it undesirable, that is different altogether. That means that you are in desire of change, not that you have embraced the undesirability. Let us be very clear about this. If you want to change the situation, then go for it.

Q: I have tried this and nothing happened. Is it because it...

P'taah: Beloved, you have just answered it yourself. It is called 'trying.'

Q: Well, what else can I do?

P'taah: Desire it and know that it is already done. You do not have to do anything. You will not do it by trying. It will not do anything because then you are in the doing and not in the allowance. It is to say, "I am desiring to change this situation and now I am in allowance for the change to occur."

Q: Are you saying it just takes some time? I have to be patient?

P'taah: Dear one, it does take time in this reality of yours, particularly because you do not really take for granted your own power. You say, "I know I am indeed a wondrous and powerful manifestor—I think, I hope. I know, indeed, that it is done—I hope," therefore you are creating doubt. And when you are in doubt then, of course, it takes time.

When all of you truly understand that as you think and as you desire, that in that knowing it may be instantaneous, then it will be so. How do you think the holy men may manifest matter out of thin air? It is because they are in the absolute knowing that they may do so. There is no doubt. It is not called intellectualization. It is not called thinking about. It is called absolute knowing within the heart that it *is* so. It is in this fashion that you may change your reality.

Q: It sounds great, but how can one feel something so strongly that one has no doubt? I think and say all the right things, but still nothing happens so subconsciously I still must doubt.

P'taah: Indeed. So it is and so it is with everybody else. Some may be a little faster at it than others in terms of manifestation, but the bottom line is you are all in doubt of your own power. You may reinforce your own knowing as to when it is that you manifest what you want. When you are in your own power, you may say congratulations to self. You may give thanks to self for being so wondrous as to manifest exactly what it is you desire. That is reinforcing your own power base.

Q: It has been said, "Let go. Let God." It has been said, "Let God be your life. Let God act and perform as you and through you." How can we best achieve this most beautiful state?

P'taah: Know indeed, beloved, that God is not outside of you. If you say, "Let go and let the God I Am," that indeed is more powerful for you because, you see, as you are saying "let God" and you think that God is outside of you, then you are simply creating separation.

Now, who you are is an expression of Divinity. It is the God You Are. In truth, it is the God/Goddess you are. So it is to let go the intellectualization. It is to let go the shield in front of your heart and let the God/Goddess of your own being shine forth, to indeed allow your heart's desire. That is how you may do it, but do not put it outside of who you are. It is you who is the God/Goddess.

Q: P'taah, it is estimated that we are entering the photon belt. Is the photon belt like a gigantic gimbal which our consciousness more or less attracts according to our depth of knowing?

P'taah: It is in a fashion like this, dear one, but it is also more. You are requiring one answer to what is multidimensional, beyond human consciousness of this time and place. It is as it is with your Goddess, the Earth. The Earth herself is a reflection of who you are, but also it is a co-creation.

So we may give you one answer, but in truth there are many answers. It is not black and white. It is not one dimension. The whole of the galaxies are involved in the photon belt. It is not only the consciousness of this humanity. It is also the consciousness of the Goddess, your Earth. It is also the people of your Inner Earth. Also the unseen energies of this plane, of this planet that you as a species are not aware of. Do you understand? So it is more than just the consciousness of humanity. It is a co-creation.

Q: To simply create freely through our soul gifts without any further drama, what question would you ask that may take us to the next step that we may not know about?

P'taah: What is your soul gift, beloved?

Q: Expressing healing energies.

P'taah: For whom?

Q: Primarily for myself.

P'taah: But you do not believe it.

Q: I do now. There is no doubt that many of us have neglected ourselves to be there for others.

P'taah: Beloved, do you know why it has always been for others and not for yourself?

Q: Probably underneath the pain has been too great to look at.

P'taah: That is correct. And, beloved, that is not only for you. Indeed, the desolation, the fear of not being enough, the agony of being alone or being invalidated, of being overlooked, hmm? It is too difficult for humanity to bear so it is very simple to extend the compassion to other people and the desire for the healing of others because to go to the place where one's own healing is to occur is just too terrifying. There is always the fear of annihilation.

It is more difficult in this time for the male gender. We are truly speaking generally here, but for men the fear and pain of who you are and of who you think you should be to be worthy is of a very different frequency than that for women. The women have no less pain, but have a different direction and manner of embracing this.

So, as this time of change is occurring, dear ones, you will find there is no escape. What you do not embrace, what you do not transmute, what creates the pain and the anguish in your life, you will create again and again, perhaps with a different storyline, until you have transmuted it all.

It is to know that if you allow it to be, it need not be great drama or great anguish. When you show forth the intent that you will, indeed, welcome whatever it is that comes forth in your life that you may come into the embracement, into the allowance, to come into the state of non-separation, the ecstasy of transmutation, then you may make it very gentle.

And you will find that, as you resist it, that is all right. You may put the lid on it— and you are all very good at that—but, indeed, the pot will again boil over.

Q: Given that we have the will and the love not to put the lid on it but to say, "I am sick of this. Let's clear this for all time," then is there a deeper step of transmutation other than you have given us or…

P'taah: Dear one, when you may indeed use the steps we have given forth, I will be on my knees before you in homage. You see, what you are doing in your head is to make it more and more complex.

What we are saying to you is that it is very simple. In its simplicity, you do not truly grasp it. It is to say, "I understand. I take responsibility for everything that I have created in my life." It is to know that there is no victim, that you have created it. It is to align the judgment of yourself, of other people, to align the judgment of the judgment and feel the feeling.

Well, we forgot to say, and put your head under your arm. Get your mind out of the way, and the only way to do it is to say that it is perfectly all right for that very busy mind, that very busy computer, to allow it. When you can do this, you may come to the stillness within.

Q: From an early age we are fully implanted with information. Later on, by various degrees of reflection, we might find that 99% of it is not only useless but also destructive. So we are in a constant state of unwinding. Then we sense and feel an influence that is essential to our growth like what is happening here tonight. We have such a residue...

P'taah: Dear one, it is not only that which you know to be destructive and erroneous and useless baggage. It is also the stuff you do not understand that you believe. That is all right, you know, because it is all a moment-by-moment choice.

What it is all about is not about thinking. It is about feeling. It has nothing to do with your head. Woman is more familiar with it than man. If you can look at your life and re-experience the joy, then you will see that it has nothing to do with the head department. It has nothing to do with rational intellectualization. It has nothing to do with intellectual knowledge.

The intellect is wondrous, indeed, but it is your servant. You are not the slave of your intellect, beloved, unless you choose it. The rational, your intellect, your intellectual knowing, is here to serve you. What is called the ego is here to serve you, not to rule you, but you do not change the enslavement by the denial, by the pushing away. You change it only by the embracement.

The ego becomes very terrified of annihilation, of non-existence, of the change wherein it is not needed anymore. Well, you do not change that by saying, "Be gone. We do not need you," because indeed you do. You change it by saying, "It is all right. We shall do it together."

You are a product of feeling. It is really feeling that creates the wondrousness in your life. It is not your mind. You are not your mind. You are more. You are not your body. You are more. What you are is Divine expression, indeed.

Q: Why has the Christian religion not mentioned the Goddess or feminine energy?

P'taah: Because, beloved, the cycle of Christian religion has come in a time where it has been chosen by all that it be of masculine energy. Men, mankind of male gender, have been very terrified of the power of the Goddess, and still are.

Q: Do crystals have a part in the arising of feminine energy?

P'taah: They are a tool, that is all. What has to do with the arising of feminine energy is called consciousness. It is also called cyclic change. Crystals are merely tools to use, but the power tool is really who you are.

Q: P'taah, I have been going through a lot of changes lately. I was wondering if I left the place where I am living, the farm, would I be putting the lid on what I would have to do inevitably, eventually?

P'taah: Dear one, it does not matter what you do. You will indeed create a scenario for yourself, with perhaps a different story line, which you may embrace.

It is also to know, beloved woman, that you need not be a victim. It is your choice to do and to be and to travel as you will, whatever it is that makes your heart sing. It is called heart's desire. If you desire change, then go forth. Do not worry that you will miss out on the lesson. Do you understand?

If you desire to give your power away to another, then so be it. When somebody tells you how it should be for you and who you are and how unenlightened you are and what you must do to become enlightened, beloved ones, if it is your choice to give your power away, then so be it.

Nobody else can tell you how it is for you. Nobody. All the grand enlightened masters who are very happy to tell you how to live your life, indeed it is all right and you may say, "Certainly" and then you may do exactly as you feel. That is called having one's power.

Q: This word embracement which you use a lot. Would you like to define it?

P'taah: You know, it is very easy for people to say, "I don't understand why there is no change because I am embracing." It is about allowance. Whatever is in your childhood, you will find repeating itself in your life until you embrace it.

Now, we understand that it is very difficult for you and so we give you an analogy of how it may be. We are speaking particularly of your grief of childhood. You know, everything else is merely another repetition of that grief to you, of the desolation and invalidation of your childhood.

You may be in your very still time and in it you may imagine a very beautiful place. You may put yourself into this beautiful place where it is very peaceful, very natural, and you may imagine in this place the child you are. You may look at the child who is totally in grief and in terror, and you may pick up the child and hold it in your arms to still it and quiet it so that the child may understand that there is no longer anything to fear. In this embracement of the child you are, you may change how it is. That is truly how it is when we speak of embracement.

You see, if a situation is displeasing to you, if it involves people with whom you feel discordant, it is indeed to understand who this person is for whom you feel hate, discordance. It is to go to this place and see how the person truly is, because it is a reflection of you.

It is to know who they are in their heart. To know that really the terror, the desolation, the pain and the anguish are indeed the same as yours. In this fashion you may go forth to that one and you may embrace. To know, "I understand how it is because I am in this fear. I am in this pain and anguish myself." Do you understand?

It is in this fashion that you may effect embracement to create the change. That is why we say to you that you will not effect the change by pushing away. You will not effect the change with hatred, by getting rid of. You may only effect the change by embracing the fact that everybody and everything is a reflection of who you are. There is no difference.

Who you are is like the lights on your Christmas tree. Each light is strung together with one another with one current so it is light. If you take one light away from the current, it no longer lights up the tree.

The current is the thread of Divinity which runs through every atom and molecule and every unseen energy, through everything in the imagined and unimagined worlds. There is no thing outside of who you are which does not belong to you. It is all you, dear ones, it is all you.

Dear ones, sufficient unto this time. You may have a break now.

(After the break, the session resumes.)

P'taah: And so, let us continue.

Q: Good evening. We had a question before about people carrying out healing practices when they themselves are not even healed. This is a fairly common occurrence. We have psychiatrists who really need psychiatric help themselves. There are doctors who are not in the best of health themselves....

P'taah: Dear one, what these people are teaching and what they are giving forth is what, indeed, they are most in need of themselves and need to come into an embracement and understanding of.

Q: Well, what are the ramifications of these practices where you have these people treating people for various reasons, yet have their own problems?

P'taah: Let us speak about healing because there are many involved in this search for super consciousness who are involved in healing.

Let us be very specific. There is only one person who can heal you and it is called you. However there are people with the sincere desire to bring forth a healing and they may indeed ignite the desire for self-healing.

When you go to a doctor, very often it is merely that you have set forth the desire for healing which can ignite a knowing within you. In what is termed New Age healing, there is much mumbo-jumbo. It is perfectly valid, beloved, else it would not be in existence, however it is to know within the heart of you how it may be.

Many times we have said to you that the barometer of truth is your heart. If that which we speak forth does not ring true in your heart, if it does not sound like the clarion call for you, then walk away.

Now, there is much which is called 'shield of the heart.' You can imagine that many people wear a shield because they are afraid. So you may also say that intel-

Conversations with P'taah   Session Three   ▼   55

lect is often used as a shield. So there is that which says, "I will not hear. If I hear, if I allow this to come into my heart, then it will turn everything around that I have known in my life."

You know it is often very difficult for humanity to say, "I am prepared for change." When people are coming forth to such as I, and there are many entities, many beings coming forth at this time on your planet, then it is to say, "I desire change. I desire to move toward an expansion of some kind. I wish to change direction. I wish to come into my own knowing. I wish to understand how to be my own power-sourceness. I wish to understand how the universe operates. I wish to be healed. I wish to understand how I may be more effective as a healer or teacher," etc.

All of that is valid because the mere fact that you are here is to say, "I desire change." However, beloved, sometimes it is like a child wanting to go very much into the ocean or into a swimming place. Then it discovers that the water is deeper than it first anticipated and it reacts in blind panic.

You all know this well. It is called grand retreat. "I will go this far but I will not go any further because I might drown," and that is all right. It may be a very gentle process.

The healing of self may also be a gentle process. It may be, in your terms, a slow process. It is to understand, beloveds, that what you consider to be a long time is very often merely a blink of an eye.

It is not to worry how your politicians are running your country. You are your country, dear ones. That is the bottom line of it. When you are focusing on the dimwittedness of your teachers and politicians, that is all very well, but know that it is a reflection of how you are with you. What you focus on, you give power to. You are the central sun of your universe. Your universe truly starts and ends with you. How it is for anybody else is their business.

You may say, "It is not so because we have to inhabit this planet with everybody else who is intent on destroying the planet."

Well, I will tell you this, you may change it all. As you focus on ill health, as you focus on the devastation of your planet, as you focus on the fall of your economic structures, so it is that you give power to these things.

As you come more and more into the understanding that you are the power-sourceness, that it all comes from you, and as you focus within to create the change, as you focus indeed on the wondrousness of your planet and not on the devastation of it, so you are reflecting the focus of who you are and how you are within.

It is like a spiral. As you are within, so it is without. As you understand how it is without, so you are absolutely in understanding of how it is within. Do you understand that?

So the healer may indeed be in desperate need of healing. You may take what is offered, but it is never to lose sight of the fact that you are the healer.

Q: How do we know that we are getting the right guidance?

P'taah: Listen to your heart. You will know. You always know. The ones of masculine gender are coming now into the allowance of listening to the inner voice, of listening to intuition. It is to say, "Never mind the rationale, the intellect, but how is my heart? How does it feel?"

Dear ones, it is not your intellect which will bring you home. It is your heart which will bring you home. It is feeling, what you are feeling. What you are is called emotion, imagination. That is how you create your reality. You will know if it is right for you because there will be an ignition within your heart.

Q: So what you are saying is that our heart is going to tell us when the information is not right for us?

P'taah: Absolutely.

Q: And what happens then? Does one reject that?

P'taah: Indeed. You may say, "Dear one, I am respecting
your view. It is your right because you are a sovereign
being. I also am a sovereign being and choose another
way."

Q: Fine, you answered my question.

P'taah: And it is not to be in judgment of what you
understand to be mumbo-jumbo. It is merely to say, "I
choose another way. I choose to listen to who I am. I will
do what makes my heart sing." That is called sovereignty,
free dominion. It is called power.

Q: P'taah, you are talking about power and that we create everything but I often find that things are happening in
my life anyway and I just feel myself helpless in a situation. How do I deal with that?

P'taah: You are speaking of that which is discordant?

Q: Not necessarily. It is as if life is greater than I am and I
do not feel myself to be in charge.

P'taah: And so it is. (P'taah turns to the audience.) Do you
recognize it, dear ones? So it is even when something
wondrous is happening. You say, "I have nothing to do
with it."

It is because humanity is programmed to be without
its own power. When something wondrous occurs in
your life, it is to say, "You see what I have done!" in the
understanding that there is no accident, no coincidence.

Whatever it is in your life, whether it be of discordance
or whether it be of wondrous exciting joy, it is you who

have created it. Indeed you may say, "I have nothing to do with it at all; somebody else did it," is the same as saying, "I am a victim; somebody did it to me."

Q: So I am simply not aware why things appear...

P'taah: Dear one, it is merely that you are forgetting that it is you who is responsible for everything that is occurring in your life. Everything. That which be of wondrous joy and that which be of great disaster. It is all yours. People have said forth to me, "Did you create this wondrousness in my life?" and I have said, "Am I to be blamed for everything?"

You see, dear ones, you are so eager to give away your power. If something wondrous has occurred in your life, it is you who have created it. So it is even with the world events you feel so remote from, those which touch the heart of humanity. You say, "Is it not wondrous that this occurrence has come into being?"

But you see, if it had nothing to do with you, you would not even be conscious of it. There is nothing occurring on this planet that you are not involved with.

You think that you are powerless. You feel helpless when you hear about the earth changes to come and the transition and everything therein. You feel small and insignificant. You do not understand that there is truly no separation. It is you, beloved ones. There is nobody else.

Now, we may say that it is a leap of faith. As a species you have been told over eons of time to have faith. So humanity has enslaved itself in an act of faith, believing in something that somebody else is telling you. We are speaking of religious dogma, etc., where you are told that if you are not doing it this way, you are going to suffer. You will be punished.

What I am saying to you is that you will know. It is certainly an act of faith to understand that you are the Source. That you are the power. That you are the reflection of Divinity. That everything and everybody in this universe, in your known universe, is part of who you are.

There is no greater or lesser. There simply *is*. That Is-ness is called Divinity and as you are in lack of respect, lack of honor, lack of love for self, so you project that exactly outside of who you are.

But do not take what I say on faith. How does it feel? When you are taking the principles, the concepts which we are speaking forth, into the choice of your every now moment, how do you perceive it? If it does not work for you, dear ones, turn away. Walk away. Find another way.

When I say to you that you are coming into a time of expansion, when I say to you that you are grand and multi-dimensional beings, wondrous entities, that you are coming into this time of power, of knowing, then as you come into the knowing of your heart, the feeling is igniting the crystalline brain—the computer that lives in your head.

When you understand that you do not end where your skin ends, that you are beyond, that you are part of every-thing, so it is then that the pieces of the puzzle, the technology if you like, will all fall into place. You will come into concepts beyond imagination. You will come into a knowing that is so grand. Why is it, do you think, that the star people of your prehistoric times were called gods?

You see, dear ones, it is you. You are the Gods/God-desses. But you must take responsibility and when some-thing wondrous occurs, look at your eyes in the mirror and say, "I have done this. I, this grand and multidimen-sional being, have wrought this." It is called salutation.

It is to know that indeed you deserve every good thing. You deserve the wonder and the happiness. You deserve the joy, moment-by-moment. You are worthy, else it would not happen.

Do you understand it? You are worthy! You deserve it all. Every wondrousness that you can imagine, you deserve, else you would not be here. Every part of who you are is an expression of Divinity, else it would not be. It is you.

Q: Thank you.

P'taah: Indeed.

Q: P'taah, speaking of not hearing earlier on, could you please repeat the advice you gave me earlier about our animals living in harmony?

P'taah: But of course, beloved. It is called the lion lying down with the lamb. But you see, it will not occur until the lion within and the lamb within will lie down together, and that is called coming home. That is called the balance of masculine/feminine polarity.

As you are desiring for yourself harmony, and as you embrace and allow the blending of what is the masculine of who you are with the feminine of who you are, so it is that the lion and the lamb will embrace and it will be reflected to all. Within your day-to-day living perspective, so it will be.

We said before to write a letter. Well, you do understand really who you are writing the letter to. So it is.

Q: I understand that there are a lot of us who are terrified to open up our hearts to love and you answered it. It is for fear of annihilation. My question is, where does this fear come from?

P'taah: Do you want the short or the long version?

Q: *(Smiling)* The short one.

P'taah: Again it is multidimensional. We will speak of what is pertinent for all to understand without going too far back in time and how it has been with the genetics, etc. We will speak of how it is pertinent to everybody at this time. We will only speak of this life because what has not been embraced in all your other lifetimes, all your other incarnations, you will certainly bring forth. There is no need to delve into past lives. Whatever the story was, it will come again.

Now in this life it is twofold. When you are birthed, you are tapping into the collective consciousness or morphogenetic resonance of the whole of humanity. We have spoken many times of this and so the material is available for you to read, but we will give you an encapsulated version.

Is it important that you understand how it is. Every cell, every particum, has its own aware-ized electromagnetic energy or you could say consciousness.

On the cellular level, the cells have a knowing of like cells. Within your body these cells organize themselves into organs and the organ has a knowing of every like organ and may reproduce itself, in terms of cells, in its own integrity. So the body has its own morphogenetic resonance that is of like bodies, human for instance, and masculine or feminine.

Then there is the collective consciousness of a family and the family lives in a town and the town is in a country. Within the country there may be different cultures and the cultures have their own resonance, their own collective consciousness.

So the energy is of its own but existing within the same space as the other resonances. You may say it is a nesting, where one rests within the other. Your Earth has her own resonance, her own consciousness.

So as you are birthed into a family, in a town of a country, of a culture, all has a resonance, a collective consciousness. At birth you are not only tapping into this consciousness, but also you are having your own personal experience.

There are those things coming forth in a life which have not been embraced before, so you have a master game plan. That is you say, "I am birthing within a certain culture," etc., that you have chosen before your birthing.

Very soon after your birthing you have brought forth the experience of certain invalidations of your beingness. That invalidation will continue throughout your life until it is transmuted. Until you are in understanding of this, that everything in your life that is not of harmony and joy may be changed by transmutation, you will continue to bring forth a reflection. Do you understand this?

Your reality is founded on your belief structure. The belief structures that you are not consciously aware of are those that you have tapped into within the morphogenic resonance of humanity, however that is. This is how it occurs both on a larger and a personal scale, that you have brought it forth but for only one reason—to embrace it, to transmute the pain, the fear, that you may come into harmony.

All of the things, beloved ones, that are harmonious to you are on line with universal energy. So when you are in joy, in happiness, that is being on line.

It is when you are feeling the discordance, the pain, then you understand that whatever the reason, whether it is something you have created from your personal experiences or something you are tapping into of the collective consciousness, it is only there to be aligned.

It does not matter, in truth. It truly is for you to understand that when what you believe about reality, what you believe about your universe, are on line with universal energy, it will only be harmonious. Where it is not, it will create chaos in your life. It is so simple.

Q: P'taah, I would like to thank you for what you give us. You give us so much joy. I have this feeling that my stomach is turning over and over. I think my heart just sings for joy. Thank you for being with us. The question...

P'taah: Beloved, you know you are also making my heart sing with joy.

Q: The question that goes around in my head when you are talking about cells is, if our cells are replenishing themselves by the second, how come the brain cells do not replace themselves?

P'taah: But they do replace themselves in a fashion. Now, everybody is concerned with the loss of brain cells. When they die, that is it, hmm?

It is as well, beloved, that you are more than your brain. Once there is the crystalline ignition between the pituitary and the pineal gland, then it will be a very different story. It will be an opening of channels which will create a change within the cellular structure of the brain. Indeed that is called enlightenment, dear one.

Q: I have a question about what you said before. I am quite familiar with looking within and feeling the pain inside. What happens from time to time is that I pick up on the pain of the whole Earth or groups of people. It is like a wave washing over me.

P'taah: But of course.

Q: Part of me says, "It is none of your business. Just get out of it. Forget about it…"

P'taah: You see, dear one, what you are doing is tapping into the pain, but we are saying that the story is not important. You know how we have said to you before that what anybody is thinking of you is none of your business?

The story beyond the self is not important. What is important is how it feels. And indeed, beloved, taking on the pain of the world is impossible to resist. All of you tap into the agony of your universe.

Now most of you have very good shields and as soon as it becomes too painful to bear, you find another wonderful diversion. There are not so many who are willing to go there, to the pain. But you see, dear one, like everything else, it is transmutable and as you transmute the pain, so it is that you create the change in your universe.

Q: P'taah, this question is about the concept of karma and reincarnation.

P'taah: Dear one, what do you say is karma?

Q: The accumulation of past thoughts and actions and emotions over many lifetimes.

P'taah: But you see, it is all occurring at the same time so perhaps it is tapping into what is occurring in your other realities.

Very often when people are speaking of karma, they see it as a punishment for what has been occurring in other lifetimes. But there is no judgment beyond this plane of reality. It is not a question of punishment or reward because there is truly no judgment.

There is no such thing as good or bad, right or wrong. There simply *is*. So we would say, use the word karma in the absolute understanding of this. There is no judgment, no right or wrong. There simply *is* in the Isness of Divinity. It is all valid, else it would not be.

It is to know that however it is for you in this focus of reality, in this lifetime, you will certainly create the patterning of what you have desired to experience in this life. That it is a choice. It is not that you are forced to come here. It is simply that you desired to experience, to bring into alignment. Anything which is not aligned, you will bring forth.

But do not think of it as punishment and reward because that which you judge to be so bad, such pain, such fear, such anguish, such desolation, truly you have created to find the jewel within. So you see, how can you imagine that it could be punishment when in truth it is an opportunity to bedeck yourself with celestial jewels?

Q: P'taah, I listened to people talking about suicide and from the conversation, I gathered that the ones who were left had to go through the guilt of not saving the person. I was wondering, is this set in the game plan that one should take one's own life?

P'taah: Dear one, it is rather like losing the plot and you know, it is valid. There is no judgment, truly. Suicide is not truly of harmony, but it is always a valid choice, as is every choice. Do you understand?

Now, guilt is a lesson not learned. Blame is a lesson not learned about responsibility. It is to understand that it is everybody's own responsibility, moment-by-moment, to create this life however you choose it to be. It is sovereign choice. There are no victims.

If somebody is worrying that they did not do enough, so it is. Never mind about suicide. It is also when you are losing somebody you have not shown enough love and they have died. You think, "If only it had been different. It only I had shown forth the love I truly felt."

If only, if only, if only. I should have, I should have, I should have... But you see, dear one, it is only there that you may come to understand that there is no right or wrong in it. There simply is isness. There simply is.

When you are so tied up with your ideas of death, it is that you do not understand that death is only a grand illusion. It is not the finish of everything. It is merely moving into another experience of reality. Love goes beyond all barriers, to every universe, to every plane of reality.

So it is certainly not to be in judgment of suicide, and it is to understand what guilt truly is. It is called not being responsible. Blame, dear one, is not taking responsibility. Blame is judgment, and when you are blaming yourself, you are in judgment of yourself.

Understand that whatever it is that you have done has brought you to this place within, to this consciousness.

However it has been for you, it simply is, and it is valid. You may say, "I do not find it harmonious to behave in such-and-such a manner. So indeed in the next Now moment of choice it will be different." And so it will be.

Q: P'taah, could you elaborate on the effect of suicide on the person who has suicided? Does the person then choose to come back and is behind the baseline, as it were, and learns the same lessons over again?

P'taah: They may choose to come back to recreate an experience that they may come into harmony rather than losing the plot. But you know, in a way every death is a suicide because you always choose it.

How do you think it is for somebody who is dying of a diseasement called cancer? How is it with any diseasement within the body? It is called suicide because you have created it. The only difference is with the body's integrity. That is that the cellular structure of the body readies itself for the separation of soul energy and cellular energy.

It is to remember, beloved, that you choose it all. You create it all, however it is. There has been grave judgment in your religion about suicide. Those who are suiciding are certainly out of control of the enslavers. If everybody did it, good heavens, there would be no one left to enslave. We are joking, you know!

Q: So everybody chooses to die? Is that to move on to experience other lives?

P'taah: Indeed, dear one. And that which is called child—there are many who do not wish to experience beyond childhood. And some wish to experience no further than gestation and not even birth.

So we are speaking about abortion. There is grave judgment about abortion, but it is to know that it is all a co-creation. There is nothing that you do not co-create in your universe. You know, it all comes back to you.

Q: The bible speaks of people who lived to be 900 years. They must have had to enjoy life to the fullest of every moment to do that.

P'taah: Indeed. But also, beloved, we would say to you that the genetics were different. It is now coming into a time where people may choose a longer physical life, and we are speaking of hundreds of years, not an expansion of 20 or 30 years.

Indeed it is sufficient unto the time of this evening, and so it is certainly wondrous to be with you. We are to have a short break in these sessions[1], but we will be in joy to see you on the full moon. (Referring to the Christmas party planned for the following week.)

Q: Will you be there, P'taah?

P'taah: But of course. You could not keep me away! This is called a P'taah-ty and we are going to be having many drinks and we are going to watch you dancing. We want to see your bodies moving in joy with lots of music! (Laughter) We want to see how you make beautiful lights for your Christmas party.

So it is, dear ones. Our thanks. Go forth in joy and we shall be seeing you in the soonest of time. I love you indeed. Good evening.

---

[1]   Christmas holidays

▼ Fourth Session January 8

P'taah: Greetings, dear ones. So it is greetings for this New Year of your time. It is called putting the best foot forward. So this time is a grand step forward. There is much change upon your plane of reality, much change upon your planet, much change within the heart and soul of humanity.

(P'taah addresses a German visitor who is returning home the next day) Grand journeying, dear one. In Europe, many changes are to come. It is to know, beloved, that what you observe outside of who you are is a reflection of how you are within.

Also, as you observe discordant occurrences in your surroundings, it is a measure of how the consciousness of humanity is stepping forth. You will come again to this place and indeed it is a joy to be with you.

(To the host) Happy New Year, dear one.

Q: Thank you and the same to you, P'taah, although there are no years where you are.

P'taah: Well, in a manner of speaking, and all years are happy.

So, dear ones, without further ado we shall invite query. Indeed if there is no query, we shall celebrate that there are no questions left for humankind.

Q: We have been talking about the imbalance the cane toads[1] are producing in the north of Australia. What does this reflect in us and this most beautiful part of the country?

---

[1] The cane toad originated in Hawaii and was introduced to Australia as a predator to keep the cane beetle in check. This toad is very poisonous and Australia has no natural predator to keep them in balance. Those predators preying on the cane toad (birds, snakes, etc.) pay with their lives and that creates a further imbalance among the native fauna.

P'taah: What is the cane toad representing? What is it doing upon your plane which is creating the imbalance?

Q: It seems they are destructive and there is no natural predator to keep them in balance.

P'taah: Indeed. What other creature upon your plane goes and destroys everything without balance?

Q: Is that specifically reflecting Australia?

P'taah: It is not, dear one, because in this your country, where the cane toad imbalances nature, it is a co-creation. In other countries there are other predators who are reflecting to mankind what it is like to be without balance.

Q: To love the unlovable?

P'taah: Indeed, to love the unlovable. The toad, in truth, is a dear creature. It is only acting according to its nature. In another place, in the early cycle of the cane toad, the balance would be taken care of in the water before it would become a toad. In this place there is nothing that takes care of the egg of the toad.

In other countries there are different species, but the outcome is the same—imbalance. And that is a reflection of humanity. As you embrace the imbalance within each and every one of you, so a natural balance may be found outside of who you are.

Q: P'taah, I wonder if women generally can comprehend how deeply a man can love and what occurs when the woman tries to attack what they cannot control and the suffering that is caused?

P'taah: Dear one, everything that you experience is a reflection of how it is within you. You know, there is no difference between man and woman. You have been both. When you may align the masculine and feminine energy within you, then you will find that it will be very harmonious.

It is not only for you, beloved, but for all people. We said before. What you call relation-ship is in truth what is called relation-shit. Always, always it is reflected forth because the masculine/feminine energy within each and every one of you is still of polarity and non-acceptance.

As you are in judgment of woman—indeed it is not even woman, it is people outside of who you are—in your own terror and fear, so it is reflected back to you. Dear one, know indeed, what is brought forth to you is a gift.

You know, it is not only you who is suffering the pain and the anguish. It is all of humanity.

Q: After the transition to fourth density, the normal situation will be a co-creation of companionship, of equality, will it not?

P'taah: It is now, dear one. Fourth density is not issued forth as a panacea for the ills of your time. Fourth density is the result of how it is that you may be in the embracement of every facet of who you are so that there is no judgment and there is only now.

There is only now. There is no future, only this moment. Every nDow moment is a choice-point of how you react, how you judge who you are. So as you come into each moment, there is the choice that may issue forth embracement, acceptance, and love of who you are.

As you love who you are, how can you bring forth anything else? That is called living in honor and love and integrity of who you are. In this fashion you may create wondrous jewels of every moment.

Q: P'taah, you said perception is a reflection of what is happening inside a person. I have had some experiences

with telepathic people who can detect when a person is
dying and I wondered how such an ESP experience could
be a reflection to them.

P'taah: Very well. In fact what you are saying is two-fold
because every human has within that which you call
extra-sensory perception. Some have developed it more
highly, but as you are allowing feminine energy to arise,
the Goddess, so you may tap into intuition and ignite
extrasensory perception which is normally not available to
humanity.

Now this is different to what we are speaking of when
we say that everything that you perceive outside of who
you are is a reflection, a mirror.

You see, beloved, humans believe they finish where
their skin finishes but it simply is not so. You are not
separate from anything or anybody. Who you are is grand
and wondrous. You are multidimensional beings who have
chosen to experience this dimension of reality, known as
third density, simply for the experience.

Now, we will not launch into our usual elaboration
about the how's and what's. If you are interested, then you
may read about it because we have spoken of this before.

What we will say to you is this. Your soul, the greater
part of who you are, has one desire for you and that is for
you to know, in your conscious mind, in this density, that
you are God. Who you are is an expression of Divinity.
Every particum of you, every facet, every thought, every
action, every word is called Divine expression.

But you see, beloveds, you live in judgment of who you
are, and by saying 'you', we speak of the whole of humanity. As you judge yourself, so you send forth the judgment
to what you deem to be outside of you. But we say to you
that whatever it is that you see outside of yourself is a
mirror of who you are.

We are not only speaking of what you judge to be bad
because, beloveds, when you are watching the most glori-

ous sunrise or the raindrops sparkling on a leaf in the forest or the sun catching on the waves of your beach, when you are awed and breathless with such beauty, we would want you to know that what you are looking at is a reflection of you. You are awesomely beautiful, but you do not know it.

All of you possess what is called extrasensory perception. For many of you, it takes a little bit of practice to tap into ESP. Women very often find it much easier because feminine energy, womankind, is much more in allowance of intuition due to much conditioning.

Man has been programmed to regard intuition, dreams, and imagination as not quite manly, as not quite the thing. So in terms of social consciousness, it has really not been acceptable in this culture for several generations. But we are very joyous to observe that this has been changing for you.

Q: I as an entity start spiritually. Does that mean that I choose my parents?

P'taah: But of course, beloved. You have chosen your family, not only your parents but also your brothers and sisters and children. It is all decided upon before. For most of you, these relationships have been going on many, many times, for many lifetimes.

However, we would remind you that what you term to be past and future lifetimes are really occurring at the same time outside of this space-time continuum. Indeed you have known each other before in very different roles. In this life mother, daughter, father, and son may have been father and son, mother and daughter, etc. Very convoluted relationships. Do you understand?

So it is that when you meet at times with a human and you feel you know this one and it may not be of immediate familial connection at this time. It is possible that this one has been a familial connection at some other level.

And, dear one, we understand that there is quite an obsession with soulmates. You know, as you are meeting people and you feel you know them, know that you do. It is not essential to know the why and how of it in whatever other lifetime it may have been. Merely recognize the warmth, love, and connection and take it from there.

Very often groups of loved ones come together in family situations to have fun and to work out whatever it is they did not quite finish in another time. That may be what you term to be past or future lives. All right?

Q: By choosing those parents, do I do this myself or do other people help me?

P'taah: It is called co-creation because none of you are alone. We understand that all of humanity feels very isolated. At some time, in fact most of your life, no matter how much you love or are loved, there is still the feeling of isolation. Very often it is the feeling of not belonging.

We would remind you that all, all of it, is a co-creation. It is not that you decide and somebody else is forced to accept. It is that everybody decides one way or another to co-create in a fashion.

You know that you are never so isolated that you may not call upon help, and we are speaking of the Now moment, indeed.

Q: How far do we go back when we create things? I cannot keep up with things popping into my life and I wonder why I created this for me. I take responsibility for whatever I create, but how do I know how far I go back in this lifetime? When did I ever create a situation which I do not really want at the moment?

P'taah: You know you do not have to go back very far because when you decide that you really do not like something, that you hate something, that you will not put up with it, then what do you think occurs?

You may look upon it as a wondrous blessing, dear one. It is a gift to you. As we said before, it is all an opportunity to adorn yourself with celestial jewels, one way or another.

So for everybody who is stampeding toward enlightenment, we would say to you, slow down the stampede. It is as if you wish to throw aside that which is called uncomfortable, that which is called unpalatable, unlovable, unembraceable, unacceptable, that which you bloody hate.

Ask yourself why? Why is it that you hate it? Why is it unacceptable? What is it that is unlovable and what is in it for me in these people who are my mirror that I will not see?

It is all an opportunity, beloved. Never mind about why you have created it and when. You have, hmm? Every time you think you have got this one licked, your soul, which is very persistent, will simply present you with something else.

So you may congratulate yourself in this fashion and you may laugh about it. Know that as you have more trials and tribulations, it is your soul bringing forth these situations for you to embrace. That is called stampede and it need not be chaotic. It need not be discordant.

Q: There will be a lot of embracing to be done.

P'taah: Indeed you will be very loving peoples—much embracing.

But you know, the one who needs embracing is yourself. That which you are finding discordant, that makes you unhappy, that brings you pain and brings you anguish—that which is called broken heart—is merely that within you which is not loved, which is not embraced. We have told you many times, there is nothing which is not transmutable.

We shall call a break at this time. We ask that you are very quiet for two minutes during the transition.

(After the break, the session continues.)

P'taah: And so, dear one.

Q: P'taah, in reference to dreams. One night you said to record our dreams for at least 21 nights. I have been doing it now for about 10 nights. Should I be looking into that for some pattern or meaning?

P'taah: You may, but as we have said before, after a period of approximately 21 of your nights, you will see that a pattern will begin to emerge. But you may, with every dream as you are in recall of it, look for the personal symbolism within.

Q: Should I expect to be able to gain some direction from these dreams?

P'taah: You may, but it is not that you may expect every dream you have to be of incredible significance because some may be just for fun, hmm? With some, what you are recalling is only a fragment, and some may only be part of a puzzle, a larger puzzle, and that is why we have said to record your dreams over a period of time that you may come to understand the underlying pattern.

Q: Will it then be up to me to say, "I like this pattern," or "I don't like this pattern?"

P'taah: It is not even to like or not to like. It is to say, "What does it represent to me? What is it that I may learn from it? What is it that the greater consciousness of that which is I is putting forth for me to look at?"

Not that it is bad or good, but merely that it is perhaps something to learn from. It is not that it may be disagreeable.

Indeed you may find that your dreams are 'congratulations', that they are bringing forth peace and harmony, that you are coming to understand that which you did not understand before, but that it is of fulfillment.

It does not necessarily have to be some deep dark mystery. It can be quite light-hearted and joyous.

Q: We are manifesting moment-by-moment. Why is it necessary for us to eat food if we are manifesting moment-by-moment?

P'taah: You do not need food, but you believe you must. You know there are people upon your planet who do not take food at all and they live. They take nourishment from the ether. That is called tapping into universal energy.

Q: How do we actually use that energy within our souls?

P'taah: Are you speaking about tapping into universal energy?

Q: No, the energy of food. How do we then use that energy to convert that to the energy required…?

P'taah: You understand what it is biologically? You are ingesting what gives nourishment to your body.

If you are tapping into universal energy, you are not using the intermediary of food. You are taking the light energy directly as nourishment for your cellular structure, as well as igniting, that is balancing, the energy within the body with the energy outside of the body.

That which is food, be it animal or vegetable, is a co-creation. As you are partaking of foodstuff, as you will give thanks and honor to the food, so you are changing the substance you are putting into your body. You are creating harmony.

We have spoken before of the races of your people who are in understanding of this. When they go to hunt, they are calling upon the spirit of the animal to come forth. It is given great honor, great thanks, with song, with dance, with words. It is called heart-felt honor. In this fashion, the meat is enhanced.

It is no different to that which you call vegetable. There are people who say it is not fitting to put animal food into the body, but they do not understand that, in truth, there is no difference between vegetable and animal.

So, indeed, as you are putting anything into your body, it is to give honor and thanks.

Q: P'taah, in regard to problems, is it correct to say that forgiveness should have our predominant attention? Jesus stressed forgiveness very much, so is it correct then that we should look at forgiveness as being predominant?

P'taah: Dear one, what is forgiveness? You see, if you understand that you are responsible, absolutely, for everything you create in your life, and if you are understanding that everything is a co-creation, then what is there to forgive?

When you are speaking of forgiveness, you are speaking about the polarity of blame. Understand, if you are blaming somebody else, you are not taking responsibility.

Q: Does that mean the same when Jesus said, "Father, forgive them for they know not what they do?"

P'taah: It does not in truth, but we will say this to you. That which was written 2,000 years before of your time was also for a different consciousness.

Really hear what I say to you. You create your own reality, absolutely. There are no accidents, no coincidences. Your whole reality is a co-creation. You do it. If somebody runs you over with their car, you have created it, beloved. If somebody becomes very angry with you and commits a violent act upon your body, you have created it. If you have created it, who do you forgive? You see what I am saying?

Now, you are not a victim. You may be, if you choose, but we are speaking about the expansion of consciousness, preparing yourselves in your stampede for enlightenment.

When you say forgive, you are really saying that you have blamed somebody for doing something to you. But you see, how can anybody do something to you when it is you who creates the reality? So we say, perhaps it would be appropriate to make the word forgive belong to another vocabulary, not of this age.

Q: I understand you and I thank you for that answer, but I still want to find out how we go about solving problems.

P'taah: Take responsibility, align the judgment and feel the feeling—transmutation. We are speaking here of pain. When you say problem, you may say every day is a problem. What is a problem?

Q: Some difficulty with a person or circumstances.

P'taah: Well, beloved, it is to know that when you create your reality absolutely, you are also creating abundance, harmony or discord, as you choose.

Whosoever you come in contact with represents a mirror of who you are. It is to look within. It is not a problem, but an opportunity to come into the knowing of who you are and to love who you are.

You know, it always comes back to you. If we are to say what solves the problems of the world, then we say to everybody, look into the mirror and love who you see. If you are truly in honor and love, if you are having a grand love affair with you, then indeed, you will automatically have a grand love affair with everybody on your planet.

Q: P'taah, I cannot really believe that I create my reality absolutely because there is no proof. For instance, I would

like you to come in your own body and have Jani partici-
pate here, but this is not happening.

P'taah: No, it is not.

Q: If I would create my reality, I would create it that way.

P'taah: Indeed, dear one. If you know how to manifest,
indeed knowing how to manifest what it is you want, then
you would not be on this plane of reality at all. Then you
may come and play with us among the stars and then you
may take whichever body you want for yourself and then
you may perceive who I be in any body that you would
perceive.

Q: P'taah, if a person is in a situation which we deem to
be unfavorable, does that mean they are really enjoying
that starvation or whatever form of suffering they encoun-
ter?

P'taah: We understand exactly what you are saying. It is
very difficult to understand how it is that everybody creates
their own reality absolutely when you watch babes in starvation, murder and war and discordancy upon your planet,
when you see your forests devastated, etc. You say, if it is so
that we create our own reality absolutely, why would anybody choose these situations? Is that what you are saying?

Q: I realize that they choose, so therefore I think something in them must be saying, "I am enjoying this starvation experience because this is what I want, otherwise I
would be surrounded by food."

P'taah: On one level this is absolutely correct. But you
see, everybody in this room has known what it is to starve
to death. In your perception of how it is at this time, your
focus so exquisitely fine-tuned to this life you are not

perceiving what is occurring in your other lifetimes and in other probable realities of this lifetime so it is that over thousands upon thousands of lifetimes, you choose what you have not experienced, not embraced before.

So persons creating themselves in a land of famine have indeed chosen it for the experience. Those who create themselves as children on this plane of reality in this time of your country who would find death in childhood have also chosen it.

In one of your previous cultures, when the man died, his woman would be burned on a funeral pyre together with that which was her husband. Very barbaric indeed and you say, "Why would anybody do it?" Well, you have done it. You do.

Q: So in summary, I can never say that I really do not want the situation I am in because if I really, really did not want it, I would not have it. So whatever awful situation I am in...

P'taah: You have created it for the experience.

Q: And if I really do want to get out of it, I have to just be serious with myself and say, "I do not want this."

P'taah: Dear one, it is also to say, "However it is, it is all right." Because you see, it is the dichotomy, the grand paradox indeed.

It is all very well to say, "I do not want it." But when you can say, "I understand that this situation of discord is being created that I may garner the pearl of wisdom within," and as you embrace the discordant or painful situation, so you create the change.

By saying, "I hate it and I will not have it and I will be very furious," what you are creating is resistance. What you resist will most certainly persist because by resisting, you are giving it energy. As you may embrace and take it close unto your heart, then you will create the change.

It is somewhat like your bank. There will not be any bother giving you a large loan if you have money in the bank. If you have no money in the bank, they will not give you any loan. That is the paradox.

As you say, "This is no good and this is good," you are in judgment. As you give energy to that which you judge, so you are creating it.

Q: But then, when does one get to choose? It almost sounds like all we need to do is accept. When does the choosing come in?

P'taah: Because, beloved, you are choosing in every Now moment how you may perceive it. You may say, "I wish to go and create thus and thus," and suddenly the God up there steps forth with a big hammer and goes bang.

Then you say, "What has happened now to my beautiful plan? What happened to all that wonderful money that I was counting on? What have I done to create this situation that I do not want?" Then you may say, "What belief has brought it forth? What is it that I need to embrace? What is it that I am in judgment of?"

You may decide—and a decision is a choice—that you do not want to embrace it. You may decide to go and scream out to God and say, "You swine. Why did you do it to me? I did not deserve it. I am a wondrous victim and I am very sorry for myself, but if you make it all right, I will forgive you." You see, that is your choice.

Or you may choose to take responsibility and as you have embraced everything and created the change, then you step forth and you create your next Now moment.

You know, beloved, you are becoming a wise one, indeed.

Q: P'taah, back to embracing. Often I find I embrace something in order to get rid of it and I get the feeling that that is not the idea of it.

P'taah: No escape, hmm? You are quite right. It does not work. You cannot do transmutation to escape the pain. You cannot embrace something to make it go away. It does not work that way.

If you are truly looking to self, give forth blessings of that which you have brought forth so that it is not that you are trying to embrace something outside of who you are.

You may take yourself to your quiet place within. Look at who you are to truly give forth blessing. To know that who you are is indeed Divine expression. To understand that all of you are Grand Masters who have chosen to experience this dimension of reality.

Give thanks to who you are, and in this fashion, you may embrace who you are, and that which you have created outside of yourself becomes part of you by extension. Then you are not striving for the change outside but change through acceptance and acknowledgment inside.

Q: Can you give us a talk about the significance of the Harmonic Convergence?

P'taah: Very well. You know, there are many who do not truly understand the significance of this time. The major significance is that people gathered together all over the planet to send love and the desire for harmony and peaceful change. So, if it were for nothing else, it is significant for assisting to create filaments of love and light across your plane.

That is one story, and as usual, there are many answers. Now we will enlarge a little. We spoke to you of the significance of this time. There are changes to come leading to a new age of humanity and, indeed, a new age intergalactically. What is occurring is planetary. Your Earth is only part of what is occurring in these changes.

So, a door or portal is shifting into place that is of communication, of love—it is many, many things. Many of the things occurring are truly not yet within the consciousness of humanity.

There is much hocus-pocus spoken about this time and about many of the occurrences to come, including talk about flotillas of beamships to come to lift you as your Earth explodes under your feet. It is not truly to be thus.

What we are going to put forth on this day is to join each of us together, and with your brothers and mine who are beyond this star-system, in a fervent desire that the transition may be one of harmony, of great joy, and in the knowledge of the God/Goddess within each and every one of you. So indeed, it will be also a day of fun.

Q: One of the questions raised tonight concerned problems. If one is starving and wondering why all this is happening to one, am I right in saying that while one is concentrating one's energies on thinking about one's problems instead of on good things, one will always have these problems?

P'taah: Indeed that is so. As you are focusing on the have not, you are not focusing on the have. So whatever it is that you put energy towards, that is what you draw to you.

We understand that it is very difficult when you are worrying day and night because there is no abundance of money and because the relationship with the husband or wife is a constant ache of the heart, or when you worry about your children or about loss.

It is very difficult for you to be able to say, "Who I am is Divine expression and all of this I have created to find the pearl within. And who I am is judgment, that I judge one to be good and one to be bad, this to be right and that to be wrong."

While you are struggling very much to be non-judgmental, we would tell you that it is very subtle. It sneaks up on you. It is like your belief structures where you do not understand that you have a belief. You have been a prisoner for so long, you do not see what it is that you are looking at and where you are looking from.

It is not to make any of it wrong. It simply is. You are simply creating this from your own Divine power. But as you can come into acknowledgment of that Divinity, of the non-separation, of your own power, so you will find that what you regarded as a problem will change its face.

As you do not focus on the destruction and the not-having, you may create the change in this fashion without pulling to you what you fear. Do you understand?

Q: Yes. The next question probably relates to that, too. What can you tell me about the two hemispheres of the brain, the left and right. I am told the left side is the materialistic side and the right the intuitive.

P'taah: That is a way of speaking of it. There are some who would say that it is masculine and feminine. The bridge between is rather crumbly.

So, the left brain is masculine, organizing, logical, directive, you may say materialistic. That which is feminine energy, the right brain, is allowing, nurturing, receptive and intuitive, that which is creative within your art form, that which springs untrammeled from the heart. As you bring forth feminine energy, and as each and every body allows the Goddess to arise within, it ignites the crystalline structure within the brain so that it is in harmony, in balance.

Q: How do we achieve this balance?

P'taah: Love who you are, beloved. Is that simple enough for you? Know that you are Divine expression.

Q: But that does not answer my question.

P'taah: Beloved, what we have been talking about ever since you have come to these evenings is really about balance, is really about how you come into who you are. Who you are is masculine/feminine energy united. I have been telling you nothing else for these many weeks.

Q: Are you saying that I am thick?

P'taah: Dear one, I will tell you this. You are no different than anybody else who hears with the ears and who does not truly know. That is why we are here.

There is no judgment that it takes time to come into the knowing, that it comes in its own ripeness of time for the ignition within the heart. But you see, I am very patient. I will keep coming until you truly understand.

Q: Yes, I understand that. Is it true to say that most humans put too much emphasis toward the left rather than toward the creative side?

P'taah: That is what we have been saying. Humanity has been operating from masculine energy for eons of your time and now is the time for the arising of the Goddess which is called right brain.

It is merely that the brain is the computer powered by the energy. That is all your brain is. It is only a computer. It only operates according to the operator.

You create your physical embodiment absolutely according to how you are. We spoke before about physical dis-easement and how you create physical dis-easement from emotional dis-easement.

The computer within is empowered by the You of you. You are more than your brain. You are more than the body. You are more than what is called ego. You are more than the subconscious. Who you are is Divine expression. When you know that it is the truth, then your computer will operate in a different fashion and so will the rest of your body.

Q: Does that mean females are creative and males are destructive?

P'taah: It does not. What is female of your gender has also been operating from masculine energy. However, there is also that in the morphogenetic resonance of woman which makes it easier for her to tune into feminine energy. Even to the extent that they are receptive and creative in the physical body, they are able to be more in tune with the body and the intuition about what occurs outside their physical bodies.

However, let there be no mistake about it. Woman is in truth also coming from masculine energy. Your whole era, your whole Earth is geared to that at this moment. That is one of the changes of this New Age. It is called the arising of the Goddess. It is not just in woman, it is also in man.

Dear ones, it is sufficient unto the time. I love you. Good evening.

▼ Fifth Session
January 15

P'taah: How are you all this evening? Indeed, you are looking very beautiful.

(P'taah walks around the room and looks at each person.)

Q: Namaste[1], P'taah.

P'taah: Namaste, dear one. Indeed we do salute the Lord God of your beingness.
   So it is. Now, you have some wondrous questions stored?

Q: For myself and also others who may be in the same position, would you comment on better or perfect vision? For some reason I keep losing or breaking my glasses. I think there is a message in that for me to improve my vision without glasses.

P'taah: It is no accident and that you know full well.
   Vision—you know humanity of your culture certainly taps into the collective consciousness about how your eyesight should be. Now this varies from person to person, however it is certainly that an impairment of vision starts, of course, inside.
   So if it is that you desire to see, so you may. But it is not to judge that which is called defect of vision. If you make it so that it is no good, that it is bad, what you are doing is focusing on impaired vision.
   It is perfectly all right to have vision which is impaired. But if you acknowledge that it is all right, truly, and desire the change, then you may create the change.

---

[1] Sanskrit word meaning "The God in me salutes the God in you."

However it is also to show forth the intent, and the breaking of spectacles is showing forth the intent. Now you may start to exercise the eyes and know that truly you do not see with the mechanics of the eye. There is grander seeing. How is it that you think that people who have no sight may see, and they do. You understand what I am saying?

So it is merely that you put forth the desire and show forth the intent. That may be with creating physical exercises for the eyes. There are many adventures you may have to correct physical vision, however the correction does not really come about from the physicality of the organ called eye. Openness to see. Open the heart to see. Open the eye within. It is very tricky.

Q: It does not have to be, though, does it?

P'taah: It does not. We say that only to remind you of the multidimensionality of it all. All right?

Q: Greetings, P'taah. I wonder. All of the people who are drawn to us here, are they all family? Well, I know we are all family but do we all have something in common with the Pleiadians?

P'taah: But, of course, or you would not be here.

Q: The Earth people come from different places?

P'taah: Indeed, from different star systems, but ultimately of course it is all from the same. There are certainly different energies that you may say, now, in your time, are of different star systems. Those who are drawn to this gathering and other gatherings of Pleiadian energy are drawn to a resonance of being. They are of Pleiadian family. That is certainly so.

Q: Does that also include that we are part of the whale and dolphin family?

P'taah: Indeed, and that which is the whole of humanity is part of Cetacea. Cetacea also has a resonance with the different star systems.

Q: P'taah, is one of those different systems Sirius B?

P'taah: That is so. This is not to say there is not harmony.

Q: I understand that. Is there equally an expansion of consciousness among the star beings from Sirius? Would there be Sirius-consciousness beings who have incarnated on this Earth?

P'taah: Indeed, but if you are with people who resonate to different star systems, it does not mean that you will not be of accord. As we have said, ultimately it is all the same.

But we are speaking specifically of this place, this time. There would be, for instance, many people who have heard about the gatherings here in this place and may feel drawn to come but for one reason or another do not. This is not necessarily their conscious decision and that is all right, beloveds.

It is to remember that everything has its own timing, its own validity. And as it is that you resonate with what we speak of, it is not to think that other people who do not think in this same fashion do not have the same validity because they do.

Q: I have heard and read that at this last stage, there is an Anti-Christ. What is that?

P'taah: Dear one, it is merely a name that you may give to energy. We speak to you of Christ-consciousness. Now, we speak this name because it has a meaning to you in your culture. We may also speak of positive/negative energy. When we speak of Christ-consciousness, we are speaking of that consciousness which embraces both polarities.

Your world, your universe, is made of positive/negative polarity, without judgment. When we are speaking of positive/negative, we are not speaking of right and wrong, good and bad. It is simply the isness of positive/negative, as in your electricity.

But it applies to everything. When we are speaking of Christ-consciousness, we are speaking of that consciousness which is allowing, which is of negative energy, that which is female energy. Goddess energy arises that the polarities may be embraced.

In these days, it is gathering momentum for the changes we have spoken about so often to you. In these times, there is the rising of both polarities, that which you judge to be positive and that which you judge to be negative.

So it is very well when you are seeing the expansion of consciousness—wondrous harmony within groups of people, world events where people come together for the greatest benefit of mankind which is so warming for the heart.

Then you turn on your television and see that which chills the blood. War, international incidents which seem to indicate that all is not well, that the warring factions become larger, that the devastation becomes more, and indeed that indescribable chaos is just around the corner.

This is what may be called the rising of the Anti-Christ. This is why we have said to you that as you regard this, know that it is only an indication of the rising of the polarity of the Christus. It is not what you would judge to be negative. It is the rising so that the culmination of the embracement of both polarities may occur.

Each situation you observe that you judge, it is truly to know that it is an opportunity for you to embrace in the knowing that as you are without judgment, and as you may love the unlovable, so you are creating the change that you desire as you desire it upon your planet and upon this plane of reality. Indeed?

So, in fact, as you are looking at what other people regard as dire circumstances, so you may say to them to regard the dire circumstances as an indication of how far you are moving towards fourth density.

Q: That happened last night when I turned on the news. I had to turn it off in the end because it was all quite disastrous.

P'taah: Indeed, and it is not necessary to focus on disaster. It is to know that the vibration of disaster coming forth on your airwaves is resonant in the very air that you breathe. It is to know consciously that you do not wish to focus upon this, that you do not wish to give forth energy to this.

Q: So, following that, P'taah, each individual, sooner or later, is responsible for their own transition.

P'taah: Absolutely, beloved.

Q: Because the motive is to activate the individual to respond, to find balance within himself?

P'taah: That is why we are here, beloved. That is what we are attempting to have you remember. That it is only you, and as you may create the change within you, so then you create the planetary change. Each one of you individually has the power to change the world.

Q: That is to change the world, as in one's self?

P'taah: Dear one, there is nothing outside of you except a reflection of who you are.

Q: P'taah, these days I rely very often on a bicycle and I caught myself recently feeling very uncomfortable about locking up the bicycle. In fact, I even lost the key. The reason I feel uncomfortable is that while I am putting the chains around the bike, it is as if I am saying to the people around me, "Look, I am in fear that you will take the bike away from me." That feels wrong.

P'taah: Dear one, it is not wrong. It is merely not necessary.

Q: My heart tells me that I should not lock it and my brain listens to the newspapers talking about how many thefts there are. Now, am I stupid if I follow my brain? It is a tricky situation because if I do not trust, it will be taken away.

P'taah: But you know the answer. Why do you ask?

Q: Because I need reinforcement from you.

P'taah: Very well. It is not so tricky. You know that which is absolute trust in the universe is called absolute insanity by the brain. Who do you trust, heart or brain?

Q: The heart.

P'taah: Indeed.

Q: P'taah, the other day at the meeting, I saw around you a pink glow. I have never seen colors around people before. Is this something that is developing, that we can see the colors?

P'taah: Indeed, and as you allow it, you will see more and more. Now where it is a situation which is highly charged, where you are very open in your heart, the energy ignites the eye within so you may see energy and colors.

The colors change. As you become more aware, you will notice the fluctuations of color around people and you may read many stories about the people merely by reading the colors.

Now it is all right if you do not see the colors. There has been much talk over the years about being able to see the auric field and other people feel like complete failures because they cannot. That is all right. There are times when you do and other times when you are desperately trying to see and you see nothing. All a matter of allowance.

Q: The colors represent different chakras? Pink would be love?

P'taah: You may say that pink is the emanation of love, but it is not the only color of love. It is a feeling. It is more subtle than to say this color is this and this color is that. Other feelings and the density of emotion change and so do the colors.

Q: So it is a shade?

P'taah: Indeed, but it may also be that you see a very wondrous green which is also the color of the heart. Then there are the colors of the beautiful waters of this place, the beautiful blues and greens mixed together in various degrees of change. It is not merely one specific color meaning one specific thing.

Q: P'taah, are the colors an extension of the body?

P'taah: Not of the body, but of the light body.

Q: Is heat the same as the light or a lower form than the light?

P'taah: It is what you would call a different spectrum. Color is of the same spectrum as sound. You may say that every sound has a color and every color has a sound. There are people on your planet who may touch the flowers, and without seeing, will hear the sound of the flowers and know the color of the bloom.

Q: So words have sound, therefore they must have color.

P'taah: Indeed.

Q: Is there meaning derived from that?

P'taah: There is, but when you are speaking of the words of humanity, they are also colored by emotion.

Q: So sometimes if I do not understand what a person is saying, I should listen to the tone.

P'taah: You may listen to the tone and you may listen for the color and you may feel the color. It is not necessary that you see the color with your physical eyes. It has a feeling. A person who is not able to hear may gauge the emotion by the vibration of the emotion which has nothing to do with the sound.

You see, dear one, you have more than what is called the five senses. When you speak about extrasensory perception, you very often limit that to very small boxes, but it is more. As you become broader in your consciousness, so the senses become more and more sensitive and you are feeling what is occurring around you. It is only a matter of being open, of allowing yourself to hear with your heart.

Q: P'taah, I have a little challenge here. I feel that I am somewhere in between making a choice of going for my spiritual development or going for what my heart desires, which is riches. Now, somewhere the belief system is there that one should seek the kingdom of God first and then riches will follow.

P'taah: Dear one, you are already within the kingdom of God. You are God. That which is called spiritual development occurs every moment of your day, whatever you are doing. It is not necessary that you put aside living to become the next Christus. You may pursue what you call business and every moment of your business life is an opportunity to expand your consciousness. It is not a matter of doing that or that.

Q: You see, I read in a book something about people in this world busying themselves making money as their sole concern, as the be-all and end-all, so I had the feeling that if you go for making money, it seems to stop you from developing.

P'taah: Dear one, there is nothing in this book which states that there is anything wrong with making money.

Q: That is true.

P'taah: Indeed? Let us be very clear about this. Now there is also a great school of thought among what is called spiritual people that money is no good and that people who have money cannot possibly be spiritual. Well, it is nonsense. It is called poverty consciousness. So go for it. If it is the desire of your heart to play the game called making money, do it.

Q: (Jokingly) So I can have my Porsche?

P'taah: But of course you may, and then you may take me for a drive.

Q: I promise.

P'taah: And our woman, too, except that she would want to drive. (Laughter)

Q: Oh, I don't know about that.

P'taah: Oh, she is an all right driver. I am witness.

Now, you know we tease you sometimes about your stampede for enlightenment. We would remind you that enlightenment is not to be won by striving. It is by allowing.

And to those of you who are very busy with all your intellectual pursuits of spirituality. It is all very good. It is all valid, but it is not enlightenment. Spirituality is living. It is playing. It is allowing the laughter to bubble into your living.

Q: It sounds wonderful.

P'taah: It is. And you know, that which you strive so desperately for, you truly have no idea what it is. For many, you are thinking that once you are enlightened beings, it is called perfection, finished.

It is not. There is no finish. There is no end. You are perfect now, at this very moment. You are in the fullness of your own Divinity, without a future. There is only Now.

So when you find yourself in a quandary about what you should be doing, there is no should. There is merely to do that which makes the heart sing so that every moment can be in its fullness, and out of that fullness comes the next full now moment.

Q: P'taah, I have just one question. How do I overcome fear?

P'taah: Love it.

Q: It is easy to say, but for me it is very hard to understand.

P'taah: Indeed, dear one, if everyone could understand it as we speak forth, you know there would be many thousands of enlightened beings in this country of Australia at this moment in time, and indeed throughout the whole world. You see, fear is only a polarity. What do you think is its polarity?

Q: Peace.

P'taah: It is called love. There are only two expressions in your whole universe, that which is fear and that which is love.

Everybody is driven by fear. Not all of the time, perhaps. The fear is very subtle. It goes under every other name which is not love.

But, it is valid. It is also a Divine aspect of who you are, else it would not be. Do you understand that? The fear is only there as an opportunity for you to allow and embrace, to step into, to know, to love it as an opportunity to transmute it to love, to ecstasy.

Truly, if you allow the knowing of this to permeate your being, you may step forth from the fear, into the fear. It will never go away while it is invalidated, while you are running from it, while you are trying to push it away, suppressing it. While you are in desperation to change it, you are giving focus to it. You are feeding it, in a way. Do you understand?

So, each time a situation arises where you are in the flutter of the belly, that is, in fear, you may imagine that the fear is really the child within you, the babe you were, hmm? You may pick up the child and embrace it, know it. You may tell the child that you are there to care, to love it, that you will never allow it to be harmed. In this way the child within you who is frightened will be frightened no more.

Q: Thank you.

P'taah: All right, dear one? (Very soft and tenderly) Indeed.

Very well, now we may call for a break. So we would ask that you would create stillness within as we are completing the transition. Our thanks.

(After the break)

P'taah: So, let us continue.

Q: P'taah, we all felt the benefits of the meditations you took us through last week. Is it possible that you could do this again for us?

P'taah: Indeed, dear one. We have said before that in this year we will, from time to time, create a situation wherein those who are interested may come together for expanded meditation.

However, for these nights, we are creating an opportunity for you to come into an intellectual understanding to ignite the remembrance and knowing within your heart. Also it is that those people who have not been with us before may take the opportunity to have their questions answered.

Q: For us to grow teeth back, or replace a limb that has been amputated, will it happen at the moment of ignition between the pineal and pituitary glands?

P'taah: It will happen with the ignition of the crystalline properties between pineal and pituitary, and indeed it is an affair of the heart. It is also that the changement of the heart creates the change within your DNA structure.

However there is only one answer, really, you know. It is called, love who you are. You see, beloved, I may take you on a meditation every day of your year, but in truth you are the only one who may come into an embracement of fear and acknowledgement of who you are. I may assist you, but it is you who creates the reality.

Q: P'taah, the visualization we did on Saturday, is this a way of putting forth our consciousness?

P'taah: Indeed.

Q: I have sort of summarized that making images in our mind is just casting reflections of one's self.

P'taah: It is certainly that, that is quite correct. But it is also more because as you are casting forth your own reflection as you did on Saturday, so you are also in allowance of expansion within you.

Now, it is likened unto creating the balance within the body—and we are not only speaking of the physical body—a balance within and without so that you are creating an expansion which may receive more.

When there is no difference between what is within and what is without in your perceptions, so it is in reality. So it is then that you have changed your plane of existence. It works on multidimensional levels and you may do this without me.

Q: I realize that.

P'taah: So you may go forth and have adventures of many different sorts. Explore. Explore the reality outside of that which you perceive yourself to be as well as the reality within you. You may conduct an exploration of your own body. That is always a good one.

Q: Right down to my cells. There is a universe within each cell.

P'taah: Exactly. And then you come into multidimensional knowing about universes.

Q: Thanks, P'taah.

Q: Can you tell me about the relationship between the animal kingdom and humanity on a spiritual level and what happens to animals? Do they go anywhere after death?

P'taah: What you regard as animal is what you may call second density awareness. That which you call animal certainly has existence outside of physicality. Their awareness is different to human soul energy, but human soul energy may experience fragments of itself within the animal kingdom or vegetable or mineral. We are speaking of what is the greater soul energy, the expanded you.

As for the connection, beloved woman, there is nothing that you are not connected with. You are part of everything that you behold. There is not a molecule of which you do not have awareness. Everything you behold as outside of yourself is as you are, a reflection of Divinity.

Q: Do they reincarnate?

P'taah: Not in the same fashion, really. But you know, that which is called pet or animal which you are loving so much, is indeed a grand reflection. It is part of you. You have created each other and there is no separation, beloved.

When it is that you love somebody, or when it is that you love an animal or even a blossom so much, it is never lost. That connection goes on into infinity.

Q: Thank you, P'taah.

Q: P'taah, can you tell me about the use of mineral crystals?

P'taah: You may say that it is a power tool. It is a magnifier and point of focus. You may program the crystal, as the crystals in your machinery, in your technology, to store information and to release information, to magnify energy. You may use crystals for anything, but we would say that in the usage of which you speak, it is not really necessary but it may be a very powerful aid.

You know, dear one, the only reason we say this to you is because we do not wish humanity to give away their own power. In the technology to come, crystals will play a very important part, as indeed it does with your own technology of today in computers, etc. However, concerning the usage of crystals by people for healing and the like, the same result may occur by using the computer that lies between your ears, powered by thought and emotion.

We are not decrying the use of crystals at all. There will be coming forth truly wondrous discoveries as to the use of crystals. There are many, many of what we would call the Board of Directors[2] coming forth to talk to humanities who give very specific information on the use of crystals and also how to build certain machinery which can be a magnifier for use in new technologies.

However, at this time what we are concentrating on is how you may use your own power. It is so with humanity that you have been programmed to use everything but your heart. Humanity has indeed forgotten how powerful the computer is which you have between your ears, and you have forgotten what powers it.

So people are very obsessed with gaining this information that is wondrous. You may go forth and you will find it, but we will say to you that there is nothing more important than to understand who you are, to understand that your greatest power is love of self. It is knowing that you are indeed an expression of Divinity, to know that your whole world is created by judgment and you may create something quite different.

When you have created this wondrous difference through acceptance, through beingness, through love of self, all, *all*, of these other things will fall into place for you and you will not need a crystal to create a whole new body if that is what you want. Do you understand?

Q: Yes, I do now, thank you. I was uncertain before because so many things have been said about them.

---

[2] Other channeled entities

P'taah: Many of the things you read are perfectly valid. Be aware also that many of the things that you read are what is called fairy story.

Q: P'taah, if one is a businessman in tune with the universe, it has to be a win-win situation, doesn't it?

P'taah: Absolutely. You know, when you are thinking about business, the major concern is called profit and loss, hmm? Well, you know, in this wondrous and abundant universe, there need not be loss.

Your universe has abundance for all people, all people. When you are in the knowing that you may have abundance, whatever it is that you desire, you will understand that you do not need anything.

When you are in understanding of this, you may create the abundance and so you may be aware in every moment, with every transaction, that as you are in honor of self, and knowing that you may create whatever it is you want, without need and without desperation, so you create the win-win situation.

Q: It sounds wonderful. Thank you.

P'taah: But it is wonderful, so do not think of business as profit and loss. Think of it as wondrous profit always for everybody.

Q: Thank you. Could you please explain to me the difference between the Family of Light and the White Brotherhood? Is there a difference or are they the same?

P'taah: Well, indeed, there is a difference perhaps in the consciousness of humanity. That which is called the Light Family or White Brotherhood is on the side of expansion and peace and love and harmony. In other words, it is the opposite, the polarity, of what you would call the Illuminati.

Q: Who and what are the Illuminati?

P'taah: They are the power brokers of your planet, and
not only of your planet. They are the people who desire to
enslave all of those who would be enslaved, but it is all
choice.

You need not be enslaved. You need not buy into it.
When you are in honor of self, when you may honor all
things, when you are in free-dom, in free dominion of self,
then you are allowing freedom for all—for all men, for all
creatures.

When you are not in need and desperation because you
know who you are and you know that you are an expression of Divinity, how indeed can you be enslaved? And it is
to know, dear one, that those who would desire to enslave
humanity live in fear of being enslaved. It is only fear like
any other.

Q: I understand that people from the Light Family have
come down to assist in the transition.

P'taah: In a way you may say this, but you see, there have
always been the people, the beings, to assist humanity.

Q: If one person wishes to manifest a place for their own
purpose and somebody else wishes to have the same
place for their own different purpose, what happens when
they are both in their own Divinity?

P'taah: They create something wonderful, beloved.
What else do you think would happen when two Divine
beings desire to create something? It is called wondrous co-creation.

Q: I don't quite mean that.

P'taah: I know you do not.

Q: When each has a different purpose, what takes place?

P'taah: But you see, that is the thought which says it can only be this or this. The truth is that there can be this and this and this in harmony, in love, in Divinity.

Q: So if one does not finish up with what they originally wanted, they are likely to finish up with something better?

P'taah: Dear one, it is always that whatever is occurring will be for one's benefit. What you are saying is regarding a judgment of better, best. Do you understand?

It need not be such. It is to know that whatever occurs in your life, you will create the opportunity for the greatest benefit to you. That is called soul integrity. However it occurs, you may profit without loss because loss indeed is a judgment.

Q: Or something not happening?

P'taah: That can be of wondrous benefit, dear one. All of it is that you may learn about judgment.

But you see, if you are in your Divinity, beloved, if you are that enlightened Master that you so yearn to be, then there will be no judgment and all will be created in the greatest possible harmony. A win-win situation. Indeed it is always a win-win situation, if only you would understand it to be so.

Q: P'taah, I thought you could talk a little bit about when we cease to dream, or when we give up the need to think that we are separate from God and separate from our brothers.

P'taah: You will never cease to dream because dreaming is merely a creative process. But when you come into the knowing that there is no separation of anything, then indeed you will change the universe.

You see, many of you certainly have that knowing for moments at a time. Grand times of illumination. You will notice that when the moments come again and again, they will last longer and longer, until indeed there will be no time when you will not know that you are truly God.

When that time comes, beloved one, your planet will reflect lights beyond imaginings, rainbow hues dancing like a fireworks display to light up the galaxies. The planet indeed will be a reflection of the God-I-Am.

Q: P'taah, last week I asked a question about the two hemispheres of the brain. I just want to ask, is it a definite fact that one particular hemisphere is the creative or female aspect?

P'taah: It is so. There are two separate hemispheres of your brain.

Q: But does it have to be that the right side is the creative side?

P'taah: That is how it occurs.

Q: In all cases?

P'taah: Indeed.

Q: Why can it not be different in certain cases?

P'taah: It is like saying why do you not have one ear on top of your head and the other on the sole of your foot. It is how you are programmed to re-create yourselves.

Q: Why I ask the question is that there are people who are left-handed and right-handed.

P'taah: Indeed.

Q: I have experienced situations which cause me to be-lieve that the hemispheres of my brain are reversed. Incidentally, I am left-handed as well. So could it be that the creative side of my brain is the left side?

P'taah: It is not really so much that the polarities are changed about physically. It is that you are expressing in this fashion. There are many humans who are left-handed, many families where everyone is left-handed. In fact there are whole communities where one is more dexterous with the left side of the body than the right.

However, beloved, more to the point is about how you will create the cease-fire in the war between that which is masculine and feminine within you. You see, you are only speaking about the physical body. We have said to you before that what drives the brain is your light-energy.

Q: Can you repeat that, please?

P'taah: What drives the brain is who you are, and who you are is not your brain. You understand that there is more to you than the brain. The soul energy, the light body, drives your body, your physical-ness.

In everybody there is a war between masculine and feminine and very often men have a great suppression of feminine energy, or negative energy, more of a non-allowance.

So the physical in this instance is not really of consider-ation. It is as if somebody has his heart placed on the opposite side of the physical body. There are many, of course, who are born thusly. They still function in their physical body, hmm? However opposite it is, what is occurring within themselves, within the isness of them-selves, is no different to anybody else.

What I am saying is no matter how it is within the physical body, it is your energy, your isness, we are con-cerned with. Whether you are born without limbs or with organs placed in a different manner than other people, the fact that you are in a body and functioning as a living, breathing human being means you have a heart and soul. You have two polarities of energy. All we are asking you to do is to allow the polarities to become one.

Q: I realize that, but I was led to believe that the creative, feminine side would be more receptive to abuse than the masculine side. I had an experience of a fellow abusing me. I had never experienced such verbal abuse in my life. He was blasting in my right ear and it went straight over the top. I deduced from that, it must have been the male side of the brain that rejected that. If it had been the female side, it would have absorbed it.

P'taah: That is not so, beloved. If it were so then there would not be many women alive on your planet.

It is called cutting off, dear one, simply cutting off. Indeed, there are women who cut off or else they would die, hmm? So it really does not matter whether it is women or men, because as we have said many times, humanity operates from masculine energy. It is called survival.

Q: You referred to the female energy as being negative.

P'taah: That is as we are speaking scientifically. It is only when you judge negative to be bad that people become upset. Negative energy depicts the receptive principle in your technology.

Q: How is it that negative energy can be creative?

P'taah: But you see, from the void of receptivity there comes all creativity. You judge negative to be a nothing. You judge it to be not so good. It is not so. That is called judgment. It is merely different. Do you understand?

Q: Yeah, I think I am learning a bit.

P'taah: You do.

Q: P'taah, I often experience flashes of light and some-times it stays there, although there is no light there to see with the physical eye. Can you explain what is actually occurring?

P'taah: Are you speaking, for instance, of when you are in bed with your eyes closed?

Q: No, just sometimes in my daily life, through the day.

P'taah: And there is no light?

Q: Not actually a lamp…they are just flashes. Sometimes it just stays there, like a reflection from a window and I can hold it there.

P'taah: Well, very often what you are seeing is a reflec-tion of energy, of light energy. All energy gives light, so what is very often occurring is that you are picking up on an energy concentration and you are seeing the light of it.
   It is the same when you are seeing people and you are seeing the light energy of them, the people. What you are seeing sometimes is what you would call light-beingness.

Q: Thank you.

Q: P'taah, talking about lights, I often see intensive points of lights, often whole groups of them and they float before they phase out.

P'taah: It is exactly the same.

Q: Mostly they are of either white or blue intensity.

P'taah: Indeed. You are just seeing energy.

Q: That reference to the lights, is that what one is physically seeing or is it like a visualization?

P'taah: It is what you call a physical appearance. You know energy is physical. You are just not seeing it expressed as matter, but it is expressing as light.

There are beings, consciousnesses, what we call light-beings, who do not have a physical embodiment but who are, nevertheless, aware-ized consciousness. Now, very often they are not perceived by humanity and very often they are.

Q: Is that different from light that one sees when one visualizes?

P'taah: Indeed it is. That is not to say that the light you see in a visualization is not real. Indeed it is real. It is merely a different realm of reality.

It is like looking at the physical matter of this chair. It is. If we remove the chair and place it away from your physical sight and I say to you, "Close your eyes" and you may see the chair. You see, it is still there in your reality. It is not less real. It is merely a different reality.

So it is that when we speak to you of many Earths occupying the same space. They are all real. In their own space-time they have their own solidity of matter. They are not in your focus and so for you, it is not real.

You see, dear one, it is in this cultural family of western thinking that anything that does not have matter is not real. Many of you are coming into the understanding that it is not so. Reality is much more wondrous than matter.

And so, beloveds, sufficient unto the time. It has been an interesting discussion for you this evening, and you have absorbed enough, hmm? We would not wish to think that we are putting our audience to sleep. Indeed, the minds of you all are very active at this moment, but enough is enough. We must save some of it for the next time, eh?

So it is with thanks and honor that we would leave you and to express indeed, as always, our joy to be with you.

So, go forth in great profit. It is called win-win, hmm? I love you all very much. Thank you and good evening.

▼ Sixth Session
January 22

P'taah: Good evening dear ones. It is very joyous that you are here with us. So we will call Open Forum.

Q: P'taah, back to manifesting things. I still have a little challenge with the underlying beliefs we have. I have straightened out my beliefs, but there is still something underneath which I do not know of. How can I find out?

P'taah: Dear one, you have named it before in your time. You have issued forth the words, "When I do not try it happens."

Q: When I do not try it happens?

P'taah: But you know it. In the last week we spoke to you about the concept of profit and loss and that it may be a profit/profit, a win/win situation.

Now, also when you speak about business you think about how hard you must work, how concentrated your effort must be, how you must strive—at least in your brain—to make it successful, to make this elusive thing called money. Is it not so?

Q: I found out I do not have to.

P'taah: Then why do you continue?

Q: I do like to have certain things.

P'taah: Indeed. But you see, you say that you have stopped the striving, but in your mind you are still striving. You do not know that as you have created the thought of abundance, so it is. You are still in the knowing that it is non-apparent.

You see, dear one, in all things that you desire, when you understand that you may manifest an immediacy merely by the knowing within you that it is so, then you will not be thinking of it in the future.

When you think of anything occurring in your future, it will always be in your future. That is when you say, "I have no money now, but when I am successful in business I will have money" or "I am not happy now, but when such-and-such occurs in my future I will be happy."

Q: I don't know how to get this understanding down into my soul.

P'taah: You may start, certainly, by minding your words. That is for all of you. Do not speak of how much money you do not have. Speak always in the knowing that what you desire of money is already on its way to you. It is not a future thing. It is already. It has merely not manifested itself in physical appearance, that is all.

As you have created the thought, so it is. Remind yourself that there is only now. There is no future. There is only now because it is of this now that you build your future.

Q: Does that mean that I do not have to try for anything? I do not have to do anything? Just allow and wait for something to happen?

P'taah: Indeed, but we would say that it is to show forth the intention that you know it already is, and that what you are doing is the joy of the heart, and in the knowing that the currency already is.

Now, showing forth the intent does not mean that you must strive—that is your terminology of striving. It is to show forth the intent that it already is. So if you have a business that is abundant, then you are in the day-to-day administration, not to make money, but merely to see to its continuance. Do you see the difference in the thought?

Q: If one has a business which is not successful and more money is needed, then what does one do?

P'taah: Continue exactly in the knowing. Dear one, the success of business is only dependent on how you are inside yourself. Everything outside yourself is merely a reflection of you. If you are in what you judge to be non-success, it is because you are judging yourself to be in non-success.

Now, there are many reasons why you may judge yourself to be a non-success and it is about things that we have spoken to you of before about your self-worth. Do you deserve to have the money? Do spiritual people show lack of spirituality by having money, etc., etc. So in this fashion you may come to the core belief of what it is, where you are with currency.

If you are perfectly clear that you are very deserving of much abundance and it is still not coming to you, then, dear one, look at what you are doing in terms of where your heart is. Because, if you are striving at something you do not like to do and you expect to make money, then truly you are not serving yourself very well.

Q: It surely must be that as we come more into the understanding of ourselves as the Divine One, as the I Am, we must surely therefore be worth the reflection ...

P'taah: Dear one, we will be very happy when you understand that you are indeed an expression of Divinity, that you indeed deserve everything.

Q: That must also extend to the question I asked last week regarding the ability to grow amputated limbs, etc.

P'taah: But of course. Everything.

Q: Obviously, I am free now or I never could be. I am Divine now or I never will be.

P'taah: Absolutely, and you know, dear ones, we will remind you that in this limited perception, there are times when you do indeed understand that you are expressions of Divinity, that you know within your breast that there is no separation. There are times of illumination where you truly do perceive that you are the God I Am. Then the moment passes and you are bereft of this understanding.

We would remind you that as you perceive each other, you are also perceiving the other person within the limitations of that perception. So when you are one to another perceiving the limitations of somebody else and knowing indeed that it is the reflection of your own limitation, it is to know that the God-light of somebody else is only viewed by you within these limitations.

That is all right, dear ones. It is not to judge yourself. It is not to compare who you are with somebody else, either in what you would regard as more enlightened or less enlightened, because within the limited perception of who you are, you truly have no idea.

Everybody has their own path. We have said to you before, the way to expanded consciousness is not necessarily what you would regard to be a spiritual path because most of you have what we would call heavy judgments about spiritual people and those who are not. So we would merely remind you of this.

Q: So what one is doing to another, one is first doing to oneself?

P'taah: Why do you think we say to you it is all a cocreation, with lessons to learn for each?

Q: The theory of evolution which is generally taught ...

P'taah: Are you speaking of the Darwinian theory of evolution?

Q: Yes, that humankind is descended from animals. There is a contrasting theory that says that the ape has derived from human activity in the past. Can you comment on this?

P'taah: The Darwinian theory of evolution is not correct. Man has not descended from the ape. Man is star seeded. Regarding that which is monkey, your primate. In the eons of time past—more years really than you may consider—there has been a similar genetic structure, but it is not correct to say that man was descended from the ape.

Q: The ape form was the result of the action of humanity at some time?

P'taah: It has certainly been the result of some genetic engineering, and it was the engineering of the star people, indeed.

Q: I have another question, changing the subject entirely. We don't really talk about the persona. We all operate from the persona in our waking hours, with all the inherited limitations and notions, the facade.

P'taah: But, dear one, in a way we do constantly refer to this. It is not, as we have said to you, to annihilate the ego. It is not to think of the personality self as something to overcome. It is not so. That which is the ego is there to serve you. The brain is there to serve you. The personality self is made up of what is called the tapping into the morphogenetic resonance, the collective consciousness of humanity.

It is most complex, but you see it is not to negate any of it. The polarity of complexity is merely that there is no separation. When you may allow your heart to be unshielded, when you may transmute your fears—and indeed it is the fears that keep the shield in place—then you will be operating from a different place.

However, the personality self is wondrous. It is what makes you individual, makes each one of you a facet of the wondrous jewel called humanity which is Divinity expressed in third density. It is not that you are to give up your personality self. It is merely the integration of all facets of who you are.

Q: To realize the integration of all facets of who we are would necessitate an overview. What I am talking about is a personality dogged by notions of self-importance.

P'taah: You are really speaking about the ego. It is helpful to have an overview, but we would say that those expressions of self-interest of what is deemed to be the ego are merely expressions of fear.

As far as that is concerned, it is most simple because you may take any area of your life which is not fulfilling, any area of your life where you are unhappy, non-functional, etc., etc., any area of your life which is the polarity of love, and know therein is fear. It is to recognize the fear and transmute it.

Q: P'taah, back to striving for abundance. Is it right that if we believe in our heart or mind that to get the abundance we have to work hard...?

P'taah: Absolutely, that is exactly what will occur, beloved, and it is not of the mind, you know, Knowing is not of the mind because you see, our beloved friend intellectually does know it very well, but that does not do it.

So it is the knowing of the heart, that is the absolute knowing within your cellular structure, that abundance may be yours without what you would call the work ethic which has been a part of your conditioning, and to know indeed that abundance is for every human being.

Q: Yes, that is right, but we all want a bit extra for ourselves don't we?

P'taah: Dear one, there is no limit, you know.

Q: I am just finding that out. I have carried out a few experiments, and I have found out it does, in fact, work.

P'taah: Indeed, do you think that we would lie to you, dear one? We are very even you know. We tell you that which is for your benefit, not to mislead you.

Q: P'taah, I love you. When I have contact with you, I fall in love with myself. Thank you.

P'taah: Beloved one, I love you and it is a joy to my heart that you understand what is called love for self because, in truth, that is why we are here, that every entity may come into the joy and acknowledgement of who they are.

Q: Good evening, P'taah. I have a problem with developing this love for myself, and maybe for others as well. How should I go about it, to make it grow, to understand this love for myself and others and everybody?

P'taah: Let us start off with you, hmm?

You know, love of self is really non-judgment of self and you may indeed monitor yourself in this area of judgment. When you find yourself in a thought which is limiting for yourself or in judgment and you catch yourself, you need only to remind yourself that the Source, the God/Goddess, All-That-Is is manifest in every particum.

Very often, you know, you do not catch yourself in time. That is all right. In these moments of self-judgment, or indeed judgments outside of yourself because it is the same, you need only to remind yourself that the Source, the God/Goddess, the All-That-Is, is manifest in every particum.

When you think of yourself, the persona that is you, remind yourself that there is not one part of you, not one facet, not one thought, not one action, which is not an expression of Divinity. In other words, it is allowable, else it would not be. When you may get used to this monitoring of your thoughts, so little by little, the thought becomes the reality. There will begin to be a reverberation of knowing within you that you are truly God, every part of you.

So it is not necessarily to try to make it a big hurdle for yourself. But just as a baby learns to walk, you may learn to acknowledge who you are without judgment. Each step of the way, beloved, you will find that you are supported. There is always assistance, always.

Q: So I should just accept and allow myself and everybody else?

P'taah: Indeed, beloved, and as you come into the allowance for yourself, you know the allowance will bring forth honor for self, will bring forth integrity for self. Then in the knowing of your own God-light, there will truly be love. Indeed, beloved, know you are worth loving.

Q: I sort of keep running myself down.

P'taah: I know. It is very easy. You are all programmed to do so because those people who live and were raised in this culture have been told that it is not a good thing to think well of oneself. It is called vanity. It is called self-aggrandizement, etc.

You know, your parents and their parents before have done a very good job, but it is all right. It is all choice, co-creation. As you know the separation, as you know the judgment, as you know the loathing of self, so you may come into the understanding of allowance and love.

Beloveds, it is not to worry too much about other people, because as you come into the allowing and loving of self, so it is broadcast to all and so it is reflected back to you, indeed.

Q: P'taah, you told us to make notes on our intuition as it happens. I have been doing that. In the last few weeks I have been responding to events just before they occur.

P'taah: Well, how extraordinary, dear one.

Q: It seems to be gathering momentum.

P'taah: It will. It is like every other facility. As you expand it and stretch it and grow into it, so it will expand and stretch and grow.

Q: It is quite stunning.

P'taah: Indeed, and that which you regard as paranormal, that which you regard as extrasensory perception, is really the birthright of each and every one of you.

Q: One day I thought I would ask something of somebody. Then I thought, "No, I will let them think of it," and she just turned around and said it.

P'taah: Indeed, but you know that all of you, whether or not you are conscious of it, have telepathic communication because it is the broadcasting of emotions as well as what you would call material thought forms.

Q: Feelings.

P'taah: Indeed, it is both. So we would say telempathic rather than telepathic. All of you operate in this way, one way or another. Just because you are not conscious of it does not mean that it does not happen. It certainly does, and there are many of your decisions and actions regarding other people which are really a result of that communication. So congratulations, beloved woman.

Q: Wonderful. Thank you, P'taah. It will continue?

P'taah: But of course. All of it will be on the increase and all of you will come into the knowing. All of you.

Very well, dear ones, it is time for a break that you may refresh yourselves. We ask that you create stillness within during this time of transition.

(After the break.)

Q: P'taah, after encountering the photon belt, what will be the effect on weather?

P'taah: It will be, in a fashion, as you know it now. There will be changes. There will be parts of the planet more affected than others. Super-consciousness will create complete change in your understanding of what you call weather. Your relationship with your planet will change.

As we have said, this is a time of transition. However, nothing is set in stone, dear one, even what we have called the timing of it all. So it is truly not to be too concerned with the phenomena of the changes within your weather patterning, and indeed with the changes of the Earth herself and what you regard as the stratosphere.

Q: Okay, in that case, rain-producing ground water will still be occurring, even though the atomic-structure will glow with its own light?

P'taah: Indeed.

Q: P'taah, in your perception, has the worldwide focus on the Harmonic Convergence changed any of the program that was in motion for what is happening world-wide?

P'taah: The focus, dear one, was really the focus of humanity coming together in consciousness to regard themselves as able to put forth the focus as a unified being, a beingness. Do you understand?

Now, the coming together at this time was certainly so that humanity may unite in the desire for harmony, for peace, and also to show forth intent in the Universe for what is to occur in probability. And this you have done.

But you know, it is not merely a one-shot affair. Each and every one of you are creating the new probabilities by each individual showing forth intent for communication for a shift in consciousness, for the understanding of the portals of communication to be aligned with the photon belt. So it is not that you have created this once and that is the end of it.

Many of the people of this planet who have taken part in this exercise do not understand what they are creating because they are locked into a limited box of perception of how it is and how it may be. Nevertheless, the desire of the heart and the showing forth of intent puts the probability on line. So in a way the answer is yes, but like everything else in your universe, it is not concrete. It is not limited.

Everything is of fluidity. Everything. Remind yourselves that as you regard it to be thus and thus and thus. It is truly not that but it is fluid, flowing, expanding, creating possibilities and probabilities into infinity.

You know, this is why we very often do not give you a yes/no answer. We understand that often you feel that we are being tricky or being particularly obtuse in our answers to you.

But really the answers are designed that you may come into the knowing of the fluidity of all things, including that which you regard to be solid, as your Earth, and particularly your own beingness. It is also fluid. It is also grandly expanding, shifting, changing, and moving.

You are not, as you very often regard yourselves to be, stuck in your body. In this you regard yourselves to be limited beings, and, as you would say, somewhat stuck in the mud.

Truly it is not so, and as you have more and more practice at this regarding yourselves, then indeed so you are coming into an allowance of the movement, of regarding yourselves as being far grander than that, and the limited perception you have—of being locked in your bodies—leaves you.

It also opens up the possibilities for you in changing what you regard to be physical disabilities, dis-easement within the body. Nothing needs to be set in stone. You may change everything. You have the power to change it all.

Q: Hi, P'taah. Oh gosh...well I was going to ask this question about what career I was going to go into. I was scared of making a mistake in choosing my subjects for the next two years at school, but listening to you speak about fluidity, I am not worried anymore.

P'taah: Indeed, dear one, and it is to know this—in truth it is impossible that you will make a wrong decision because there is no right or wrong.

Q: Before I came here this evening, I was speaking to my sister about this gathering. We were pretty freaked out about it. We are both Christians, and in the Bible it says that to deal in witchcraft is an abomination unto the Lord. Also we are not supposed to contact spirits from other worlds. Where does this fit into it?

P'taah: Very well. That is a very good question, you know. First, we would say this. That which is called Christian, is called follower of the teaching of Yeshwa Ben Joseph, the Christed One.

Now that which was Christ, indeed, said to the people to beware of false prophets. He also enabled his followers the knowledge of what is a false prophet. Do you know what it was that he said? He said that by their fruits ye shall know them.

Now, dear ones, we are not a prophet. We are not a holy being. And we are no more spirit than you are, because you see we are all spirit. That is what makes you human.

But you know, in all of your life, that is how you know what is harmonious and that which is not harmonious— by the fruits. And you know, beloved. You know the fruit. It is, "How do you feel?"

If you are with beings telling you to do something or to be something, and your own intuition and your own feeling says to you, "This is wrong. This is not for me," then, indeed, your integrity will say, "Turn away." But if indeed it is peace and harmony and it is love, then you may trust intuition.

We would also say this. That which were the words recorded by your Christed One are wondrous indeed, but it is to know that there have been many things recorded which have changed over the period of nearly 2,000 years that have nothing to do with Yeshwa Ben Joseph.

There are many things of Christ which are of Christus-consciousness, but you see, beloved, there is also that which is called religion. Religion is that which has en-slaved mankind and put humanity in chains. Indeed it has been co-creation, nevertheless, it has been based on fear. If you do not do what the church tells you, you will burn in hell.

But you see, there is no hell and there is no judgment and there is no God to say to you, "You have done wrong, therefore you will never go to heaven," because who you are is indeed part of God, and what is hell, is judgment of self. That is called fear.

Q: *(A very little boy about six years of age)* P'taah, you know everything, don't you?

P'taah: Well, not quite everything, but many, many things. Probably everything if we put our mind to it, just like you. Just like all of you, eh?

Q: *(The little boy's father)* This process of recognizing ourselves, learning to love ourselves, and knowing our God-Self, well what about the people around us? Are we to keep this a secret? The normal teachings from school and our parents teach us to be subservient, but if we reach the stage of being unlimited and know we are God, are we to keep this a secret?

P'taah: Beloved, it is impossible to keep it a secret, impossible because you become a radiant being. Every other of humanity is drawn to you and you will show by example of living how it is to be a God realized in man.

Q: So we do not have to tell people. They won't believe anyway.

P'taah: Dear one, if you are standing on the street corner telling people you are God, they will certainly take you away in what is called a coat with no arms, hmm? We are advocating sovereignty, not insanity.

Now we have always been saying it is not necessary to say anything, however we may guarantee that as you are coming more and more into your own knowing, and as you will speak forth your knowing of your universe and how reality operates, many people will want to know the why's and the how's of it.

There will also be those who will be frightened, who will not want to know, who will speak in derision about what you are speaking forth. However, the proof of the pudding is, 'by their fruits ye shall know them.'

The truth is that as you come into your own expansion, you will be as a prophet, and it will have nothing to do with what you will be saying. Those who are so busy trying to teach with words what they barely may truly perceive themselves is called blind leading the blind.

However, that is all right, you know, because it is like bouncing off a sounding board, that you may communicate and commune with your friends and colleagues, that you may illuminate each other's minds. So that is all right. Do you understand? We are not saying that you must not speak. What we are saying is that if you do not feel to speak, it is not necessary.

Q: In other words, other people are made aware of it by example?

P'taah: By your being, merely by your being.

You know how it is, dear ones. When you are moving into a room of people and there is one there who seems to shine more than anybody else, then sometimes there is a wondrous feeling of serenity, of harmony, of happiness and joy, of laughter, and you are immediately drawn, indeed?

And that is how it is. When somebody seems to be of joyful resonance, you want to know how and why. What is the secret? So that is what I call example—by being in every now moment, however it is.

Q: That is not to say that if we have learned by our own experiences that we should not pass that knowledge on to others?

P'taah: But, dear one, it is as I have said to you. It is wondrous that you become a sounding board that you may help others. It is wondrous. It is just that we do not wish you to feel that you must go and shout about it against your judgment.

Q: What if they do not believe you?

P'taah: Dear one, you are not responsible for how anybody else thinks. It is up to everybody. It is choice. If they do not believe you, it is quite valid. It is not their truth at that time.

Q: P'taah, we were speaking about intuition before. May I ask you about *déjà vu*? Whenever it happens to me, it leaves me in a state of confusion because it is impossible to explain how it functions.

P'taah: Indeed, you may say it is embracing the future into the now moment, that is all.

Q: But this experience makes me believe that certain circumstances and actions have happened before and I am re-experiencing it right now again.

P'taah: In truth, beloved, you may remind yourself that all of it is occurring at the same time. You are merely tapping into the probability of the next now moment, so it is as if you were experiencing past, present, and future all at once.

Q: It is almost frightening.

P'taah: But it is truly wonderful. You need not be frightened. It is merely that you have had a forward thinking, in your terms. It is that you are doing something and you think, "Now just one moment. I have already done it," and you may do it more if you desire to.

You know, in a way, you may liken it unto past life regressions, the same as when you are putting yourself into a state of altered consciousness to experience a past life. Well, you know, you may do it for lives in your future. Do you understand?

Q: Not quite.

P'taah: You perceive time in a linear fashion. Time is truly not linear. You may imagine a roll of film in a box and when you look there are many separate frames. When you look at it in this fashion, in a roll, it is easy to see there are separate frames. However, if you want to understand the continuity of it you must roll it through the projector.

So you may say that your mind is the projector and that whether you view the frames as lifetimes or moments of your life, you may, at any time, look at any frame and you will get a picture. However, to get continuity you must run it from the beginning to the end. But in truth, it is already there.

Now, to make this more fluid for you, we must also say to you that there are also probable realities. It is not truly cast in stone. There are many variables and you choose moment-by-moment which option you wish. Many of those choices are not conscious choices. Many of those choices come from the greater part of your soul energy, to bring forth what shall be of greatest benefit to you, whether or not you judge it to be bad or good.

However, the seeing of your future is seeing a probable reality. It does not necessarily make it so in this focus of your third dimensional reality. That is not quite the same as *déjà vu*, but we are saying it is part of the same. Do not think for one moment that it is cast in stone. It is not.

Q: P'taah, if our whole future is fluid, not cast in stone, it is true that our past is exactly the same and it is not cast in stone either?

P'taah: Absolutely.

Q: So it is all fluid and can be changed, like a piece of clay?

P'taah: Absolutely. You change your past by your perception of it. Indeed that which you call your reality at this moment is only a perception.

For instance, we will speak about historical writing. If you have one event which has been a worldwide event and many people write about their own experience of this event, then each experience is valid, is their reality. Yet one may have nothing to do with the other and may be diametrically opposed, not only in physical reality, but in ideology, culpability, etc.— each believing their own story is the truth. Do you understand?

So it is in your own life. For instance, there will be people who will talk about their idyllic childhood, how wondrous it was, and truly it is for them because they have changed what has been trauma, agony and tragedy because it is too painful to bear.

Now the idyllic childhood they have created is no less real because it did not actually occur in this fashion. Do you understand? So, you may say that your perceptions absolutely change your reality.

Q: When you speak about perception, is it the same as consciousness?

P'taah: Indeed.

Q: So when I change my consciousness...

P'taah: ...You change your reality, absolutely. And you know, whatever you perceive, even if you are not directly involved with it, it is a part of who you are, else it would not be within your perception.

When you think about war in which some people have had physical participation, there will be other people in other countries who do not have that physical participation. Nevertheless, it is part of their own consciousness, and in this fashion it is part of their own experience. It is different, but it is valid. It is their story.

Q: So that means even in our lives, right now, if we make an effort to see things from different angles as much as possible, we will have a better view and understanding. So our reality changes.

P'taah: But of course. You know, you can liken it to two children. One goes to school and learns to read and write and one child does not. The one who learns to read will have a broader perception about reality with an infusion of different ideas, whereas the child who has not been to school may have a more limited view of his world.

That is not to say that it is invalid because, in truth, the true perception lies within the heart and has nothing to do with the brain.

There have been wondrous masters upon your planet who have been very simple—women and men, particularly women. You know there have been many wondrous prophets who were women, but indeed their spheres of influence have been very different and not allowable in a male-oriented society. Men have been used to an authoritarian figure, a man, not in every society but in many, certainly those ones who have shaped your own cultural present.

But many of these women, and we speak particularly of the unsung heroines, did not have a public life at all. They were very much involved with what would be termed a simple life with a family, with knowledge of plants and herbs of healing, of tapping into a grander consciousness and of knowing exactly that they were of Goddess energy.

Many of these women were annihilated in fear, as were many other of your grand beings, unsung, we may say. But it is not that these people had great learning in the accepted sense of your world.

It is all valid, and we have said to you earlier, it is not to judge how anybody else is playing their game of life.

Q: P'taah, could you talk a little bit about the sun? I feel the sun is very hot recently and many people are getting burned. I feel that if we could align ourselves with the sun, we would not get hurt by it. Is it so?

P'taah: It is so.

Q: How do we do that? How does one align with the sun?

P'taah: How do you align with anything, dear one?

Q: Can you tell us?

P'taah: It is to know that it is all right. Know that nothing can harm you. Know that you live in a safe universe. Know that the sun is Divine positive energy. Without it, you would not have a world that you understand. Know that you are God, beloved. Simple, hmm?

Q: I knew, but I forgot.

Q: P'taah, if I need to talk to someone to gain some peace for myself, and in the past there has been some negativity, how can I prepare the conference room, so to speak, in myself and the other person so that there can be real communication?

P'taah: Very well. Now we would say that what you are anticipating is confrontation, not communication. Whenever you are desiring communication, it is to be tranquil within yourself, in that you are understanding who you are and recognizing who the other person is, and to show forth love.

That is all that is required. To be in allowance of the other person being who they are. In other words, if you are open, the other person may also be open.

Q: So the negativity I have been feeling in the past has been coming just as much from me as from them? Is that what you are implying?

P'taah: Indeed, but, dear one, it is not necessarily so. If somebody is very closed and you are feeling very open, you may assist them to be open also. You may say exactly how you feel about this. You may say, "I love you and wish to have a communication with you. Are you happy to have this communication?" You may speak from the heart—indeed, you will be very surprised—and you may say, "I am also afraid of what it will be if we do not communicate". You may tell of your fear, and as you are open enough to be vulnerable, you are in a position of great power.

Q: How so?

P'taah: Dear one, vulnerability is certainly the most powerful position in your universe because nothing can harm you. It is grand dichotomy, indeed.

Q: So by completely exposing myself...

P'taah: Exactly. By completely exposing who you are. It is called an act of faith, dear one. It is very difficult for humanity to do this, to say, "This is who I am," because all of you are terrified that if you show who you are, somebody will not love you and the pain will be so great, you will die.

But you see, when you truly show who you are, you are irresistible. To be vulnerable in this fashion is what is called loving who you are.

Q: I do not know if I am mature enough to handle love coming from all these different directions and not to let it be too special on a personal basis. Does this make sense?

P'taah: It does, indeed, make sense. But you see, beloved, if you are in love and harmony within yourself, it will not be a problem. It is that you cannot even handle being in love with yourself, let alone anyone else being in love with you, hmm?

You may rest easy, beloved. We have not heard of anybody dying from too much love.

Q: So I should really get all this straight now so I can plan the conference, shouldn't I?

P'taah: Indeed, to decide what it is that you desire in your heart. That is all. Nothing else.

Q: And also be accepting if it does not work this time?

P'taah: Absolutely. Desire without expectation of the outcome. To know that whatever the outcome is, it is a jewel for you brought forth by your own soul that you may come into greater expansion, greater awareness, greater wisdom. That you may come into the knowing of the judgment that has created it. Very good, dear one. It is very good.

Q: Hello, P'taah. I have heard a tape about Yeshwa Ben Joseph and I may have misunderstood it, but it said that it was not Yeshwa who was crucified. Could you enlighten me about that?

P'taah: It is so.

Q: That he was not crucified?

P'taah: Well, dear one, does it matter?

Q: No. It is just a matter of interest.

P'taah: It is a matter of great interest because that which you regard to be Yeshwa Ben Joseph has nothing to do with the idea-construct of the reality of this moment, which are millions and millions of followers of this being over 2,000 years of your time, more or less.

We will say this to you. Yeshwa Ben Joseph did indeed move across the civilized world of the time. He did not end his days at the physical age of 33 years. But you see, if there had not been the story of the crucifixion and Christ dying for your sins, there could have been no enslavement because your Christian religion is based on death. Yeshwa Ben Joseph taught about life.

Q: P'taah, how did the story get so mixed up? Was it mankind wishing to enslave mankind?

P'taah: But of course, dear one. It was a power play. It was not about spirituality, but often about the material possession of a country, about great wealth, etc.

Now, it has been a tool of great enslavement, but know that it was a co-creation. Nobody is to blame. In this day of your time the churches are great power brokers. As each and every one of you come into your own sovereignty, so you have chosen. There will be no enslavement. What has been done is valid, and from this comes great wisdom for humanity, you see?

Q: P'taah, is Yeshwa Ben Joseph still around this planet, giving us love and light?

P'taah: Dear one, but of course. He is one of many of what you may call the energy of light beings. Physical embodiment is only a facet. Within each and every one of you is Yeshwa Ben Joseph. Why is it, do you think, I say to you that you are coming into Christ-consciousness? You are already there, in truth.

Q: P'taah, one more question: The sun is divine expression. Do light beings live on the sun, or in the sun itself?

P'taah: Indeed, part of the sun. It is so. But it is not in the sun of your understanding. This is where explanation becomes difficult for me because we are trying to convey an idea on many levels of awareness.

There is that which is the physical sun in your understanding. It is rather like trying to explain the beings of your Inner Earth. In your scientific understanding, it is impossible. If scientists put a probe into the Earth they will say, "It is not possible."

Your scientists would say it is impossible for there to be life on your sun, and yet the sun is resonant to divine beings of such a high frequency—and these terms do not truly describe it—that you may rather say they are a resonance.

So it is not to say there are beings living within the sun, as you understand it, but rather there are beings who resonate with the sun and inhabit the sun and all of the galaxies.

Q: Are light rays actually light beings, part of the mind of God? Do they have consciousness?

P'taah: Dear one, everything has consciousness. But that which you would call light beings, you may say is a concentration of energy of itself, but also of everything else. You cannot limit it to one thing. You are in the habit of this. You are part of light being-ness. It is merely a higher frequency, and higher and higher. It is infinite.

Q: I have to think about this, I guess.

P'taah: Do not do any thinking about this, beloved. Do some feeling about this, that you may understand that you are also a part of this light-beingness. There is nothing, in truth, that you are not a part of and there is nothing that is not God. The more you think, the more you limit it, and what you are not, is limitation. What you are is God/ Goddess expressing as mankind, as humanity, and what you are is awesome.

Now, beloved ones, sufficient unto the time of this evening. Go forth in joy, dear ones. Switch off the brain, switch on the heart, and go forth in laughter, that the resonance may be the aligner for you and may align you with your planet and everything upon and within the planet.

Go forth in love, and know that whether you know it or not, you are certainly love expressed. Nothing to do, dear ones, only to be in each now moment in the fullness, that is all. Then truly you shall know riches beyond compare.

So, beloveds of my heart, we are already in anticipation of seeing you again soon. Good evening.

▼ Seventh Session
January 29

P'taah: So, in our usual fashion, we will be very happy to have query from you.

Q: P'taah, could you tell me how various foods affect us differently? For example, herbal tea may relax us, mushrooms may give us hallucinations, or sugar may give us an adrenaline rush.

P'taah: Much of it, of course, is according to your belief structure. As it is, there is a certain sensitivity within the body which is relating to emotional repression or emotional dis-easement.

As always, whatever the dis-easement is emotionally, it is recorded within the body. Different people will have different ways to express that dis-easement. For some it is an allergy. For others it would be a mutation of cells, etc.

The properties within the food, for example in mushrooms, or the inhalation of marijuana or other natural substances which create a different state of consciousness, are all there for however you desire to utilize them. You wish for more information?

Q: Yes. I was thinking more in terms of where we might feel sick or come out with a rash after eating a certain berry or brushing up against a certain plant. Why would the body have that reaction if we were not aware of the consequences before we ate the berries?

P'taah: Ah, but you see, dear one, the properties of the plant have nothing to do with the fact that you have attracted it. It is that you are attracting something to look at. However, dear ones, we will say to you always, it does not have to be that difficult.

Q: Greetings, P'taah. Yesterday I was watching a flock of lorikeets[1] flying and moving with absolute synchronicity and that is all well to understand, but what happened— and this may sound funny—is that they all pooped at the same time. I was wondering what kind of consciousness it is and how we can tap into that consciousness which is in a harmonious flow and motion with everything, with a complete understanding of each other.

P'taah: Well, dear one, you have put yourself in contact with such in your observation. Human consciousness works in the same way, but you are normally not aware of it. If you were to have an overview, you would see how the core belief about your reality creates a mode of behaviour where everybody re-acts in the same way, that is for those who are tapping into that consciousness.

Now with an overview, you may perceive that there is an ebb and flow within the consciousness, and indeed the movement of humanity may be likened unto a school of fish or flock of birds. Merely the desire to come into this perception will heighten your awareness.

Q: So it is just to allow whichever energy comes to me, whether it is good or bad?

P'taah: Energy is energy, beloved. It is only judgment which says it is good or bad. It is all merely energy.

Q: I have friends in the animal liberation movement who say that violence is justified to free imprisoned animals, also to free people.

P'taah: Use of violence is valid, but it is not the optimum. There is always another way. It is certain that cruelty to animals is co-created so that humanity may come into

---

[1] An Australian parrot.

compassion. In this fashion people are touched in the heart more than if it were humans who are ill treated.

It is quite common that people who would normally be non-violent become raised to such a pitch that there is much violence within the heart where animals are concerned. If everybody would understand that it is a co-creation and why, then there would be the understanding and knowing that it need not be violent.

In every moment, beloved one, there is a choice of how you perceive and how you react to the emotion. Of course, on one level you may say it is never necessary. It is not desired.

When you are saying on one hand that what humanity desires is peace and harmony, to give forth love to all, then it is not to such an end that one would employ violence for anything. However, beloved, it is valid because it is. In the is-ness it would not occur if it was not valid.

Q: P'taah, in the last session you mentioned that Yeshwa was not crucified. Jani was under the impression that you had stated at some other time that he was. Could we have a clear answer if Yeshwa was physically crucified or not, please?

P'taah: A yes-no answer? Well, I will certainly tell you this, and then we will get into a grand discussion.

You see, dear one, it is called will the real Yeshwa Ben Joseph please stand up? The idea-construct—that which you, as the humanity of Christian culture, have created as Yeshwa Ben Joseph who was crucified for the sins of humanity—is real, dear one. That is real.

Let there be no mistake about it. That which you have created within the collective consciousness of humanity is a reality, and what has occurred over these hundreds of years has created it larger and more defined than was the original because of the energy that was put forth in this fashion.

Now, Yeshwa Ben Joseph, the man, has been put onto the cross. He was not annihilated by this. We are speaking of what humanity imagines came after—there was death, resurrection, and ascension. There was also the return.

There are many myths about the life of Yeshwa Ben Joseph. We would say to you that he was a very happily married man with a family. In truth, he had quite a normal sort of life in the fashion of his day.

The mother of Yeshwa Ben Joseph was a normal woman of her time, one who was very gifted, one who was quite famous within her own community. She would have been very surprised at how she has become Isis, hmm? And the man Yeshwa Ben Joseph would probably be very appalled to know what has occurred in these centuries with the perversion of everything that he imparted to humanity.

However, beloved ones, it is all a co-creation, you see. The bottom line is it does not matter. There are many stories. Each one is valid. Each one has its own reality. But you see, the greatest reality of all is the myth that humanity has created. It is concrete. Very much larger than the event itself.

Q: Thank you. I am very aware that knowing the historical facts does not bring us one iota closer to the God within, but we are conditioned through our entire lifetime with a certain truth...

P'taah: We are in understanding of your desire to have the knowing of the validity of what we speak forth to you, and that is all right. That, dear one, is called discernment, indeed.

Q: What was the nature of the star which guided the three wise men?

P'taah: It was not a star. It was a ship. The name Bethlehem is the name of the craft.

(The man continues to question P'taah about historical events concerning the biblical timeframe.)

P'taah: ...You are presuming that history all started with your own book[2]. It did not. There is more of the pre-history before this recorded time than in any time since.

Biblical history was only of one small civilization. There were grand civilizations on your other continents, far older than this. Your mind is set in this block of history because it has been your cultural heritage. It is time to stretch from this heritage.

Q: Can you explain to me the process of speaking in tongues?

P'taah: I do not have any idea. It always seemed quite extraordinary to me.

Q: To me, too.

P'taah: Dear one, I am teasing you in a way. Whatever is, is valid. If it feels good, do it. If it does not, do it not. It is as simple as that. It is not that one has to lie on the floor and speak in tongues, but it is as valid as being in your garden.

As you are in your garden, you are certainly experiencing God. If somebody wishes to make a dogma of gardening, then it is as valid as making a dogma of speaking in tongues or not eating meat on Friday or to confess all of your sins to some man who is your intermediary with God. All is valid however it is.

Q: Greetings, P'taah. I am in a fury at the moment. I thought that I had cleared it only to find that the mention tonight about the Christians brings on fury.

---

[2]   The bible

P'taah: But of course, dear one. It is igniting memory, hmm? And it is of this lifetime also.

Q: It feels as if it is all happening simultaneously. I cannot get beyond the fury to whatever the pain is behind it.

P'taah: That is all right. There are many who feel this fury at the injustice, the enslaving, and what is called, "Look what those bastards have done to me," hmm? Why is it you have created it in the first place?

Q: To feel the feeling.

P'taah: Indeed. To know the dichotomy called separation and unity. We have spoken to you about forgiveness. When there is not blame, when you take responsibility knowing that you have created it for the wisdom, then the fury, the anger, the pain beneath may be embraced and allowed. Indeed, you will know that it is what has brought you here. Do not judge yourself for not transmuting it all at once.

Q: In terms of judging who we are, I have done some affirmations for my daughter who has great judgments of who she is. She asked me to put affirmations on a tape and felt it may be of assistance to her. I really want these affirmations to work for her. I still feel great guilt and pain regarding her. Can you talk about affirmations and how they take us through the beliefs about ourselves?

P'taah: Dear one, we understand. Many people regard affirmations to be a magic wand. It may certainly be so. If you desire to work with affirmations, you may find that the repetition may ease the way into the knowing. That as you become more and more familiar with an idea, then it becomes part of your belief structure. So in this fashion it can be very supportive. Whatever it is that creates support

for you is wondrous. If it is comfortable for you, then do it.
So it is all right. Indeed.

Q: *(Coughing)* My question relates to this cough, and it is
probably a silly little question. I do believe that as we are
in our mind, it will show outside, in our body. I have had
this persistent little cough for weeks and I feel it is trying
to shake me around to say, "Hey, look at something or do
something or say something," but I am not sure how to
pinpoint it or what I should be acting on.

P'taah: It is to voice what it is that disturbs you.

Q: All the things that disturb me?

P'taah: Where you would deem it to be appropriate, beloved.

Q: So until I deal with it, the cough will persist? Or if I
think it will, it will persist?

P'taah: Very probably. It is you who create your reality,
beloved, not I. It is merely a suggestion for you.

Q: If I were to feel there was nothing to come to grips
with or to work out, then the need for the cough would
disappear, would it not?

P'taah: Indeed. Merely have a play with it, hmm? You
may ask yourself what area in your life you would really
like to bring forth.

Q: Is there anything behind the fact that I can go for five
or six hours on my own without coughing, but the minute
the phone rings or people knock at the door, the contact
with another person starts off the cough?

P'taah: What does that tell you?

Q: That I don't want to communicate?

P'taah: Exactly. That you feel obligated to be with people, to communicate. And when you are with them, you are perhaps not speaking forth as you may, even if it is to tell them to get the hell out, hmm?

Q: Should I possibly need to be alone for a while?

P'taah: Very possibly, beloved.

Q: I have a friend who is a clairvoyant who has interesting things to say about the future. I know this is valid because she believes in it. If I give it power then it will also be valid for me, but how much power can you give to these things?

P'taah: As much as you want, beloved. You see, a clairvoyant is somebody looking into a probable future. Now, you may change it. Very often when you are with a clairvoyant and they are telling you something which is very beautiful, you do not want to change it. Indeed you are very happy to give power to this thought.

That is all right dear one. If it is a beautiful thing, you may indeed give it power, but it is also that it may not be exact. That is why many scientific people will tell you it is not valid. They will say this and this did not happen, although it was predicted. We would only wish you to be aware that it is a probable reality, so you may change it according to your decision at any choice-point.

Now you see, if you had not seen the clairvoyant and had no idea what is mapped out for you, it is still you who makes each choice. You would ask, "Is it still a probable reality?" Do you understand?

All through your life from your childhood when you begin to make decisions based on an emotional desire, re-action, etc., you make a choice of one situation as opposed to another. While you have given focus and thought and desire to the other choice, you have given it its own reality, which is as real, as valid as the one you are focusing on. So by the time you have reached maturity, there are many probable realities, each as real as this one.

So it is merely that somebody may tap into a future probability and then you may choose. If it is something dire, you may indeed not choose that reality but desire something quite different.

Q: It is amazing that she can see into the past when she would have no way of knowing.

P'taah: Dear one, it is no different. It is all occurring at the same time. It is all there.

Q: If I understand you correctly, we have chosen to come on this Earth at this particular time, or many times over, to have different experiences.

P'taah: That is correct.

Q: So we choose the things that happen to us in this life?

P'taah: You do.

Q: So if I choose to be born a cripple, I am born as a cripple.

P'taah: Indeed. For the experience.

Q: So if I get fed up with one experience and I want to change it, I can, can't I?

P'taah: But of course.

Q: How? By desiring it?

P'taah: By knowing that you may.

Q: If I am ill, I can change it by using my brain, by doing certain things?

P'taah: It is to know what caused the diseasement in the first place.

Q: Which can be physical or emotional?

P'taah: Dear one, it is only emotional. We are not speaking here about choosing, before birth, to have a body which is dysfunctional. We are speaking of diseasement created in the body during your life. It is always emotion which creates this because everything is a reflection. The body is merely reflecting what is in the energy of the person.

Q: So I can change the illness by changing the emotions?

P'taah: It is to embrace that which is creating the pain.

Q: Loving it.

P'taah: But of course. And it is to love the dis-ease as well. And you may do this when you are in understanding that you have created it all to come into non-separation, to come into the knowing of who you are. Knowing, loving, being, so that whatever it is in your life which is not harmonious, you may change to harmony, to light, to live within the God-light.

Q: So to accept and love, in spite of everything else.

P'taah: Indeed. But it is to love self—all of it. Dis-ease-ment is created out of lack of love of self, because if you were in love of self, then the body would be in wondrous peace and harmony.

We would ask that you hold your questions and we will take a break. Our thanks, dear ones, and we will return very soon to you.

(After the intermission.)

Q: How can I get out of the circle of my life? I feel trapped. I have no motivation, only frustration. How can I truly find myself?

P'taah: Indeed, dear one. Now, first we would give you an exercise. It is for all of you when you are feeling in this fashion. It is to say in the morning when you awake, "What is it that I desire for this day? What is it that will bring me joy?"

You know, dear ones, even if what you desire seems totally impossible for you, acknowledge what it is. You may say to yourself, "I desire to go forth and do that which makes my heart sing." Do you understand? It is called acknowledging that it is you who has power to create whatever it is that you want.

Now, you may say, "I desire from the God/Goddess of my beingness to bring forth joy, to bring forth love, and I understand that I, indeed, am the central sun of my universe. I may have whatever I desire."

You need listen to nobody but you for you have all the answers within. When you ask other people, know that they are usually as confused as you. You have every answer within you, and indeed, beloved, fear is valid.

You have created yourself at this time that you may come to know how you may embrace the polarities of fear and love, to know non-separation of self from Self. In this fashion you will come to love and honor who you are.

When you are brushing your hair in front of the mirror, look into your own eyes and know that you are looking into the eyes of the God/Goddess, the All-That-Is, expressing in third density.

Dear one, you have created yourself here. It is you who have done it, for the experience, and you may choose however it is you want the experience to be. You are very powerful. Humans do not understand their own power.

Know that when you are feeling power-less, you are merely experiencing a polarity. Where one exists, so does the other. It is not to judge it. It is to embrace it.

As you fear, you may imagine that the fear itself is like the child you are within. You may hold the child, soothe it, comfort it, and say, "It is all right. I will never allow you to be alone. I love you." This way the fear is embraced and is changed to love. In this love you will know the power. Is this helpful to you, dear one?

Q: P'taah, is eating processed and man-made synthetic food as valid as eating natural food?

P'taah: Dear one, it is as valid.

Q: I do not understand how it can be equal.

P'taah: I did not say equal. I said valid. Now certainly you may be sensible about what you put into your body, hmm?

There is that which you have co-created with your mother the Earth. Bountiful nature that is here to support and nurture you. So indeed it is to offer love and thanks for all that which you ingest. It is to have natural food where possible, and that which is pleasing to the eye and pleasing to the senses, but really, it does not matter.

Now, we will explain this further to you. The truth is you do not really need food for your existence, but you believe that you do, and so indeed you die if you do not eat. But as we have said before to you, there are those among humanity who are indeed aligned in the knowing that what sustains the body is the God-light, the light-beingness of you.

It is truly not necessary that you ingest material. To eat is very pleasurable for most people. Food, the color, the smell, the flavor, is an art form. Is it not so, dear one?

So, enjoy your art form. Enjoy your food. It is wonder-ful. You certainly have a belief structure about what will affect and what will not affect your body in such and such a manner, and of course as you believe it, so it is.

Q: If one is aligned, in balance, would one feel the effect of drugs such as marijuana or mushrooms?

P'taah: Indeed, there would be no adverse effect. Now there are certainly physical results from many of your chemicals. Much of that depends on the why of it. For many people drugs are a form of escape, for some will do anything to escape the pain of their life. For some, it is for the thrill of it, a sense of curiosity, and that is all right.

Then there are people who will use drugs for what they believe is mind expansion, to be on the spiritual path. Well, we will say there is no shortcut. It is perfectly valid. There is no judgment, but we would say it is sensible to exercise discernment. It is not that you will become enlightened masters when you are taking drugs. Where it is physically detrimental, then it is sensible that you do not do it.

Q: In the last months I have found myself to be very sensitive to noise. Is that a normal thing?

P'taah: It is what you might call a by-product of fine-tuning. When you come to have heightened perception, then you may find loud noises discordant to you. That is all right. When you make it not all right, then you will find you become more sensitive and it will become very aggravating for you.

Very often you will find that you develop areas of sensitivity in your body, also allergies, etc. It is merely that as you are coming into an understanding of how you operate within your universe, you will create situations faster and faster to embrace.

Q: Sounds wonderful.

P'taah: You do not think it so wonderful at the time, but I assure you, it is all right eventually.

Q: P'taah, is there a multi-dimensional doorway[3] on this continent?

P'taah: Indeed there is.

Q: Where are the doorways?

P'taah: There are new doorways. They are really an expansion of what is already in existence. But you know the energies change and shift, and it is not what you would call a geographic location.

What will occur is that the doorways become broader and broader in these next years of your time, so this expansion will become faster also. It is part of the change. As the electromagnetic energy of the Earth is changing, so the portals change. In a way it is a vortex of electromagnetic energy.

Q: I look outside myself and everything seems calm, even my cat, but inside I am really prickly. I do not seem to have any judgment about the person I am looking at when I get this reaction.

P'taah: Are you sure about that, dear one? You know it does not have to show itself outside when you know perfectly well inside of yourself how it is. Hmm? The judgment outside is really a reflection to show you how it is inside. When you know, you do not need the reflection, and I think you know very well how it is within you.

Q: Yes, I have done the compromise to allow.

---

3 An etheric energy gate or portal.

P'taah: Dear one, it is not the compromise and allowance outside. It is the allowance inside. It does not have to be a compromise, you know. Compromising is always to give your power away. You do not have to compromise. However, if it is your desire to keep the peace, you know it is always your choice. If you cannot enjoy it as it is, then change it.

Q: Were the Australian aboriginals star-seeded?

P'taah: But of course, dear one. The aboriginals do have mythology relating to their connection with the star people. However, like most of the truths which have become mythology, it has become so disguised that the fact of the matter merely becomes another beautiful story.

Humanity was star-seeded and there has been much genetic engineering in the eons before your time. There have been changes and much coming and going which has resulted in the beautiful stories that you have of the gods and goddesses.

It is also that remnants of the civilizations before your history are not in evidence. However, that will change because what will occur in the time to come is that some of the artifacts of these civilizations will come to light. Then your scientists will very quickly do an about-face.

Q: Can you tell us about the aboriginal Rainbow Serpent?

P'taah: It is symbolic of the early understanding of the aboriginal people of energy as a tangible. In the early memories of this race, they were able to manipulate energy in a fashion that humanity has forgotten—to manifest matter from energy and to put forth energy in a tangible form. From this the lovely story has risen.

There are many levels of the Rainbow Serpent. It is also representative of the layers of density created in colour. It is that humanity lives in multi-dimensions at the same time. In this understanding of energy, in creating energy, it is tapping into the multi-dimensionality of humanity.

Q: How long ago was the ability by the aborigines to create matter from energy lost?

P'taah: About the same time as the rest of humanity on your planet, dear one. But there are, of course, people who have a natural ability to do this now, people who are named masters.

Really it is a wondrous teaching. It is by example, to show people it is a possibility about your own power. Indeed, it is the knowing within that all is possible, that you, indeed, create everything, and you may in an instant create matter, move matter, merely by the thought. There are many of your people who know how to do telekinesis, to move objects without touching them physically.

So there are many things which you all have facility for. It is as we were speaking about extrasensory perception and what is called paranormal in our last gathering. It is for you to come into an understanding that it is quite normal. These abilities will become more and more wide-spread. As you become increasingly aware of your own possibilities, so you will develop your own abilities.

Q: I saw on a TV documentary what appear to be ruined abandoned cities in the north of Australia. Can you tell me what period of time were these cities inhabited?

P'taah: We are speaking about the time of Lemuria, dear one.

Q: Many years ago I was initiated into a method of Balinese self-defense. If someone tried to attack me, I would say certain words and make certain gestures and the attacker, leaping through the air at me would seem as if he had hit a wall of energy and fall on the ground without actually touching me. Can you tell me how this is done?

P'taah: Dear one, it is exactly as humanity may walk on fire and not be burned. It comes from knowing that it will be so.

Q: From inside, you mean?

P'taah: But of course, beloved. It is just the knowing. That is how you do everything. That is how you create your day-to-day existence, by the knowing. Now your body has the knowing within each cell, cellular integrity, and so it is within you.

Q: That really gives us incredible potential in a short space of time.

P'taah: Ah, beloved man, your potential is undreamed of by the humanity of this time. Who you are is limitless, wondrous, powerful people...powerful. It is within these exercises of doing what seems to be logically impossible that you show yourself time and time again that you are not limited beings.

(A man questions P'taah about certain hieroglyphic symbols found in Australia.)

P'taah: Indeed, they are the exact same as you would find in the pyramids of Egypt.

You know, in your pre-history there was a great exchange of knowledge among people from one area of the world to the other. Australia in those terms was very close to the continent of Lemuria and there were land bridges connecting all the continents of your planet. There was also travel by craft from one planet to another, a method of transport which will come again. Hieroglyphics also come from the star people.

This area of your country was indeed a seat of power and a seat of great learning. People would come to this place, as they went to Egypt, for great schools of learning. There are a few artifacts left not uncovered as yet, and when they will be uncovered, it will be a great puzzle to your scientists.

Q: Getting back to the aboriginals creating matter from energy. Why did they lose this power?

P'taah: Not only the aboriginals, but all of humanity understood this. Humanity has simply forgotten. In a way it was also a choice to come into a different experience, to come into separation to understand non-separation. The knowledge was long gone before Europeans came to your continent.

It is the same with the shaman magic and knowledge of the Native Americans. It was once common knowledge. It is no longer, although there is much effort being made to restore the knowledge. It is the same with the druids and many of the old orders of learning. The knowledge is no longer there. You see, it is always such when knowledge is held secret, withheld as a power tool, as a means for enslavement. Then indeed it will be lost.

It is occurring now on your planet with governments. Where there is non-appropriate use of power and knowledge, it will cease to exist because it is not of harmony, not for universal benefit.

In the days gone by, where the knowledge was held secret for the enslavement of others, to keep people in bondage, where it became a matter of secret societies, the knowledge is gone. Vestiges remain, very tantalizing pieces of knowledge that people are trying to fit together.

What is occurring within your governments and scientific circles at this time is really very secret in regard to advances in technology.

However, it is all right, dear ones, because you will never be enslaved if you are free within. It does not matter what they do.

The knowledge now will not be withheld. You will come into the knowledge. It will be an unstoppable force, the power of the people. The power of humanity united in love, in the desire for peace and harmony, the desire for technological knowledge which is not for warfare and then the means of enslavement and empowerment for small groups of people. You are unstoppable.

Q: What is the difference between daydreams and night dreams?

P'taah: There is not much difference. It is really only that what you think of as night dreams is certainly a reality. But the extended scope of the realities is quite fantastic so you are having the adventures and travels and learning on many levels and many dimensions of reality, whereas when you are daydreaming, it is rather a gentle excursion of imagination. Do you understand?

Q: Sometimes the dreams are ridiculous, unreal.

P'taah: It is really that what you are bringing back into consciousness are fragments. It is not at all ridiculous in truth, you know. It is not really so farfetched. When you are in the reality of your dreamtime, it is this that is the dream. This life that you understand to be real is much more the dream.

As you come into a greater knowing, the division between reality and non-reality will start to merge. Then you will truly understand what it is to be in many dimensions at the same time. That will indeed be a grand adventure.

Q: P'taah, I was in a situation yesterday where I felt that I had been totally ripped off. I was in instantaneous fury, then suddenly I just accepted it. What happened there?

P'taah: You have accepted responsibility, beloved.

Q: I just embraced that horrible situation and said, "This is all my own creation."

P'taah: Absolutely, and you see what has occurred since you first heard of this concept? You hear the concept, "You create your own reality, absolutely," and you say, "What sort of bullshit is this?"

So what I am saying to you is that the concept becomes part of who you are. You are not even noticing the change until there is a situation like this. Where before, as you say, there would have been blood all over the floor, now you are in an understanding of accepting responsibility. It is your creation. It is wondrous.

Congratulations indeed, beloved. In this fashion you have shown yourself how far you have stepped in what you would perceive to be a very short time, that you are coming into a new understanding, broadening perception, changing your consciousness.

That is how it is to be, and it may be gentle. It does not have to be that you create hard lessons. All of you may say that you desire to bring forth your experiences in a gentle fashion. It is not necessary to have blood on the floor. You do not have to put yourself through the wringer, the mangle.

Very well, dear ones. Sufficient unto the time of this evening. Our thanks indeed for this exchange.

(P'taah thanks the host and hostess.)

So indeed, dear ones, little by little you are creating the changes. Truly we would remind you that it is simple. It is truly simple. As you create these grand intellectual exercises for one reason or another, it is all right, but we would remind you that it is truly simple.

I love you indeed. Good evening.

▼ Eighth Session
February 5

P'taah: You are well-come indeed. How are you all this evening? We shall declare Open Forum and you may query forth.

Q: For two years I have been following the path of an Indian master who says it is to go beyond the mind, to dissolve the ego. I have observed in myself how controlling and manipulative my mind is and how destructive it is of all happiness. It is certainly destructive of love. So the path I have been following is that of letting go, of allowance, not to take an active role. Part of my mind judges this path by saying that this is not taking full responsibility.

What is the line between consciously creating one's reality and not allowing the mind to come in? I cannot seem to manifest successfully. For example, if I decide to have a particular pizza, I can be guaranteed that either the shop will be closed or that that particular pizza is off the menu. Why is this so?

P'taah: Dear one, what do you think it is?

Q: My feeling is that it is the judgment.

P'taah: Absolutely. Now the I that is the persona does not need to be dissolved. It is to be embraced, and in the embracing and non-judgment, you will then have alignment. Then indeed there will not be the fight. Your mind is your servant. Your ego is your servant.

If you desire only to be passive, then so be it. But you see, in truth, what you are is a grand creative being. If you believe that everything you try turns to ashes, then indeed, beloved woman, it will.

However, the lesson for all of humanity is *being*, not to be a human doing. Nevertheless, as you desire something, then you may show forth intent. That is all right, but it is also not to be hung up on the outcome. Because you see, beloved, when you are hung up on the outcome, you go into great judgment because it is not exactly as you have written it. Do you understand?

It is not necessarily only to be a re-active being. You are indeed action personified even when you are sitting doing nothing. Your body is the most wondrous of active, creative organisms. It is like multitudinous galaxies creating actively at every microsecond. So is the brain. It does not shut off, not ever.

It is to allow this busy-ness of mind. You will find that if you judge the busy-ness of mind, and if you are trying very hard to turn it off, nothing else will be accomplished.

It is to let it go. It is a busy brain. Make it okay. Whatever your consciousness is, it can exist simultaneously with the busy-ness of the mind. Even when you are asleep, your mind is still busy.

Now, the state of being and the state of doing are polarities. It is not to make one wrong and one right. It is to embrace both.

We have noticed with humanity that you become very bored when you are not doing something. So it is to be joyous in what you do. Have we not said to you, do what makes your heart sing? Judge it not.

And as you are in the doing, it is to be in the joy of the moment. In such a fashion, there is no past and no future, just the beingness. It is not required that you just sit on your posterior and do nothing. Go forth and dance!

Is that clear for you, beloved?

Q: I don't really want to do anything, but I find that I am stagnating. I have no interest in any activity.

P'taah: Then that is all right if that is what makes your heart sing.

Q: The problem is I have to earn a living. I have some money at the moment, but it will be gone in another three months.

P'taah: A rock and a hard place, eh?

Q: Could you talk about that part of us that is controlling and manipulating?

P'taah: Dear one, for as long as you judge that part of you which controls and manipulates, you will just bring it forth more and more.

It is valid to be controlling and manipulative, you know. It is a Divine aspect or it would not be. But it does not have to rule your life. As you are in fear of it, as you are rejecting it, as you are pushing it all away, so you are giving it so much energy, you are merely drawing it forth.

Q: Could you talk about duality? My understanding is the mind is based on duality, therefore when I say I want to experience light, I automatically attract darkness.

P'taah: Dear one, your whole multiverses, as you understand it, are polarity. That is your universe. It is to embrace both polarities that they may be brought into the light. It is not that one is right and one is wrong. Both are valid. Without one the other one would not exist. You are polarity. You are masculine/feminine, you are positive/negative ions. You are all things. You are love and you are fear.

Q: I would like to know why I have manifested 90% unhappiness in my life.

P'taah: Dear one, do you think you are alone in this? Would the 10% please stand up?

You see, dear one, every one of humanity manifests pain and anguish. Why do you think it is that we say humanity is dying of a broken heart?

It need not be so. What we are giving you is a tool for you to be able to create the change you desire in your life. We are what you would call a recipe-giver. If we were to write a cookbook, it would be a best seller. And so we give you the recipe and how you cook is your business.

That is in fact the most wonderful part of the creativity that you have at this time. That is why you are here. That is why you have created yourselves in this place at this time, so that you may witness what is called duality, polarity, change.

As it is occurring within you, so you are observing it outside of who you are because everything you observe outside of who you are is only a mirror. It is all a reflection. There is nothing in existence outside of who you perceive yourself to be which is not a mirror. No thing.

So, dear one, we would say do not worry about how it is that you are perceiving it. There are two expressions, love and fear. It is your choice at any moment how you perceive it to be, how you choose to live it. You may cower in fear or you may dance into the light.

I will tell you this. The time will come when you will be very bored with living within fear, of being paralyzed into a no life. One day, beloved one, you will open your eyes and say, "This day I will step forth into the light."

Q: It seems that I cannot do this as an act of will. It seems that it will happen when the moment is right. This is the confusion. This is the judgment. So how do I do it?

P'taah: Dear one, I have told you already. To make the judgment all right, yet to know that it is judgment not to be pushed away but to be embraced. That is what alignment is. We will speak to you further about this if you desire.

Q: Namaste, P'taah. St. Germain has talked about the Gene of Isis, and stimulating the pineal and pituitary glands. How do we do that? What do we stimulate it with? *(Lots of laughter)*

P'taah: Heart light, beloved. In truth the channel, the crystalline structure to be ignited so that you may step forth into super-consciousness, is stimulated by embracement. So in every moment you have a choice whether to allow the stimulation to occur or not. It is as simple as that.

Q: So whatever I think is the stimulation?

P'taah: Dear one, at all times in your life internal you are choosing, and what do you choose? Love or fear? Embracement or rejection. Do you understand?

Q: Oh yes. It is so simple.

P'taah: But of course, beloved. We do keep telling you this, you know.

Q: The young lady who spoke before talked about soon not having any money. I just want to get something clear in my mind: As long as she is concerned about the money running out, it will run out, is that right?

P'taah: Indeed.

Q: Because she is directing her energies ...

P'taah: ...to the not having. Absolutely.

Q: The other part of her question was about allowance. Should we not rather direct our energies toward making things happen?

P'taah: That is so, dear one. There is certainly what is called showing forth the intent. As you are in desire of something, then you may show forth the intent that it is already in your reality.

Q: It sounded to me as if the lady was expecting everything to happen without any input from herself. It seems that you can take this allowing a bit too far.

P'taah: It is not taking it too far, beloved, because if our dear lady was in the knowing that there is nothing to do and that all will be provided, and if she were sitting doing nothing in joy, then indeed it would be creative.

What we are saying is that when you are in the paralysis, then it is truly the paralysis of fear. So if you are saying, "I desire the change," it is to show forth that the change has already occurred.

In that instant it may be to take the body into sunshine and listen to the birdsong, to walk and to feel the grass underfoot. You understand? This in itself is called showing forth intent to change. In the showing forth, the change is already created. It is dichotomy, indeed.

Q: Last week someone asked a question about not locking her bicycle, of having universal trust. But it is not the universe that we are not trusting. It is the thieves out there who will steal the bicycle.

P'taah: But you see, dear one, it is not so. As you are grounded in the knowing that all is secure and all is safe, so it becomes a co-creation. You are not in any way isolated from the rest of your universe.

Q: How do you get the message across to the thief of the bicycle?

P'taah: Dear one, it is merely that the bicycle or vehicle is not within the field of consciousness of those who would steal. It is simply that.

Q: *(The lady who finds it difficult to generate interest in any outside activity.)* In response to that I would like to share something because I have been developing great trust. The night of the workshop I was driving back down the mountain from Kuranda and I had the feeling I could trust everything, and that everything was made of love—that the car, the road, the trees, everything was made of love, that there was really nothing whatsoever for me to do.

In that moment, without thinking about it, I took my hands off of the steering wheel. I looked out of my driving window and I was going down the mountain approaching a bend. In that moment I was prepared to die rather than live in a state of fear or in the feeling that the universe is not taking care of me.

In a way it was a test, but it was not consciously so. It was something that just happened. For about five seconds I was completely unconcerned. I looked out the window and just trusted that the car would steer itself around that bend in a controlled way. That was exactly what happened. It went around the bend for about five seconds, and then I looked forward. In that moment I came back into my mind and grabbed hold of the steering wheel. Somewhere I really do feel that the less we do the better. That this is possible.

P'taah: But of course it is possible, beloved. When you say you would rather die, you know that is the greatest illusion of it all. There is no such thing, in truth, as death.

Our thanks for sharing this. It is always so that as you are totally in the knowing of being in a safe universe—so it is. Always.

Q: I do not think I really care about becoming enlightened. I just want to feel confident about myself all the time, or at least some of the time.

P'taah: Try all the time, beloved. Be practical—plan a miracle.

Don't want to be enlightened? What do you think it is to be in the light of knowing who you are? That is certainly what you would call supreme self-confidence, hmm?

Q: Fair enough. It is the same thing, then.

P'taah: You know, enlightenment—that which you are all quite concerned about, one way or another—is already who you are. You already encompass enlightenment. You already encompass total love. That you can include the polarity, that you can include everything else is wondrous.

Q: So I should not be concerned about what happens, whether it is good or bad. It is all the same, really.

P'taah: But, indeed, it is all the same really. It is only your perception, your judgment which makes it good or bad, right or wrong.

Q: So I should really develop better judgment, shouldn't I?

P'taah: Why would you not just throw the judgement out of the window and practice discernment instead?

Q: Discernment means that I can see what is what.

P'taah: Indeed. Without judgement.

Q: Changing the subject a little. The current theory of the origin of the phenomenal universe states that it originated with what is coined the Big Bang. In other words, an explosion of energy culminating in an extension apparently endlessly. The counter theory is that it then contracts. Do you have a comment about this theory?

P'taah: You may say it is called the breath of the Source.

Q: Philosophically, yes. Still, it is said that the breath is the ultimate analogy. Incoming and outgoing. In the micro sense within us human creatures, the breath symbolizes the macro incoming and outgoing. Mathematically, how you appreciate the scale is one thing. Simply appreciating in feeling is something else.

P'taah: Ah, indeed, beloved, because you see, you may take every mathematical equation and you may create most elegant designs about the hows of the beginning of the universe and the end. But you see, dear one, the only important thing is you. You are the central sun of your universe, and what creates you moment-by-moment is feeling.

Q: Underlying that which creates us moment-by-moment is not only universal, it is constant. It is sustaining all manifestation in every conceivable context.

P'taah: Of course, dear one. But you see, you do not know about anything else. You do not even know about yourself, and we are not speaking only of you, beloved, we are speaking about all of humanity.

When you know who you are, when you may feel and love, you will know everything. Then you will understand the macro-universe, because you will know micro. To know one is to know the other.

Q: As you referred to very often, we do know, but not in the sense that is relative.

P'taah: There are no words for this knowing, beloved, and if you truly knew who you are, you would not be sitting here.

The knowing is that you are enlightened masters. You are knowing all things, but you will not tap into this knowing without total embracement of who you are.

Q: Greetings P'taah. After a lifetime of deceiving myself, I finally have to admit that what I want most is a love relationship as in the most wondrous fairy stories, but I do not seem able to create it. Maybe you can give me some support.

P'taah: Yes indeed, dear one, we would be delighted to give you the support. Now, you may create the most wondrous love affair that indeed is the basis of all the fairy stories, but you see, beloved, first you must have it with you.

Q: So how can I gain it myself?

P'taah: How can you love yourself?

Q: I think I have started to love myself.

P'taah: Indeed, you have.

Q: But I think I am the only one loving me. *(The audience is amused and touched at the same time)*

P'taah: Ah, dear one, that is not so. You know that I love you, not that it is much good for you. *(Lots of laughter)* It is certainly not warming your bed.

Beloved one, who you are is most beautiful, most worthy of love. But you see, you do not really understand yet that you are worthy of love.

Q: I thought so.

P'taah: Beloved one, you are worthy of all things. You are worthy of love. You are worthy of loving, but it is to show yourself day-by-day how much you love yourself, how much indeed you do honour who you are. Have integrity in the fashion in which you treat yourself, and then you may have a wondrous romance.

Q: It is not just romance. I want it all.

P'taah: And you may. You may indeed. Have we ever said to you, beloved, that you can only have a little bit and not everything? We have said to you, "You may have it all." Indeed, I insist.

Q: Greetings, P'taah. In regressions I have gone back to the beginning of my spiritual journey to see what I have been and I agree with you. I was a Goddess, still am. But what caused me to turn away from this and come to such a miserable condition where I have become detached from my Self? Was it an ego trip? What cut me off?

P'taah: What detached all of you, because all of you, *all*, have been and still are Gods and Goddesses? It is, you may say, that the Source in desiring to experience itself, created separation. So it is for each and every one of you.

It is truly a wondrous game. It is merely that you have forgotten the rules. You have forgotten that it is only, as we have said before, a roll of film. Your movie, beloved. It is you who says it is all shit. That is called the judgment of how it is.

You may also say that it is the most wonderful way to be able to adorn yourself with the celestial jewels of the knowing of the Goddess. It depends entirely on how you choose to view it.

Q: I want to make a last comment to that. After seeing what I had been, I cried for one and a half hours. It was a mourning process. I was mourning my loss, then from the depths of myself came the knowledge that I will become what I have been. I will come back again. I enjoy what I am now, but it was horrible to see what I have lost.

P'taah: It is mourning indeed, but you see it was for the whole of humanity. That is what we mean when we say the whole of humanity is dying of a broken heart, beloved.

Q: P'taah, you have spoken about the fear, but I have experienced an ecstasy which was so great I almost had to beg it to stop. Are we afraid to receive our full kingdom?

P'taah: But of course, dear one. In this fashion it comes in little bits and pieces. You know, it is very difficult to give up what you know so well. It is almost as if the neurons cannot take the charge.

Q: Yes, it is almost like a disintegration point, yet it was so ecstatic.

P'taah: Indeed, and yet if you had gone with it then, indeed you would be an ascended master.

Now dear ones, we shall call for a break. We ask you to be still for the transition and we shall return very soon.

(After the break.)

P'taah: And so, dear ones, you may query forth.

Q: P'taah, could you discuss with us forthcoming Earth changes for the next ten years, and is it profitable for those who wish to stay in the body for the next ten years to be here on the Atherton Tableland during these changes?

P'taah: We have given forth much information in these months about Earth changes and we would suggest that if you are very curious about the details you may read this information. It is available here for you.

Now, we will say this. Certainly the Earth changes which are coming are not to be regarded as catastrophic, although indeed it may appear to be so for many people. There is always, as we have said before, the moment of

choice of how you may perceive what is to occur. If you
are in fear of what is to occur, it does not matter where
you reside. If you are not in fear, it also does not matter
where you will reside.

But we will say that this place, this area of your continent,
is quite wondrous, and we have said before that the energy is
of gentleness, of healing, of nurturing. And we have also
congratulated before those people who desire from the heart
to reside within this area, and not only on what is called the
Tableland, but in this northern area of your country.

Q: In line with this: I have been residing in this area for
over twenty years and I have had a feeling that I cannot
really describe, but I usually say to people, "This is where
it is," or, "This is where it is going to be," but I don't really
know what it is, but it is. Now do you know what I am
talking about, because I don't? (Peals of laughter.)

P'taah: You have really said forth the words of our woman
also, and it is so. You may say this is where it's at, hmm?

Much of this is also because the area is constantly
visited by star people, and so it is that many of you—and
we are not necessarily speaking of the people in this
room—without understanding why, are drawn to an area.

It is because of the desire for close proximity with the star
people, and in a place of these energy leylines, you may say
that it creates its own vortex of energy. So people will arrive
without intention to live within this area and find that they
really do not desire to leave and they do not know why.

It is magical, dear one. This area has a magical feel.
The energy within your rainforests, what you call your
nature spirits, are very busy indeed. It is an area where
there is an abundance of growth, of fertility and the
people do indeed have great love of their land.

Where people are living in very large cities, they are not
allowing themselves the communion with the Goddess.
So it is like attracts like. Do you understand?

Q: P'taah, I would like to share something. When I lived in Sydney I felt rather pulled to the Sunshine Coast where I lived for a certain period of time. Then I visited the north and I knew I had to live here one way or another. Last year I came to Tully[1] and even there I did not feel at home. I knew I had to go somewhere beyond Cairns. Now I am indeed north of Cairns, and although my friends at the Sunshine Coast want me to return, I feel this here is my place.

P'taah: Indeed. It is certainly so that the energy north of your city becomes intensified. Although you may say that it starts south of your city in an area called Tully and intensifies north of this place.

Q: This is the first time that I have attended a gathering like this. Recently, during the past few years, I began to ask myself some questions and began to seek. It is all getting a little confusing for me. Is it reasonable to ask someone for a sign to confirm that there is something after death or that there is a spirit life?

P'taah: But it is absolutely reasonable, dear woman. You know, you do not really have to ask anybody except you. Who you are, the larger of you, is very happy to communicate. In this fashion you may be sure of the answers.

Q: How does one do that?

P'taah: You may place yourself in stillness and merely ask. That is all. Know that you will certainly get answers.

Q: What if I ask you?

---

[1] A small sugar cane-producing town south of Cairns in North Queensland.

P'taah: But indeed, you may ask me anything you desire.

Q: Right. Well, the sign that I have figured out that would confirm another level or dimension is if you could tell me my late husband's pet name for me. If anyone could tell me that I would believe.

P'taah: Dear one, you know, if you send forth an explanation of how it must be, then it is really to call forth no thing, because as you are in expectation of how is must be, you are closing down one million probabilities.

You are requiring to know that there is indeed something beyond this third dimension of reality. But you see, you really do know so. What you regard your own three-dimensional reality to be—can you not trust it?

Q: I do not know.

P'taah: Indeed, you *do* know. All of you do know. Because if you could trust it, you would not be here. You would not be a seeker. You would be saying, "There is nothing in existence except what I can touch, smell and hear and see with my own eyes."

Q: That is exactly what I did until recently.

P'taah: It does not work, because the greater of you knows that there is more. You may deny it, but if it were not true, why then are you looking?

Q: I don't know.

P'taah: Well, I will tell you. What humanity seeks is called fulfillment and nothing outside of who you are will fill the dreadful hole within you.

It does not matter how satisfactory your relationships are, they are never satisfactory enough. Great wealth does not do it either. Investing your life in children will not do it, neither an absorbing job. There is still the ache of the void within.

The void, the ache, is separation and it is the separation of the self from the greater Self, the Source. It is the non-understanding that who you are is the Source expressing in this dimension of reality.

You have lost touch with your power. In that void of separation, there is intense pain and anguish and yearning because all of humanity understands that there is more, always more. This understanding that there is more is called intuition.

The deep-seated knowing—it does not lie to you. It is the only thing in truth that you may trust because you certainly cannot rely on your external senses.

Q: Is it the knowing or is it a hope?

P'taah: There are many who are saying that what is called spiritual seeking is nonsense and would have you believe it is just a hope and that spirituality is a crutch. How often have you heard it?

Q: Quite often.

P'taah: Indeed. But you see, dear one, it is the proof of the pudding. As you come into an understanding of what we are saying—and it is not merely we who say it—as you desire the change and the knowing, as you desire to come into non-separation, so we give you a recipe.

As you start to practice what we are giving forth, so you may know great changes in your life. (*P'taah addresses a man whose change in understanding has created profound changes in his life.*) Is it not so, dear one?

Q: Certainly.

P'taah: And so as you are experiencing the change and as you discern that this change creates more joy, more laughter, more freedom, and as you are coming slowly into the love of self, as you come into the knowing of the concept that everything outside of you is a reflection—as you come into the understanding that you are truly a microcosm of the multiverses—so you will know that there is nothing that you are not part of, that you are indeed the breath of the All-That-Is, that you are a multidimensional, powerful woman.

You and all women of humanity are indeed stepping forth into a grand adventure called knowing the Goddess within, realizing your own power, sovereignty. This indeed, beloved, is called the proof.

Q: I hear what you are saying, but I am not sure I fully comprehend.

P'taah: That is all right, beloved. There are many new concepts that you are stepping into and as you are stepping forth you will know within you.

And you see, we are not a soothsayer. The only proof that means anything to humanity is what humanity proves to itself. You know we could create paranormal miracles and humanity would say, "Give us more. Show us. Show us your power."

But you see, dear one, I am not come forth to show you *my* power. I am come forth to show you *your* power. I am come forth to show you who you are. I come forth in honor, in love of humanity, and we do love you. We come to show you how you may come to know your God-light, and indeed, you will light up the galaxies.

Q: I have one further question. I have had trouble with my throat for a few months. What is causing the irritation and can you help me?

P'taah: The throat is about communication. It is to come into the allowance of that which you desire to communicate.

You know, the communication is not even so much a communication outside of self. It is also to allow yourself to be open to accept communication.

Listen to the voice within, dear one, and it need not be tight within your throat. You may relax and understand that there is nothing to fear, neither from your own communication, however you desire it to be, nor is there anything to fear from what you hear, whatever it is that is coming to you.

Q: The aboriginal population of this area is getting much publicity at the moment. It seems to arouse a lot of discrimination. There is always talk about the last 200 years since the white race discovered the continent.

I spoke to aboriginals who were 100 years old and who lived separated from the white civilization. These old purebloods do have the ability to integrate with us white people. They show no animosity. There is none of the aversion as is the case with the ones who were exposed to the white population.

Eighty-five years ago they were okay. Since then they slowly developed their problems. The basis of their problem is the same as it is with everyone else—one cannot love someone else until one can love oneself. In my view this is strongest with the mixed race aboriginals and not with the pure-bloods.

P'taah: It has nothing to do with that. It is a co-creation and is called not taking responsibility. It is called not being worthy.

Q: Why is it then that the old people have enough self-esteem...

P'taah: But you see, that is exactly how it is, that they are still steeped in their own tribal heritage.

The aboriginals of recent time have no tribal heritage. They do not belong anywhere. They are invalidated from the time of their birth as not being worthy, not good enough. They have nowhere to go, no place to hide. So of course, they do not have any self-worth in what is called knowing who they are.

Also, they do not understand at this time that they have been the co-creators of their reality. When they accept responsibility, then they may create the change they desire. For as long as they do not take responsibility and judge the Europeans as the cause of all their ills, it will not change for them. It will only become more and more and more. When they can take responsibility and know, indeed, that they have co-created the situation, then they may come into the knowing and create the change.

Q: P'taah, can we look forward to a vigorous and rapid dismantling of the American nuclear arsenal or is it necessary for our space-brothers to give the US military a good kick in the backside?

P'taah: It is rather that governments will come more into an understanding that weaponry will be of no gain.

Q: Good evening, P'taah. I would like to hear your view on fear as a desire to escape from a threat. This is what I understand fear to be. That uses much energy and the body becomes worn out.

P'taah: You may say that whatever is not love is fear. There are many expressions. However, in the body itself, the emotion of fear causes the body to release adrenalines of various kinds.

If there is no physical release in the fleeing from fear, then diseasement is created, as can be seen by the classic syndrome of your cancer. But it also manifests in many other ways. However it manifests, it is always the result of fear.

Q: There follows, as I see it, a vicious circle. My form of escape takes the form of thinking about the future and trying to plan it so that there is security. Now that prevents me from experiencing the present, but I also become aware of my body and the physical manifestations of my attempts to escape, so it seems to be a vicious circle.

P'taah: Absolutely, dear one. I have been watching it with great interest for many hundreds of your years.

Q: So how do we break that cycle?

P'taah: It is always the choice of the now moment. At least you understand what is occurring and that is what you may call a very positive step.

Do not judge your desire to escape, beloved woman. Fear is to be embraced. It is not to run from it. It is not to push it away. It is not to invalidate it. It is to say, "It is perfectly all right to be fearful." As you can make it perfectly all right, you have already chosen.

Q: But fear is still the desire to escape.

P'taah: When you embrace the fear then there is no desire to escape.

Q: So embracing the fear means not trying to conquer it.

P'taah: You see, beloved, when you are trying to conquer something, it is because you are in fear of being over-taken, paralyzed by fear. It is such with all of the manipulations—the desire for control. Do you understand?

Q: Yes, because I have allowed myself to feel fear for hours.

P'taah: But of course and that is all right. When you understand what you are doing, the next time around you may choose something different.

Beloved ones, do not ever be afraid of not getting another chance. *(Laughter)*

Q: When I am in my still space, I can feel my energy moving. How do I define that?

P'taah: *(Softly)* We will give you a little tip, dear one, do not define it. Now you can tell me why!

Q: Judgment.

P'taah: Limitation. Dear ones, we come among you week after week and we put forth word after word and in this fashion we are limiting you.

These words are really a sop to your intellect. What we speak forth you may imagine like specks of light dancing around the edge of an abyss—a void of nothingness wherein is everything. I am attempting to bring you concepts which in truth cannot be taught.

We are attempting to ignite a feeling within your breast, to stretch you a little, so that you may come to understand that you are limitless.

It is not necessary for you to speak of every experience you have. It is not necessary for you to define every feeling. You cannot. It is beyond words. Your flashes of Oneness—you cannot speak of them. Words do not convey the feeling of non-separation. There are not words to describe the God/Goddess, the Source. Even as we speak to you of energy, it does not really do it.

So we would simply remind you—you are truly limitless. Feelings are feelings. It is not necessary to judge how they are. I know that if you had a meter, you would all be rushing around measuring every thought and feeling you have. *(P'taah faces the amused audience.)*

That is all very well, too, but you see, it does not get you any closer to the God/Goddess. After all, beloved ones, let us not lose sight of that. That is the only reason you are sitting here on your bottoms in this room and week after week listen to us burbling on at you. The only reason is because you want to be closer to the Source of who you are, because you want to live in your own God-light.

You want, with a passion, to understand your own power and sovereignty, and above all you want love. And nobody else can do it for you. It does not matter how much somebody may love you, it is not enough. You are the only ones.

When you feel so alone, nobody can truly change it for you, but it is you who has the power. You know, I am, in truth, a wondrous magician, but I am not more powerful than you.

Sufficient unto the time, dear ones. We are never further away from you than your next thought. We would merely have you remind yourselves that who you are, I am indeed in love with. I desire for you also to be in love with who you are.

And so, dear ones, be joyous. Be in allowance of your God-light. We expect you to be dancing. (*Teasing*) Anybody who does not will go to the bottom of the class.

I love you. Beloved ones, good evening.

▼ Ninth Session March 4

(P'taah greets the audience and walks around the room, acquainting himself with every face.)

P'taah: The nature of your universe is called polarities. Everything is a polarity. What you are, each of you and all of humanity, is in judgment of polarities, that which you judge to be negative.

We would indeed remind you that what you regard to be enlightenment is merely the embracement of both polarities to create the light. It is that simple.

In this regard we will say to you that it is now time for query. If there is no query then I am in great joy and we shall have a cup of tea and I shall leave you.

Q: In the last few days, I experienced two instances of instantaneous manifestations. I would like to share one of them.

On a recent trip to the United States, I was impressed with a zinfandel wine. Back in Australia I tried to obtain this wine, yet the person in charge of the shop had never heard of a zinfandel and tried to sell me a different wine instead. Standing in the aisle between hundreds of different wines, I glanced across the man's shoulder and stared directly at a bottle labeled zinfandel and, lo and behold, it was even the exact brand of wine that I had tasted overseas.

Now I know these things happen when we are at peace and somewhat in tune, but how they happen, the mechanics of the process, escape me.

P'taah: But you know perfectly well. You know there is no accident. There is no coincidence. As you desire it, so the whole universe rearranges itself to fulfill your desire, and I hope that you purchased a bottle for me. *(Laughter.)*

Q: Sure, our greater Self is all-knowing, but technically then it must even have knowledge of such fine physical detail to lead us to the very spot where that wine in stored.

P'taah: Dear one, it is only you who judges whether it be a small or a large detail. You know, in terms of energy, in terms of the universe, it does not matter. It is all the same. Your greater Self knows it all. It knows everything.

So, that which you regard as the most important factor in your life, and which you give much energy to create what you desire, takes no more energy than what you regard as insignificant and create without even thinking about. Is there not a little lesson in there for you?

Q: P'taah, it is said, "Seek the kingdom of God within you first and everything will be added to you." The Bhagavad-Gita says it. The Sermon on the Mount says the same. On the other hand, there is, "Ask and ye shall receive" and "Whatsoever you desire and believe it is yours, you shall have." Now, is there not a contradiction in there some-where? Is it all right to have a desire?

P'taah: But of course, dear one. Do you not have desires every day of your life? Do you think it is wrong?

Q: No, definitely not.

P'taah: There is no contradiction. Know Thyself and you know God. That is when you know who you are, when there are no areas in your life which are unknown to you and unaccepted by you, everything acknowledged without judgment—aligned—then indeed it is called knowing the greater Self. In this fashion, all is made manifest.

In the meantime you are creating, creating, creating moment-by-moment. You are creating your existence every microsecond. You are holding your body together and replenishing every cell. You are creating your reality, so as you create your reality, you have the choice of how to do it.

When you desire something, it is merely to put forth the desire and it will be made manifest in truth in that instant. Yet in physicality you may well experience a time-lapse. As you become easier with the idea of creativity, so you will notice that the time-lapse will become less and less. So, in fact, there is no contradiction.

Q: P'taah, you say regardless if a person makes a decision born of intuition or intellect, if that person puts enough yearning into it, the universe will bend to come to his aid. Where is the place for intuition here? I thought it is better to base one's decisions on intuition.

P'taah: One does not replace the other. You may act on intuition, moment-by-moment. It would be very good if everybody did so, nevertheless there are times when you would say, "I would desire this." It may well be that your intuition will bring it about quicker than if you are striving and not listening to intuition, using force of will trying to manifest what you desire.

We shall give you an example. You desire very much to go to a far-away place and the far-away place will cost you much money which you do not have at this moment. However, it is your earnest desire to do so and you would say, "This is my desire. I would desire this to occur."

And then you say, "Now I must work and work to get the money." Your intuition says, "Do not work. Take it easy," and you say, "I cannot take it easy or I will not have the money." So you work and work and work.

In the meantime there is a very fond aunt who will say, "Dear one, I have heard that you are desiring to go away. We will give you this money and have a good time." So in this respect you have manifested the money and your intuition said, "Do not work hard. You will manifest the money."

Q: If your intuition said, "No, next month is not the time to go on holiday," but the travel brochures look good...

P'taah: Dear one, if your intuition says, "Do not go," then do not go.

Q: But will the universe bend to make the trip a success, even though your intuition said, "Don't go."

P'taah: Dear one, what do you think? If your intuition says it is not the ripeness of time for you to go, and you do go, you will indeed find that it is not the ripeness of time and you would have well stayed at home.

Q: But if I put enough energy into it, then...

P'taah: Dear one, you are not listening. This is called force of will. It is all very well to have the desire, but it is to know absolutely that it will be brought forth in the manner of the greatest possible benefit to you. If you have the desire, if you have the thought flashing across your mind, and your intuition says, "No, no, not this time," who do you think is saying that to you?

It is called the greater Self. It is the self who knows what is of greatest benefit. Now, in truth there is no wrong decision, however in your life you may do it the easy way or you may take the longer route. Is that clear?

Q: So if something does not feel good, it is not going to work?

P'taah: We always have said to you, "Go with the feeling." Intuition is never wrong, you know. When you desire something, the moment there is doubt, you have a spanner in the works. The moment you have expectations of how and when something may occur, you have limited the millions of possibilities. In other words, you are stifling your creativity.

Q: P'taah, some time ago you said that the learning course for children will be very much different from what it is now. Can you give us an outline of how it will be?

P'taah: People will be more in community living. We are not saying commune, in your understanding of how that has been. There will be gatherings of children who will be instructed in more creative beingness.

Also, the consciousness of the parents will be different. It means that in the home environment, in all homes, there will be much more sense of harmony. The parents will understand how to allow the children to be more creative day-by-day without the restrictions of social consciousness, without the don'ts.

In the early years, the formative change-over years, the communications centers—computers, although not quite as you know them now—will have information which will enable children to learn in a different fashion.

It will not be from a teacher in the classroom with a blackboard where the children are learning parrot fashion. In other words, the learning will be of a broader spectrum. The children will be learning creatively who they are and how they are related to their universe.

Now there will be technological expansion which makes this more viable than you can understand at this moment so that the learning process will be not so much a schooling, as you understand it, but rather a learning in terms of play.

There will be children who understand the manipulation of matter, and it will be most creative to play with sound and color. In this way, the children will learn the harmony and the sameness of humanity and the flora and fauna of your planet, and indeed of other planets, too. So it is really that the learning will become vertical instead of horizontal.

Q: P'taah, how do we protect ourselves from micro-waves, radiation, electricity, and other forms of electro-magnetic energy which is harmful to the cells?

P'taah: Dear one, for as long as you will be afraid that all of this energy about you is malignant, so it will be. Of course, it is more harmonious to the body in this present way of your being if you are aware not to overload your-self. We do not desire to speak of this too much because people will rush out and become what you call totally paranoid, and that is not necessary.

It is necessary only to know that you may be in har-mony even with that which you regard to be microwave, electricity wave, radio wave, television wave, and all of the countless other waves that at this time you have no knowledge of.

Your universe is made up of waves, and so you may practice all of your wondrous methodology of using your energy, conserving your energy, having your en-ergy whipping round and round, and it is very good. In fact, it is very beneficial, but you know all of this is not the ultimate. The ultimate is transmuting the pain in your life. The ultimate is to come into acknowledgement and love of self.

You know, dear one, if you become bored with hearing us say it, I will remind you that you may scurry about in your stampede for enlightenment. You may try every trick in the book, and indeed, in the millions of books.

That can be a wondrous adventure and may be won-drous entertainment and that is very good. But the bottom line is to take responsibility for everything that you create in your life, align the judgment, and feel the feeling. To indeed have a wondrous love affair with who you are.

Q: And deepen the presence of love.

P'taah: Dear one, it is automatic. You are love. You are light. You are the God/Goddess. There is nothing else.

Q: Yes, I know.

P'taah: Well, we would desire that all of you really did know. We understand that you all have wondrous flashes, hmm? And it is wondrous. You will find that the open-hearted knowing that you are it will become longer and longer. The black holes that you fall into after these realizations, after the feeling seems to have passed, will become less and less.

Q: P'taah, we have marriage and laws and systems in our present life. When the change comes, what will happen to those laws? Can you give us an outline?

P'taah: Well, dear one, marriage is really called 'sign a piece of paper.' It is of your government and your religion. True marriage has nothing to do with a piece of paper. It has only to do with how it is with somebody else at that moment.

If the moments continue on year after year, that is wondrous. If it does not, then that is also wondrous. The rending asunder of a marriage when one is aligned is not that one is separating because there is no love or because of violent dispute, etc. It will be that the relationship is based on love of self, so indeed, where there is true love of self, there is no jealousy, no possessiveness, fighting about possessions, or indeed, possession of children.

Humanity will understand that every child in the universe belongs to every one of you because the belonging is only called loving without ownership. So each person will care for each child and there will not be children of neglect. A child, indeed, is only another person, another

soul with, albeit, a smaller body. So it will be that humanity will look back on this barbaric situation that humanity
has in this culture at this time and they will feel very sorry
for you all.

You know, when you truly have a love affair with who
you are, dear one, you will be having a love affair with the
whole world. And when you are not living any more with
somebody with whom you have lived before, it is perhaps
that you are desiring to explore a different avenue of life.
But the separation will be of harmony, not discordance.

Q: P'taah, I was more concerned with the children recognizing who their parents were, and for the parents and
children to recognize the new system.

P'taah: You think the child will be lost and not know its
mother or father?

Q: No. The new system will make so many changes.

P'taah: Dear one, it is no different now. What is the
percentage of your people who marry, have children, then
in a very few years the marriage is split asunder in great
discordance. The children do not see their father, may not
see their mother, very often do not live with either parent
but with relations or in an institution which does not
really care about the soul of the child at all.

Do you think this system is better? Do you think it will
be such a dreadful transition to be in a community where
all children are loved absolutely because they are simply
another wondrous being? Where there is never discordance and fighting between mother and father? We do
not really understand your question, beloved.

Q: I understand the problems with the system we have
now, but with the new system, things will change so
much.

P'taah: Children will still have parents, dear one.

Q: We will still have children similar to what we have now?

P'taah: The children will not change. They will still be little beings who are fully developed souls, who are sovereign, exactly the same as now.

Q: Although it seems simplistic and wanting things in little boxes, with all this focus on moving up to fourth dimension, it seems that everyone will move up and I would like to see you in the flesh, so to speak.

P'taah: Indeed, we were very amused and we will recount this. My beloved friends were in a discussion about what will occur when your third density reality becomes fourth density. One of our beloved friends asked, "Do you think that everybody, including P'taah, will move up one?"

Our woman said, "It would be very disconcerting. You think you're going to get there and it's, 'Oh, shit, they've moved up one, too, and we're still behind'" (*Laughter*) You see, dear one, when the change occurs, you will be able indeed to flit between dimensions, so do not worry yet.

Q: People talk as if this transition is just around the corner. Are there people who have already made this transition?

P'taah: Indeed.

Q: And yet they are still appearing in this third dimensional form that I may meet them in the street?

P'taah: There are some.

Q: I am not a great judge—what foresight have I—but I cannot see that the world is going to expand that quickly that we will pass this physical state. Is that what fourth dimension means?

P'taah: It does not.

Q: Perhaps I just do not understand the terms.

P'taah: It does not matter. Neither does anybody else, really. Further dimensions of reality in the understanding of the changes to come does not mean lack of physicality. It really means that you become lighter in your physical vibration.

Q: Meaning that we are not limited by the third dimension?

P'taah: Indeed. You will be in understanding of manipulating matter. You will be in understanding of greater technology in terms of intergalactic travel. You will not be confined to the body, that is, you will be able to travel without your body, as well as with your body, in grand craft. (*P'taah smiles at the host*) Some are already planning for their own craft. So the four-wheel drive will be replaced by a little beam-ship.

So, dear one, it is not that you are going to go forth in a puff of smoke and leave all of this behind. It is merely that your perception of reality will change because the vibrational frequency that is you will change. Time and space will have a different understanding for you.

Q: Is it likely to cause much division within the community?

P'taah: It will indeed create quite a division because when you accomplish what is called the shift, it does not mean that third density does not exist any more. It only means it does not exist for you, although you will be able to perceive it.

You know, dear one, to talk about this is like describing to the fetus within the uterus what life will be like after birth. So it is also when we speak of life after death. In a way, I may as well be standing here speaking mumbo-jumbo, for all the sense it really makes because you have not experienced it. The wisdom is really garnered after the experience, not before.

Now, dear one, we will call for a break. We would ask you to create stillness for two minutes during the transition and we will see you very soon.

(After the break.)

Q: P'taah, do you come of your own accord, feeling that we are in dire need of some assistance?

P'taah: You know, humanity needs nothing. Also, every word we give forth has been given forth many, many times before.

Certainly there is limitation in communication because we are speaking to you, of necessity, within the limitations of your own consciousness. However, our being with you is twofold. It is that which is the joy of my heart. It is also in this regard not only a personal decision in terms of that which be I, but larger than that. You may say it was a decision of the Board of Directors merely to give forth assistance.

Now it is certainly a choice within the heart of humanity whether or not that which is given forth is acted upon. There is in no way any force involved. We do not force. To do so would be to deny your sovereignty. If we denied your sovereignty, then we would also be denying our own. Do you understand?

You may say in a fashion that this communication is called a joy, fun, that which makes my heart sing. Who you are is a gift to me. Indeed, in knowing you, I also know the richness of who I am. Does this answer your question, beloved?

Q: It does, and I have to give you a compliment. You are the only Being with whom I have experienced that once you looked into my eyes for a few seconds, I had no questions and at the same time, I felt a warmth, a physical warmth.

P'taah: Dear one, the time is approaching when you will have it with everyone. More especially, you will have it when you gaze in the mirror into your own eyes because what you will see reflected there will be utter beauty.

You see, who you are, beloved ones, is absolute beauty. Who you are is Divinity. Who you are is wondrous beyond compare. You simply do not recognize it yet, but you will.

Q: P'taah, I have recently read that the phenomenon of Fatima was a holographic insert and that the church has kept that message from humanity. Can you tell us what the message was?

P'taah: You have already heard the message, beloved, many times. And you see, dear one, nothing will remain hidden. This is the time of the revealing of all secrets. It does not matter what your governments attempt to do and what your religious leaders attempt to hide from you, it will not be hidden.

This time frame of change, the changes to occur, you know already. We have discussed this with you at great length. Not only we, but many other entities. In fact, the information has been given forth repeatedly over a millennium.

It is only that the information given by the star people, in various guises, has been judged to be not healthy for you poor common humanity who are not of the hierarchies. Do not be disturbed. It is nothing that you do not know.

Q: Another question is what is the purpose of the ultra-violet rays surrounding the Earth?

P'taah: Are you speaking about the violet ray?

Q: The ultra-violet ray.

P'taah: Ultra-violet is different. There is also the photon belt and other wondrous phenomena all heralding the changes to come. But you see, it is not that the Earth changes and the changes of consciousness—and indeed there is not one without the other—will be in a blink of an eye. It is already in motion. It has already begun, the last phase of this, just a few of your years ago.

What is occurring now is that the Earth and humanity are stepping year-by-year into a speeding up. Do you understand? In one respect it seems to you as if it is all happening very slowly, but in another fashion it is very difficult for you to keep up with all the changes, even with the telecommunications that you have.

There will be more and more disorientation about what time really is. You will feel as if you are standing still, running very fast. Nothing is happening, and everything is happening so very fast that you can truly not really comprehend it.

So there will be this grand distortion, and so it will be in many other areas of your consciousness. The feeling of great elation. The feeling of depression. The feeling that the changes in your own life are out of control as well as those which are happening to your institutions, the socio-economic situation. That is why we say for many people it will be distressing unless they are in understanding of the what, why, and how of it.

It need not be chaotic. When you are in the knowing of who you are, and each and every one of you is stepping further into the broadness of your consciousness, then you are anchored in who you are. You will not be tossed like a leaf in the wind. You will be in understanding that it is you who are creating your own reality.

Dear one, there will be many occurrences upon your planet of which you will not even be aware until after the event. It will simply not be within the realms of your

consciousness. Indeed, there will be many situations occurring that you will not be aware of at all, during or after.
So it will be very curious for you, and in fact, it is
occurring already. We know that many of you surprise
yourselves in the sense that what seems like dire calamity
to other people seems not so important to you.

It is never to lose the compassion for the people who do
not have your understanding. It is perfectly valid. It is
perfectly valid for people to choose not to step forth. Dear
one, it is perfectly valid for you to choose not to step forth.
There is no judgment. Your opportunities are presented to
you moment-by-moment. What you do with them is your
choice. No right and no wrong in either choice.

Q: P'taah, I choose to step forth and I do have an ache for
some of my children who may not choose, although this is
judging them now, but the possibility that they will not...

P'taah: Indeed, dear one. Now, for all of you, there is a
certain fear that those who you love will be left behind.
But we will tell you this. Those who you love will never be
left behind. There are certain learnings coming to some of
your children and in the learning, there will come the
knowing because, in fact, there is already knowing within
them.

You know, humans are very stubborn people. It is easy
to stay with the known, even when the known and the
habitude of it create pain and anguish, discordancy.

But all of that is known very well to you and sometimes
you fall into the habitude of eons, and that is all right. Just
because you do it once does not mean that you have to do it
all the time. When you do it most of the time and you fall
along the wayside, that is all right, too. It is only another
opportunity. The opportunities will go on and on and on.

So it is not to judge yourself when you fall back into
your old patterns. It is all right. It is in this fashion that
you are learning. When you find yourself falling into an

old pattern and you do not judge yourself, you have already changed the pattern. You see, dear one, dichotomy works both ways.

Q: You said earlier that our intuition is always right. Well, I think that I do things intuitively, but on occasion it is not working out. What is going wrong?

P'taah: It is not intuition. Now that seems like a trite statement, but in fact it is not. Very often your intuition will tell you to do something and then in the implementation, you will use will. You will have a very intuitive feel for something and go for it, and in the going for it, you change it. When you are being intuitive, it is very easy to allow intellect to take over.

Q: You mean I am allowing my intellect to talk me out of it?

P'taah: Sometimes you allow intellect to talk you out of it. Sometimes it is allowing the intellect to take over the original thrust. Very often the intellect, the logical mind, will turn the channel into another direction, or instead of allowing the flow, you will use the intellect to push into another direction, or into a confined channel. Do you understand?

Think about those times in your life regarding business, because in your business you have been very intuitive. Now, and we do not ask you to do this at this moment, but over the next days look back to when you have had the flash to do something. Then see if you can mark the spot where the intellect took over and screwed up the whole deal. You will be surprised. Write on paper how it was, and it will give you a great insight in how you operate and how you may change it to your advantage.

Q: I think I know because what is effectively happening is that I can make intuitive decisions which will create abundance, then the intellect interferes and I am finishing up in poverty.

P'taah: Indeed, and we will tell you this also. Poverty may become a habit.

Q: It has its good points, though.

P'taah: So does everything. It is a great lesson for humanity, that which you call poverty, especially because none of you really want it. Indeed there are many of you who have been playing with the idea in your life that to have material wealth is not spiritual.

There are many variations on this theme that we have discussed with you before. We will say to you again. Poverty, lack of abundance of whatever it is, becomes a habit and so you talk yourselves into it day-by-day. Day-by-day you reaffirm that you are poor, and so of course it becomes a continuum. We will not even get into the deserving of great wealth because most of you do not believe that you are deserving.

Q: P'taah, what can I do to get out of stagnation? I try to live more meaningfully, but I find that I cannot get out of being blocked somewhere.

P'taah: It is called not being 'able to' and not being 'worthy of.' Now what is it, beloved woman, that you would do if I say to you that I will make it possible for you to do whatever you want. What would you ask of me?

Q: Perhaps to take the block away. To get more self-confidence.

P'taah: No, dear one. If I say to you, "You can have whatever you wish in this life. You can go wherever. I will make it possible for you. You do not have to do anything. I

will make it possible." What would you like to do if you
had the confidence? We would, of course, give you that.

(She ponders P'taah's question.)

P'taah: What change may I create for you in your life,
day-to-day? You can have anything. What do you want?

Q: More courage. I somehow cannot describe it.

P'taah: Very well. But if you have more courage, what
would you do with it? Where would you go? What would
you bring into your life that you do not have now? Tell me.

(P'taah's persistence has the audience spellbound.)

Q: More knowledge.

P'taah: Indeed. What else would make your heart sing?

Q: That I use my knowledge for humanity.

P'taah: Never mind about humanity, beloved. What about
you? What may I do to change your whole life, to give you
whatever it is that is the desire of your heart? For you.

Q: Perhaps to accept myself.

P'taah: Indeed. What about the things outside? You want
to go places? You want to change your mode of living. You
want a lover? More friends? What is it? I will give you
anything. All of that?

Q: Yes. I will be more modest. Perhaps a little more
money.

P'taah: More money?

Q: Yes, and perhaps the right kind of person to share it with.

P'taah: Indeed. A wonderful lover.

Q: Yes. A lover. A person who I can live in harmony with. Someone who understands me.

P'taah: Indeed, and lots of joy and laughter?

Q: Yes.

P'taah: *(Softly)* Well, beloved woman, I give it all to you. It is yours. If that is your desire, you may have it all. In this knowing, you will create it and you do not have to do anything.

Q: Thank you. It makes my heart sing—not to have to do anything. I am impatient. Thanks.

P'taah: That which I am is called fairy godmother, dear one. *(Laughter)* It is true.
  (Very softly) But you, beloved woman, are a Goddess. Which is more powerful? It is you. So go forth in joy. All of it is yours indeed.

Q: P'taah, you talked about poverty becoming a habit. Is there anything wrong with enjoying it?

P'taah: Dear one, whatever you are in joy of is wondrous. If it is that people are enjoying their life, with or without money, it is wondrous. It is also rare.

Q: Sometime back, I could not have handled lack of money.

P'taah: It has been a great lesson for you to be without money. It has been that you are without responsibility also. However it is, it is all right, beloved one, as long as you are in joy of it. And when you change your mind and it is no longer a joy, you may change it.

Q: Actually, it is quite a good position to be in because people cannot screw you. Well, that is the most expressive way of putting it. People cannot take anything from you if you do not have anything, and for me, it is very enjoyable to be in this situation at the moment.

P'taah: Dear one, the fear of being ripped off or screwed is not so harmonious. You cannot, at the moment, be screwed for money, but you can in other ways, indeed?

Q: How?

P'taah: You tell me, dear one. It is your life. We would suggest to you that in recent times, you have felt exactly that, and it has nothing to do with money.

Q: Yes. I understand.

P'taah: Money is only a label for consciousness. It is only a label for energy. It is the name of something.

It is how you feel in your life, that is how it is. If you are in fear of being ripped off, you will be. If it is not money, it will certainly be something else.

It is the same as the question about the thieves and the bicycle. If you are in fear of it, it will certainly happen. If you know absolutely that it is safe, that nobody can take anything from you, it will not occur. Do you understand? Same principle, different label.

Q: That does not mean we have to make things very accessible, does it?

P'taah: Dear one, let us not be ridiculous about this. You do whatever it is that makes you be in harmony. If you wish to offer whatever it is, even your heart, to somebody, it will not be ripped off if you are not in fear of it. If you are in fear of it, your heart will be ripped out. It is choice, always.

Dear ones, sufficient unto the time. Good evening.

▼ Tenth Session
March 11

P'taah: Good evening dear ones. Well now, in this evening of little numbers, there will be no escape. (*P'taah walks around the room greeting each person.*) And so, you may query forth and we will be delighted, as always, to reflect back to you that which you know already. If there are no queries, I will sit here and you may talk wisely among yourselves.

Q: P'taah, when a soul incarnates for the first time, can it go immediately to a developed civilization or does it have to start as a primitive?

P'taah: But there is really no such thing as a new soul. An energy may come forth in physicality for the experience, in the full knowingness of it own Divinity. There are some energies who only desire one experience. However, we may assure you that these beings are not great in number.

We would remind you that there are many who do not incarnate on the physical plane at all. We would also remind you that who you are lives in many dimensions of reality at the same time. That, in a fashion, you are in full knowingness of your own Godhood.

The soul, in your understanding, is not a limited entity only able to express in one dimension or one time frame. As we have said before, that which you consider to be linear time, and that which you consider to be incarnation, is all occurring simultaneously. In itself that gives you some idea of the grandeur of who you are.

Within you there is all knowing. As you come into conscious knowing of who you are, in total acceptance and acknowledgment so that you may fall in love with who you are, so all this knowledge will be made manifest to you. You will never feel lonely or separated again. Your loneliness, your pain of separation, is only experienced in one dimension of reality when you are cut off from your own grandeur.

Q: Is it possible that one experience in another dimension is affecting the experience in this dimension?

P'taah: Of course, because you are not really separated. You only believe that you are.

Q: So certain urges I may have could be stemming from another reality.

P'taah: In a way it is so. It is, as you may say, also the latent possibility of creativity that you will experience as a thread from one lifetime to another.

Q: If I have a particular fear or problem which may have stemmed from a previous lifetime, is there any point in trying to track that down?

P'taah: It is an adventure, hmm? In truth it is not absolutely necessary because whatever is not resolved, whatever is not embraced, whatever is still within fear and not in love, you will recreate and recreate until you are finally obligated to look at it. That is all right.

You know humanity is very, very stubborn and does not, in the main, like to look at areas which are not in the light. You will have wondrous excuses for not doing so. You will say, "I do not need to because there is nothing there." You will say, "We will not focus on what is negative, we will only focus on what is positive." You will say, "Well, I have resolved all that shit." And indeed, "Who I am is absolutely on line and I am acknowledging all of the areas which are not in the light."

You all have multitudinous ways of avoiding having to look at what is painful, to look at what you truly do not wish to bring to light. In this fashion it becomes an adventure, a journey of discovery when you are delving into your earlier life and into previous incarnations so that you may consciously contact the thread which you are carrying forth.

You know, dear ones, we have said to you before. Whenever in your life there is a defense, whenever you say 'but' in defense of what you have done or what you are about to do, you may know that there is something to explore.

There truly is no escape, you know. If you are determined to come to who you are, know that whatever is hidden from yourself is keeping you from your own Godhood, your own God-light. You know you may fool everybody, but you do not fool you.

We have watched the dichotomy of the soul, the being who is in desperation to know. The greater the desperation, the greater the defense. We say, "Surrender." It is not to surrender to anybody else. It is to surrender to who you are.

Within your birthing, as you are brought forth in physicality, as you create yourselves into this third dimensional reality, you are already in the full potential of what you may be. It is all contained within you. There is nothing outside you. It is your belief structures that build your physical reality, and as you come into the knowing that they are only beliefs *about* reality and that everything outside yourself is a mirror to you, a gift to you to know who you are, then you will find that the belief structures will change and you will flower.

Q: P'taah, I have a question about belief structures and reality. Where people believe that there is no reincarnation, and that once they are dead they are dead and that's it...

P'taah: They certainly get such a surprise.

Q: How can they have a belief which is so far from reality?

P'taah: How long is it, beloved, that you have believed there is such a thing as reincarnation?

Q: Probably about two or three years.

P'taah: Now, as you have changed your belief, so you have opened up limitless possibilities for exploring who you are, in the knowing that who you are is far grander than what you presupposed.

It is in this fashion that the change of the belief will change your reality. For those people who do not believe that there is such a thing as reincarnation and believe there is nothing after death, then that is exactly what they find for a little while because the consciousness is carried forth after the transition, after you have sloughed your body.

So for a little time these people will find themselves in a no place, in a nothingness. Then they will have a desire to experience something else. At the moment that desire is expressed in consciousness, they have already brought forth the change.

Those who believe in heaven will find exactly the same. They will find a heaven of angels or an earthly paradise. Then they will come into the understanding that there is so much more.

Q: P'taah, how would we know when we are ready to raise the dead?

P'taah: Dear one, when you have the possibility, you will know.

Q: It was presented to me quite distinctly in the reintegration of a cancer patient who was able to integrate his entire life before passing. In fact he relinquished his body into my hands. At that point, is it enough to say, "We did that."

P'taah: Had it been any other way, beloved, it would have been. When you know who you are, then you may work with somebody who is in desire of the same thing. We would suggest that you not be in too much bother about raising the dead at this time. As we have said to you before, beloved, coming into allowance of your own being is of more importance.

Q: I understand, but in a situation like that, one wonders if one has done enough.

P'taah: Why do you think it is your responsibility, beloved? You cannot heal anybody. Dear one, it is their decision. It has nothing to do with you, really. If somebody truly desires, within the knowing of their being, to change their physical situation, not to translate from physicality, they truly do not need anybody else.

Now, if somebody has called forth for assistance, that is wondrous, but it is not your responsibility. You may only do from your own knowing, beloved. And your own knowing is that you do not know who you are. You have a concept of how it may be, all right? So it is not for you to feel guilt or for you to feel that you have failed. It is not for you to take any responsibility for anybody else's living or dying. Do you understand?

The body is only a reflection. Illness, diseasement, only reflects what is within the persona. Illness is only an opportunity for you to look at how it is within you. That is all. The body will begin, very gently, to tell you that all is not well. If you refuse to look, the body will show you larger and larger lessons, and the ultimate one is called death. You know, dear one, death is no big deal. It is an illusion.

Q: Death does not exist in my terms at all.

P'taah: If it does not exist in your terms, why are you speaking about raising the dead?

Q: Because other people speak in those terms. When a cancer patient has learned that the body is printing out the lessons to be learned, how may I then relieve the pain so they can pick up that lesson?

P'taah: Dear one, we give you each week the method for changing pain, whether it be emotional or physical.

Q: Are you saying that if the patient cannot relieve himself of the consistent pain, we should not do anything about it? I want to hear it from you.

P'taah: Dear one, we speak to you about transmutation week-by-week, month after month.

Q: It is all right for me, but what about those who do not know about transmutation.

P'taah: Dear one, it is not all right for you because if it were, then you would be allowing it to occur in your own life. Then you would become a shining example, where your God-light would affect all those about you.

We have said before, a healer is one in desperation of healing himself. Now, it is also that you regard illness to be something negative. As long as you regard illness to be negative—not good—you will never heal.

Q: So what is it that I am not doing further?

P'taah: (Softly) You know, if you were truly understanding, you would perhaps not be a 'healer.' We are speaking to you. We are not saying that there is something wrong with healing. We are speaking, beloved man, to you, for your greatest benefit.

Q: *(A newcomer)* You have spoken this evening about coming to know oneself. I would like to know myself better. Can you give me some advice how to do this?

P'taah: Well, we have given you a signpost this evening when we have spoken about defense.

Q: I think I have missed the essence of that, then.

P'taah: Very well, we will repeat it. I must say that there is no one who will not benefit from hearing it again.

Humanity lives in a universe of duality, polarity, positive/negative, that which is judged to be good/bad, right/wrong, masculine/feminine, black/white, etc.

Now, the reason for all of the pain and anguish is judgment, how you judge yourself. Since eons in time you create yourselves, life after life. Each time there are areas in your life which you carry forth—it is not only from this life—and you judge certain facets of the self to be not good. You live in fear of discovery, of being found out.

Now why is it that you are afraid, dear ones? It is because if somebody knows really who you are, they will not love you. The basic fear is that you are not enough, that you are not worthy of love and loving.

So, from the beginning, you very carefully sweep under the carpet that which you judge to be not so good. As you go through your life and experience invalidation, rejection, betrayal, humiliation, and abandonment, the walls that you build to hide yourself become bigger and bigger. You become more and more defensive.

Now there are those who, with much reading and workshops, etc., come to understand the benefit of letting down the defenses, saying, "This is who I am." In this fashion, they are bringing what they judge to be the unlovable parts, the frightened parts, into the light to be embraced, to be acknowledged, to become part of the God-light. Not to be rejected, pushed away, suppressed, hidden under the carpet.

For many, it is difficult to come to those areas which are so hidden. There have been many, many years of practice in the hiding so we give forth a little signpost. When somebody attacks you and you defend, what are you frightened of? What are you defending? What are you hiding, hmm? Do you understand? In this fashion you may unearth that which you have been hiding from.

You have tucked it away behind your consciousness, but it is begging for the light. We will remind you all you create your own reality absolutely. Your whole universe you personally create. There is nothing in your perception that you do not create.

You are responsible. If the situation is one which you would not choose consciously, if it is something you would deny, then indeed, another signpost. There is no accident.

When you have created a situation that is painful to you, you have created it for your learning, for your benefit, not for anybody else's, although, in truth, it is always for the benefit of all because it is a co-creation. It is always, if you could but see it, a win/win situation for all people if you will allow it to be so. The bottom line, beloved ones, is you did it all.

Q: P'taah, earlier you made mention of defense systems and the word surrender. Does that mean if one is not enjoying a situation and one surrenders, does that mean throwing in the towel, so to speak?

P'taah: Dear one, we did say to you that it is not to surrender to somebody else. It is to surrender to who you are.

Q: Does that mean one does not have to accept the situation as it is?

P'taah: The situation that you find unpalatable simply means that there is something for you to align. Either whatever is occurring is within universal law or universal truth or it is not. When it is within universal truth, then you are resonating to your universe, then what you are perceiving is radiance, joy, and laughter.

When you are perceiving discordance, sorrow, and pain, it is because you are in non-allowance, because you are in judgment. So when we are saying to surrender, we are really saying to be in allowance so that you may align the judgment to come into your own universal truth.

It is not to surrender to somebody else. It is to surrender to you. You see, beloved, if you were really in alignment, it would not occur. How can you surrender what is already given?

Q: Depends on what is being given. If one is given a hard time...

P'taah: Dear one, that is your perception. Why is it a hard time? Because you are in fear, because you are not aligned. You are judging it to be bad. Judgment is non-allowance.

Q: But it can be bad, can't it?

P'taah: Dear one, listen to me. Listen with your heart. If you are in a situation which is bad, it is because you are judging it from fear. If there is no fear, there is no good or bad. It simply is, and in the is-ness you may perceive the joy in it.

Very well, dear ones. We shall take a break for refreshment of the body.

(*After the break*)

P'taah: And so, dear ones, we shall continue.

Q: P'taah, I have a question. Can you give us an overview on what life is like in the Pleiades?

P'taah: It will be very brief, dear one. Harmonious.

Q: I thought you would be that brief.

Q: P'taah, what is the most compassionate way to help another person who is in mental anguish?

P'taah: Show them that you love them.

Q: I feel that they almost wish one to enter their anguish to show that one loves them. Do we need to do that? Or, being really caring, would it be better to give them a very brief opinion on what the situation is and then leave?

P'taah: Dear one, you may only speak from the knowing of the heart. Indeed, you may speak forth in love and compassion in your own knowing. It is certainly to know that everybody creates their own reality absolutely, and as you know this, so you may give it forth. But it is also to say how it may change. It does not mean that you must be hooked into somebody else's story, merely to have love and compassion, to be supportive.

If somebody is in confusion, then you may speak forth and say, "Beloved, you have created this situation that you may benefit, and you know how that is." As we have said to you, the pain and anguish is created by judgment.

Q: By being supportive, do you mean to be there?

P'taah: If it is your desire. What we are saying is that to get hooked into the story of somebody else is of no benefit to you or anybody else.

Q: I am realizing now not to see it from an ego point of view but rather to say what I feel, instead of being concerned about how I would appear. If I do not appear a certain way, will they judge me as not being loving or caring? This is me coming back to the fear of loss.

P'taah: Congratulations, dear one. This is wondrous that you have come to this realization because very often humanity acts forth from social consciousness. They are afraid if they are not seen in a good light, if they are not well regarded, then indeed, they will not be loved.

When you love who you are, that consideration becomes null and void. So it is to follow the heart. If it is truly the desire of your heart to be of assistance, then you may do so by showing that you do love and you do care, that you have compassion.

Q: Each situation may be different.

P'taah: Dear one, it does not matter what the story be. Humanity is in separation of self from Self and from each other. So when the time of stress comes, of pain and anguish, then people feel more isolated. It is wondrous that you may step forth and say, "Truly, you are not alone. Truly I do care and I do love you."

That does not mean that you buy in. When you buy in, you are buying in to irresponsibility. It is only by humanity being responsible that you will come into the understanding of how the universe works and how you may operate comfortably within the universe.

If you are co-joining with people to cast blame, to affirm victim-hood, you are doing no service. Also, if you are acting only to appease the ego of somebody else, or you are acting from your own ego or social consciousness, it is called disservice.

It does not matter what words you are saying. The knowing of the heart is greater than the mind. When one is doing something from duty or to appease one's own ego, then the recipient is certainly aware on a deeper level of knowing.

Q: I have a couple of questions. Firstly, do you have a physical form on your planet?

P'taah: Indeed.

Q: Can you describe what you look like?

P'taah: Hmm…We are very beautiful. In physical form you may say we are humanoid, though of a different frequency, therefore the body does not appear to be as dense, as solid, as the human bodies of this planet, in your understanding. But very beautiful, as are you.
    Next question.

Q: I have a question about imagination. I wonder how much validity there is in imagination. Can I give you an example? If I say to George here for instance, "Imagine you are on Mars looking in a particular direction, and tell me what you see." And if I do the same exercise at the same time, would we both see in our mind's eye the same picture?

P'taah: It is very possible. Imagination is valid. Your whole universe is created from imagination. There can be no thing created in your physical reality without it being a thought first. That which is a thought without matter is indeed imagination. Even that which is war has to be a thought-form before it is manifested in physical reality. So, it is certainly real. There can be nothing in the imagination which is 'not'.

Q: If I imagine something, I understand that it exists as a thought-form, but does this mean that it has a physical reality somewhere?

P'taah: It may. But because it is not in physical matter does not mean to say it is not real. Now, when there are two people who are looking at a scene in this physical reality, do you think they see the same thing?

Q: Physically, yes, but the interpretation would be different.

P'taah: But what is the difference? They are seeing differently. Also, when you are working with imagination and you set a scene in imagination which each person sees differently, it can be that one is looking at a different time frame or a different dimension of reality which creates the difference. Very often people will imagine what is, to all intent and purpose, the same thing. Very often it is that humanity is tapping into collective consciousness.

You know there is nothing to be discovered out there that is not already in existence. It already is, it is just that you have not seen it yet. So, in even thinking about this, you are already broadening and enlarging your concepts beyond normal limitation.

That which is called thought is not limited to the inside of your head. Once it becomes a thought-form, it is broadcast to the universe. That is why, in truth, there is no such thing as a secret, even your own deep dark secrets. I promise you, they are not really a secret.

Q: Thank you. I do have one more question. It has to do with karma. I do not really know how it works.

P'taah: What is it that you imagine karma to be?

Q: An equalizing, balancing, educating force. If I put out something bad, somewhere along the line I will get something bad back, if I choose to decree it to be bad.

P'taah: That is so. You are in understanding that there is no judgment in the universe of good and bad. So we would say this. It is merely that as you would choose incarnation, it is to experience what is different to what you have experienced before.

It is not in any way to be considered as punishment, but merely that you experience the polarities in order to embrace them. Therefore, if you have been a murderer in a previous incarnation—and you have—then you will also experience how it is to be murdered because that is the polarity. It is to embrace both.

That is the lesson, but it is not a lesson in terms of punishment and there are threads that you carry from one lifetime to another in this fashion. That is all.

Q: P'taah, I used to be quite happy with my intellect and brain, but I have found recently that I cannot rely on it any more. The day I started a new career, I got a terrible pain in my neck. My brain gave all sorts of reasons for the pain, which did not help. After chiropractors and massages I finally lay down and breathed through it and got to the bottom of it and it went away. There seems to be such a disconnection there for me.

P'taah: There always is. If there was not the disconnection, there would not be the pain. Pain is resistance, so you may lie down and breathe. Somebody else may take a walk in nature or put their body in water. It is merely to allow the stillness, to bless the resistance. As you bless it, it is aligned.

Q: In my case it can never be done in the brain.

P'taah: Not in anybody's case. What we are talking about is transmutation and it does not matter whether it be emotional or physical. We have said to you, take responsibility for the creation of the pain, align the judgment, take off your head and put it under your arm, and feel the feeling.

Do not forget that your intellect is your servant. It is there to serve you. It is not there to rule you. The ego is also your servant, not to be beaten, not to be put asunder or rejected, but to be embraced so that it may serve.

Q: May I ask you, you said before there is something I am seeking that is eluding me. What is it that is elusive?

P'taah: What is it that you desire to bring forth in your life, dear one?

Q: I am completely satisfied with many areas in my life now, but I long for a lover.

P'taah: Indeed. And what did we say to you, beloved? As you will strive and seek, as you will be in need and desperation, so that which is the lover will elude you. As you will be in allowance, in non-expectation, in non-need, so you may have whatever it is you desire. That is not only in regard to lovers. That is about everything.

Q: The last question about lovers: What makes us fall in love with a particular person? If there are a thousand men, all shapes and sizes and characters, what causes the chemistry? What causes it when your pulse races and you go all weak in the knees and you feel as if you would faint? It is not by will. Everything then seems out of control.

P'taah: It is such good fun, hmm? (*Roaring laughter from the audience.*)

Q: Can you understand then how difficult it is not to strive for it? To have that experience again? Of course I want to have the same feeling again.

P'taah: The divine madness!

Q: What you call striving, I enjoy it. Thinking about it, imagining it. But I want to have it physically, too.

P'taah: Beloved, we did not say do not imagine. We did not say do not feel. (*Approaching the lady, P'taah adds very softly*) Did we?

Q: Don't come too close to me. You are such a power-house. (*The audience laughs.*) When you come near me and look into my eyes, there is so much power, you almost knock me over.

P'taah: We will be gentle with you. *(By this time gales of laughter fill the room.)* All of you know this divine madness, hmm? That which is the desire of the heart to come forth and mate, it is wonderful.

It is also called looking for the unity and excitement that you have not found within yourself. When you can regard yourself with such excitement, beloved one, we shall bow down before you.

Do not judge it. It is wonderful! Go forth in joy, but let the words tickle the back of your mind now and again and you may be in allowance and non-expectation of how and when something may occur. Then you shall manifest what it is you desire.

Q: P'taah, it has been said that love is convertible energy. If someone is in pain, you send them love. Can you explain how this actually helps them? Can you expand on this?

P'taah: We have said to you that thought-forms are not confined within your head. That which is the most powerful energy in the universe, that which makes it all tick, is love. It is that which humanity—and indeed all things, even what you regard to be inanimate objects and flora and fauna—are responding to.

Love. All resound to love. Without it there is no growth. Without it there is no healing. So, when you send forth love, the thought-form, it is like a projectile. Nobody can withstand it. And so it is assimilated. There are no barriers against love. In this fashion, love may reinforce what is called the God-light of somebody else to help them to integrate their own knowing, which is love, to create their healing.

Q: P'taah, surely people can refuse love?

P'taah: Dear one, you are speaking about consciousness. The God-light of humanity and all things is beyond consciousness. It is beyond anything. It cannot be refused.

Q: So, does it come within their aura, awaiting their realization?

P'taah: It is not necessarily a conscious process at all. If somebody is on the other side of the world in diseasement, when you visualize the person and send them love, it is instantaneous. There is no time lapse. Love is received the moment it is conceived in the thought-form. The self receives it, whether or not there is a conscious knowing.

Q: What good is it to the person if the consciousness has not received love?

P'taah: Well, now, it is not necessarily the consciousness that has created diseasement in the first place. It is that the consciousness has not taken note of what has been occurring below consciousness or outside of consciousness.

When you are hiding whatever it is that creates the disturbance in the body, your conscious mind may say, "I cannot understand why it is I am feeling so unwell. It must be the weather," Hmm?

However, outside that consciousness there is the self saying, "Wake up and listen!" It is that greater self that indeed knows love. Do you understand?

Q: If the greater Self is all love...

P'taah: We are speaking in levels. The greater self knows all things, knows all things of all universes, also. So there is this focus of energy in layers which you have separated into consciousness, subconscious, un-consciuos. But truly, there is no separation, and what we are reflecting to you, in a way, is that there is no separation if only you will allow it.

That which is subconscious is certainly aware beyond what you allow consciously. Dear one, when you walk into a room and you are meeting someone for the first time, you have an immediate knowing. Sometimes you will say, "I feel very drawn to this person and I do not know why." Or you feel, " I do not like this person." In other words, the subconscious has already made up its mind in judgment of how it is, good or bad.

If somebody looks at you with love in their heart for you, there is a knowing. Sometimes it trickles into the consciousness. Other times it does not, however you will feel very warm without really knowing why it is that you feel so good.

Q: Sending love to someone who is hurting—I must admit I am still hooked into stopping their hurting. To what degree does sending love enhance their capacity for opening up their awareness and their healing?

P'taah: It is like reinforcement. Now, if there is a small child who is neglected, who is not shown love, the child does not really flower in spite of the fact that it is given three meals per day, clothed warmly in the winter, etc. Where the child has all the physical comfort and yet there is no love of the heart given forth, the child withers. It cannot flower.

So you may say it is not really what you can touch with your physical hand, but you may certainly see the effect. Where there is love within people, it creates strength. So it is not that you take over the responsibility for somebody else's well-being, but merely that you are re-enforcing the idea-construct of good health, whether that be physical or emotional.

The fact that you have a hook in there has nothing to do with the love. It is the love that is doing it. Your hook is your business. You know, what you are is God-light. When you are sending forth love, it is God-light communicating with God-light. In truth that is how you may manifest anything you desire in this reality.

We have said forth to you that you manifest in physical reality through the idea embraced by the desire and the knowing that it already *is*. What you are really communicating with is the God-light. When you are desiring something to come forth for you, it is the Godlight that you are pulling toward you. So if you are in desire, whether it be something of physical matter or not, merely visualize it, send forth the desire within that visualization and the emotion of *knowing* the God-light of it, then the physical vision fades and you are left with the God-light. It is that which you draw to you. That is called a recipe, beloved ones.

Q: You have said no one can heal another person, but what about a person's desire to help another person with compassion when seeing somebody suffering?

P'taah: Indeed, and you put forth love, hmm? It is called the God-light talking to the God-light.

Q: So this business of laying on of hands, it does not have any effect?

P'taah: Dear one, it may be. It is merely called methodology, hmm? It is not necessary. It is not even necessary to be in the same vicinity, in truth.

Very well, beloved ones, sufficient unto the time. Our thanks, indeed. It has been a joy to share with you. Go forth in your God-light. Let it shine. Be the brilliance you are. Be the joy you are. Be the laughter you are, because you are all that. Good evening.

▼ Eleventh Session
March 18

P'taah: Good evening, dear ones. Welcome indeed. In the week past we spoke to you about manifestation, about calling forth God-light to God-light. And we gave forth a recipe. It is truly the most simple thing.

Now, this evening we are going to have a change. This evening you will reflect to me your own great knowing. So I shall ask forth of you, and as you speak with me, you will be very even, because it will be as speaking to yourself.

There are several areas which I would be most delighted for you to share your knowing. As we have spoken about manifestation in this last week, we will ask *(addressing a man)*, dear one, that you will tell me how it works.

Q: It works from the total knowing that I am Divine One I Am accepting total responsibility for what the situation is, desiring to express the wholeness of the soul. Using the awareness of I Am, I desire such and such, and that I know that it is.

P'taah: Very well, *(to a woman)* now we will ask the recipe for a particular thing in your life. If you want to have money in your life, and you have it not, why do you think you have it not?

Q: Perhaps the desire is not strong enough, or perhaps I am not working for it.

P'taah: Ah, not working for it? Do you think you must work for it?

Q: There is still a certain belief in there.

P'taah: That is all right. So when you understand that this is a belief that you hold, how will you change it?

Q: I should believe it is there in abundance.

P'taah: There is no 'should.' How would you change it? How would you change a belief structure that stands between you and the desire of the conscious mind?

Q: I have to change.

P'taah: But how?

Q: Just accept that it is there.

P'taah: But when you say you have to change, you should change, what does that imply to you? How do you feel about the fact that you have the belief that you must work for money?

You have said that it is the belief that stands between you and money. You have looked and said the belief is, "I need to work." So now that you have looked at the belief, how do you feel about it? Do you feel that you should not have that belief?

Q: No.

P'taah: What does it mean if you think that you should not have it. Does it mean that you are judging it?

Do you see where this is leading? You see, if you are holding a belief and you know that this belief is not conducive to bringing forth what you desire in your conscious mind, you say, "This belief does not serve me any longer."

When you judge the belief, you are not aligning it. When you judge it and you say, "It is perfectly all right to judge it," and when you embrace it like you would embrace a child, then you have alignment. Do you understand? So it is that you may look at all the beliefs that do not serve you in this fashion.

(*P'taah addresses a man who is always very quiet*) Now, my sweet one, you must speak, hmm?

Q: *(The man chuckles)* Good evening, P'taah. Is that sufficient?

P'taah: We have got you this time. No escape. How is your life?

Q: Wonderful at the moment.

P'taah: Why do you think it is that your life is wonderful?

Q: Because I want it that way and I am willing to accept it.

P'taah: Because you are willing to accept whatever comes?

Q: Knowing that that is how it has to be, and however it is, is great.

P'taah: You are a wise one, indeed. It is thusly that you may allow the God-light within you to expand. (*P'taah pauses, then adds softly*) You are most dear to us.

(*To a woman*) Do you feel as if you are at school? Everybody in trepidation that they will not know the answer?

Q: Yes. *(Laughing)*

P'taah: It is all right. You know there is really no right answer. What is most difficult for you, beloved?

Q: Knowing what I should be doing on the physical level with my life. My spiritual life is fine.

P'taah: We do not see the difference. You are your spiritual life. What else is there?

Q: It is the life I am following now. I chose it. Making choices...

P'taah: Ah! What terror, to make a choice. Tell me, what would be a wrong choice.

Q: Well, I know there are no wrong choices.

P'taah: Then?

Q: Sometimes I cannot work out where the good is in some of my choices.

P'taah: What about, which would be more fun?

Q: Following the heart's desire? Doing what makes my heart sing?

P'taah: *(Feigning outrage)* No! So, shall we say from this day, every time you are to make a choice, to hell with the money? Which choice is more fun? Can you be that courageous, beloved?

Q: I shall certainly try to be.

P'taah: Do not try.

Q: Do not try? Allow it?

P'taah: Allow yourself to have fun? Very good. We thoroughly recommend it.

Now, you know in the times we are speaking with you, what we are saying, truly, is very simple. As we ask the questions, it is very easy for you to give an intellectual answer. You have read all the books, done all the workshops, and yet you do not hear me.

That is all right. Sometimes we think we do not speak clearly enough for you. Yet it would not matter how clearly we speak to you if you are within the rigidity of your defense systems, your precious and most beloved ego.

There is nothing wrong with your ego. It is a wonderful, valid, divine aspect of you. It is not to be annihilated, but it is certainly for you to be aware that this wondrous servant called ego, can become in control of your life and be your master. It is very tricky. Very often you are not aware of the defense mechanism. It is that defense mechanism which keeps you from your God-light.

There is nothing to do, dear ones, to become enlightened masters. You already are. It is just a matter of parting the veil a little to allow yourselves to glimpse that light that you are. And as you have the glimpse, so indeed the curtain parts a little more, the glimpse gets broader, the knowing becomes more and more and the curtain parts yet a little more.

It is not difficult. There is nothing to *do*. You may sit back quietly and watch the ego play its little tricks, and you may say, "That is all right. It is only frightened of being dispossessed. That is all."

(*P'taah speaks to a man.*) So what is it that you do with a child who is afraid, dear one?

Q: If I look at my own children, I take them in my arms and comfort them.

P'taah: Absolutely. Well, that is exactly what you would do with your ego. Take it in your arms and comfort it and say, "Beloved, we are not going anywhere. We are not parting company, you and I. But if you will allow, we shall have a wonderful adventure together, and nobody and nothing will harm you. Together, you and I will step into the light." Fairly simple, eh?

(*P'taah walks over to the man holding the microphone.*) As you have the machinery in your hand, dear one, how is it that you recognize when the ego gets in the way? Not that it occurs very often.

Q: *(Laughs)* Too often for me.

P'taah: Do not judge yourself. We are being quite serious, you know.

Q: I recognize my ego is in the way when all I want to do is get the hell out of wherever I am.

P'taah: Indeed. *(Walks toward a lady.)* And you, beloved woman, how do you recognize when you are being held off by your ego? Do you have a method of recognizing this?

Q: Yes, when I am unable to love myself.

P'taah: Ah, but that is fairly often, not for you only, but for all people. We are speaking about a day-to-day situation when you are in re-action. When somebody says something to you which is disagreeable and the ego comes into the play. How do you recognize it?

Q: I either get angry or I want to withdraw.

P'taah: Indeed. Does anybody else have an answer?

Q: I look inside myself and notice a feeling of lack of contentment, of unhappiness.

P'taah: That is not only necessarily the ego, beloved. If it were, it would be most simple to cure the anguish of humanity. Does anybody else have a comment?

Q: I would feel tense. I would relate that to fear.

Q: If a situation would result in disharmony, then the ego would be speaking.

P'taah: What would the ego be doing?

Q: It would be in fear, in defense.

P'taah: Defense. That is what we are looking for. Defense. All of the other things are quite true also, but when you are in defense, you know that there is certainly something to look at. The words, "But I..."—sometimes, you know, we think that was another name for the ego, "But I." We hear it often enough.

Q: I went through a time about fifteen years ago when I was filled with fear and if I had nothing to be afraid of, I would create something. The only way I got out of it was when I became grateful to the experiences and surrendered to them. That seemed to solve the problems.

P'taah: Ah, and what do you think is the magic word there.

Q: Surrender. You have to surrender. There is no other way.

P'taah: Indeed. Surrender. It is called the posture of the Christus. Surrender—the ultimate feminine, negative energy. Simple? Surrender. There is nothing to do, nothing to *do*.

And so here you all are, my beloved friends, on the rack of your desperate striving for enlightenment. The recipe for transmutation is the only recipe in your universe where you do not have to do anything to get results.

The recipe for transmutation. You know, you forget transmutation. Week-by-week, you forget it. We have tried to engrave it in your heart, but we discover that we are writing in invisible ink. (*Everybody chuckles at this truth.*)

Transmutation—the ultimate alchemy of the soul. You don't have to do anything. You know those magicians of your far-off years worked very hard to change lead into gold. You may change the lead into gold without doing anything. A simple recipe:

1. Take responsibility. Whatever the situation, you have created it. Nobody else.

2. Align the judgment. That simply means bless it all. Bless the people involved. Bless the situation. Bless yourselves for creating the situation to find the pearl of wisdom within.

3. Feel the feeling.

4. Surrender. Surrender, and when you surrender, the feeling, masked by the resistance of pain, is suddenly revealed as a neutral energy which is then allowed to move from the solar plexus to the heart.

Take responsibility—align the judgment—feel the feeling—surrender. *(Very quietly)* What is more simple?

Q: This surrendering—I have a problem with it. Intellectually, no problem. It is crystal clear. But I would ask this gentleman, how did you do it? You say there is nothing to it, but what do you say to a person who is terrified, who sees ghosts everywhere, who is paranoid, is afraid of dying at any minute? How can I tell him to surrender and feel the feeling? Will he understand?

P'taah: You may have to explain that he creates his own reality, beloved. But you know, you may explain it and people may hear it, but until they take responsibility, it is called pissing in the wind. I do love these ship expressions.

Do you understand? You see, you are all so addicted to your pain and fears that it is very simple for you to be a victim. This way you do not have to take responsibility. It is very easy to be in self-pity. That is also not taking responsibility. "Woe is me." "Look what they have done to me."

It is valid. It is a divine aspect. The only trouble is that it does not bring you joy. Every time you blame somebody else, you are not taking responsibility. Every time you feel sorry for yourself, that life has dealt you a raw deal, you are not taking responsibility.

(A young aboriginal woman.)

Q: Good evening, P'taah. I would like to talk to you about this surrendering and taking responsibility in regard to the aboriginal people.

I went to a conference last week about the future of our Dreaming. In the traditional life, the men sung the land and created our stories, and that was the strength of the tribe. Now the elders and the men are not singing the same songs as before.

I have fear for the people who are only part aboriginal and who are misplaced in society. I work at a school and I can see those children suffering the same way that my mother suffered, and my grandmother suffered. Such injustice to aboriginal people. *(The woman bows her head and weeps.)* At this conference there was a new movement called the Aboriginal Provisional Government.

What I want to know, P'taah, is this the way that aboriginal people can re-identify and re-create their aboriginality so that they will not be a dying race? This is what I wonder because this is where my energy lies. I feel that I have come through this life to help the movement along, to be part of that movement, to help the young ones to identify with the aboriginality and their culture, to keep it alive.

P'taah: Indeed. Now, do you know how best you may do this?

Q: Well, I believe this provisional government could be the way because it means the aboriginal people need not be dependent on the federal government and white people for their own lifestyle.

P'taah: Indeed, and that is wondrous, beloved.

However, we would say this to you—how you will be a star leading your people is when you understand in your dreaming that who you are in creating your land is a Goddess. When you come into the light of the Goddess within you, do understand that that is the greatest dreaming of all.

When your people will understand that each and every one of them is sovereign God-light, that the dream is not even how it has been for your people because they will realize a dream at this moment undreamt of.

They will step forth and be as they have been in times gone by, before civilization was birthed. How it was when they knew no separation. Every atom of their being and every atom of their planet—their wondrous Goddess—were as one.

You know, the stories of the Dreaming, the songs of the Dreaming were really only the celebration of the knowing of all of this. It was not a thing of culture. It was birthed of a grand knowing. Do you understand the difference?

Culture is ideas and traditions passed on. The knowing is the knowing of the God-light within, the sovereignty, the unity, the Oneness of the Self in all things. To know indeed, that the God/Goddess, All-That-Is, lives within and is part of all things that exist without.

And your people knew the star people. So it is to say, "Never mind about the culture. The new dream is so much grander."

Q: Are you suggesting that I put my energy to the new Dreaming?

P'taah: Dear one, go ahead with whatever it is, but know that until you allow your own God-light to shine forth as a beacon to draw your people to you, the changes will not occur.

And this is not only for you. It is for all people who desire change. The changes will only occur from within. It is all very well for your people to say that they are in need of another government, their own government. But, dear one, what makes any of you think that this government will be any better than the one there now?

We would be very happy to see one government on the face of this planet that is doing anything of substance to help your planet, to help the people, to lessen the starvation, to lessen the murder.

What do they do? They do nothing because they do not know. Your government is not about soul!

Q: That is what I was hoping about the aboriginal government, that it would be all about soul.

P'taah: Indeed. And it may certainly occur as the people allow themselves to come into the knowing of who they really are. And who they really are is not aboriginal. Who they are is God/Goddess expressing in third density. That is who humanity is.

So indeed, go forth and enjoy the great fight. But know truly, you will create the change when you create the change within you. Indeed, dear one?

Q: Indeed. I am ready. It is happening.

P'taah: Very good.

Q: About defense and wanting to blame others. I have been studying a certain teaching which has forgiveness as the key to freedom.

Within myself I came across a very deep well of anger which came from my childhood and physical abuse. I read a book by a woman who had a lot of experience with this and she suggested it is okay not to forgive in order to help oneself release the energy.

P'taah: Very well. Now, this is what is called the interim period, to express the anger and that is valid.

You know the expression of it is only the polarity of suppression.

Q: I do not want to hold on to the anger. I do not want to be non-forgiving, and yet I am protecting myself.

P'taah: Dear one, of course you can feel free to express anger. When you are making it wrong, you are giving power to it.

Q: When I am making my own anger wrong?

P'taah: Indeed. Do you understand?

Q: Indeed. It is very important to allow my anger. This is why I am choosing not to forgive for the moment.

P'taah: Now, when you are saying not to forgive, what is the polarity of forgive?

Q: Well, the understanding of forgive in *The Course of Miracles* is the dissolving of things I have been holding on to, but it does not seem so easy.

P'taah: But is it not because what you are trying to do is to destroy that which is within you?

Q: Well, I recognize that by being humble and accepting things as they were as a child, it was a very spiritual thing to do, but I have paid a very high price.

P'taah: Who says it was spiritual?

Q: Well, it was spiritual in that it involved humility and a surrender to what was at the time.

P'taah: A surrender to somebody else.

Q: A surrender to the irrationality of somebody else.

P'taah: Well, beloved, we will tell you this. It has brought you here.

Q: I know that. I am very thankful for that.

P'taah: Indeed. Now, you created it all. You create everything. There is nothing in your reality which is not your responsibility.

Q: The only way I can be free is to totally accept responsibility?

P'taah: Indeed, but you know what you have given yourself is a treasure beyond compare.

Q: Hmm. A pearl of wisdom.

P'taah: We would perhaps suggest to you that you may care to read very soon what has been given forth these evenings which may bring you to a broader knowing, hmm? So be it. You will enjoy.

Now, it is such that there are many people who have incredible horror stories in their early life. But I will tell you something, dear one. It does not matter about the story. The pain is the same for everybody.

Q: I have believed that for a long time. Everybody has a cross to bear and I am not someone special.

P'taah: Pain is pain. You are very special. You are a unique facet in the Divine crown of life. There is nobody in the universe like you and the universe would not be the same without you. You are very special. One of the things which is so special about you all, and I could name many, is the fact that there is not another species who could survive the pain that you all know so well. But even more wondrous is your unlimited capacity for love and joy.

We shall take a break now.

(After the break.)

Q: P'taah, I am changing quite dramatically, but there is still this residual clinging on to fear. I can see it is the most ridiculous thing to do. You told me last time to love and embrace the fear. I still find that a problem.

I think we are totally conditioned to thinking we are unlovable. I know that is a fallacy, but it is so difficult to come to terms with that concept, that we are the God I Am, that we are love and loveable. Could you give me a push toward transmutation?

P'taah: *(Tenderly)* I love you. You know, you hear all the words. Every time you turn around, there is another bombardment of words about how it 'should' be. The little head does not stop working, "I know I should love myself.' 'I know I am the God I Am," etc.

Well, all of that is true. You are the Goddess, but who else you are is a frightened baby girl. That is all right. This room is full of frightened baby girls and boys. They do not really know it is all right, either.

How do you get from your head to your heart? How do you embrace the fear?

Q: A bit of a problem, whether to embrace the fear, the threats that caused the fear, or just the physical manifestation.

P'taah: All of it. Now, you say that you are aware that you have created it all.

Q: Yes. I am taking full responsibility for creating it all.

P'taah: It is to be very thankful. That which is illness is only that your body is telling you a story. When the body tells you a story, it is for your own benefit. So it is to bless it, but it is all right for little boys and girls to be afraid of dis-ease and afraid of death. It is perfectly all right.

When you try to change it—when you know that you should not be angry at fate, when you know you should not be a victim, you should not be afraid, you should be able to do this—you are making it all wrong. It is not wrong.

Embracement you may also call allowance. Allow fear and ego. If you imagine that the fear is really just a baby you, and if you will sit and go into that still place within you and see a baby who is afraid, you may pick up the baby girl, embrace her and hold her close to you. Tell her that you love her. Hold her close to you, tell her that you will never let her be harmed and just allow her to be. Hold her close to you.

If the fear is like a child, you would not push it away, hmm? You would not try to annihilate it. You would simply gather it unto you, not to do anything, beloved woman, just to be in allowance. Is this of assistance to you? Indeed.

I wish to ask each and every one of you what is that that you are most afraid of.

Q: Can I think about it for a minute?

P'taah: No.

Q: Success.

P'taah: What are you most afraid of?

Q: I don't know. I truly do not know.

P'taah: What are you most afraid of?

Q: Being alone, I guess.

Q: Failure.

Q: Being seen to be stupid and not getting it.

Q: Not achieving what I set out to do.

Q: Not expressing my soul-gifts before it is time to leave the Earth.

P'taah: Very good, dear one.

Q: Aloneness and death.

Q: Rejection by people.

Q: Fear itself and death.

Q: Aloneness.

Q: I don't know.

Q: Possibly men.

P'taah: Very good.

Q: That I may not be enough for humanity.

Q: That my bicycle may be stolen. *(Shrieks of laughter, as the audience knows the lady's on-going bicycle story.)*

P'taah: Why?

Q: Because as I said before, it is a tricky thing.

P'taah: Why would you be afraid if your bicycle gets stolen?

Q: I would become insecure.

P'taah: About?

Q: About myself.

P'taah: Indeed. About?

Q: That I do not have trust, generally. I was not making a joke. I mentioned the bike for a reason. It stands for something.

P'taah: I understand, beloved. I want you to understand exactly what it stands for. What is the insecurity?

Q: Because trust is new to me. I have entered into a new area with trust and I still feel insecure. I also do not lock the house at night.

P'taah: You do not want to doubt the validity of your own power.

Q: That is why I mentioned it to you. I still need that support.

P'taah: Indeed. Absolutely.

Q: I want to find the right husband.

Q: Actually, only fear itself. If we really knew that we have everything we need, there would be no fear.

Q: My biggest fear is not having enough time to achieve everything I want to do.

P'taah: You are afraid of not achieving everything you want before you die, is that what you are saying?

Q: Yes. I guess so.

Q: Until just recently it was about not being good enough, but I have faced that. So…I really don't know one now.

P'taah: Indeed. How interesting it all is. That which is fear, and which you are in desperation to keep at bay, you draw to you. When you can make it all right, when you can be in allowance of that which you fear, so indeed, you will have changed your world. Questions?

Q: If the world that we perceive is a reflection of us, how can we bring back what we see as occurring outside of ourselves to be inside of us, so that we can know more of who we are?

P'taah: It is all a mirror. How many times do we tell you and how many times do you say, "Oh no, this is not a mirror. There is nothing there for me to look at."

Every time your buttons are pushed, you are looking in the mirror. Now, you may deny it, you may defend it, you may tell yourself a wondrous story, but it does not work. Every time you denounce somebody, every time you say 'oh shit', you are looking in the mirror, beloved ones. You are in judgment no matter what pretty name you give it.

That is all right. It is perfectly all right. It is a valid aspect, else it would not exist, but it is keeping you separate from who you are.

And so you need to play a little game of honesty, with the self, that is, if you wish to truly know who you are. That is if you are willing to give up the bullshit. I like that one.

We are often quite amazed how many 'wise gurus' walk your planet busy giving advice to every one, but who really do not like to look too closely inside themselves. We would say to you, beloved ones, as you are looking at the guru giving forth the wisdom, and as you are in the knowing that the guru is far more comfortable in putting words out than taking the thoughts in, that is also your mirror.

Q: I like that one.

P'taah: We thought you might.

Q: I judge myself so much and maybe everyone else does too...

P'taah: Oh, you may rely upon it.

Q: ...and I find the hardest thing is being honest with myself.

P'taah: Do you know why it is? You have all lived with invalidation all of your life. You are terrified that you are not enough, that you are unlovable. You have all been told how it should be, and you are all desperately trying to measure up to your own ideal and how you think everybody else may see you and how you would want them to see you. It makes it very difficult to be honest with self.

But you see, dear ones, what is it that you really want? What you all really want is to be human being realized, in full potential, standing in full sovereignty. Knowing that who you are is the God/Goddess, the All-That-Is expressing in third density, and in this knowing you will know all dimensions of reality. So you will know all things, indeed.

Q: It is a privilege to be here with you tonight. I have also been privileged to have spent time with another channeled entity called Ramtha, and I find great similarities between you. Can you explain this?

P'taah: Dear one, we are the same Board of Directors. (*Chuckles from the audience.*)

Q: Your disposition and manner is almost that of Ramtha and if you did not have a different name, I would sit here and say, "This is Ramtha coming through another body."

P'taah: Would you indeed? But you see, we are not called Ramtha. We are called P'taah.

Q: Is Ramtha one of you, seeing that you use the word we? Are you Ramtha as well?

P'taah: We merely say, beloved, that there is a Board of Directors. Our woman says: "The Board of Directors is sitting up there, the bastards, organizing my life." And then she says, "I am only teasing," so I do not get mad at her. (*The audience is greatly amused.*) She will get very angry tomorrow when she hears this. I will get my ass kicked.

Q: How does this bring us back to Ramtha?

P'taah: It does not. The hows and whats of it, beloved, is none of your business. (*Softly*) I am only teasing you.

Q: P'taah, I think that most of us can see the beautiful pearl that you are teaching us, and what we have learned over the years from books, from gurus, from meditations. We know it intellectually, yet we are still not really there. Could you suggest to us what we have to concentrate on to see the pearl more clearly?

P'taah: Give me a word. What is between you and enlightenment?

Q: Nothing. I am enlightenment.

P'taah: Yes. We will be very happy when you know it. What is standing between you and your knowing that you are a grand enlightened master?

Q: I am searching for the answer and I cannot find it. I know there is something there.

P'taah: How about judgment?

Q: Yes?

P'taah: Yes? Is it not simple? The only thing of importance is that all of the information that comes through is the same, no matter what phenomenal means is used. It is called love who you are. Know yourself and know the God/Goddess, All-That-Is.

Q: Okay. Going back to my fear about running out of time. If that continues to be a fear, that means I will run out of time.

P'taah: You bet.

Q: In recent times I feel I am achieving something. Things I was in fear of, I stopped fearing.

P'taah: If I were to tell you that you will die tomorrow, what would be your fear?

Q: None.

P'taah: I tell you what. Your desire for achievement would certainly fly out the window. You may live every day as if it were your last, all of you. There is no tomorrow. We have said many times to you, there is no tomorrow. There is only today because what you regard as your future is built on this now moment. Whatever it is that you want will always be tomorrow. (*Addressing another man who also fears death*) Indeed, dear one?

Q: You have just answered my question.

P'taah: Indeed? How extraordinary.

Q: P'taah, it seems that one of the major fears that was not spoken of is the fear of life.

P'taah: Dear one, that major fear that you are speaking of for everybody is your fear. Fear of life is the greatest diseasement and the greatest killer of humanity. However, beloved ones, it changes, we are happy to say.

You know, you really are so wonderful. You are simply amazing, astonishingly beautiful, astonishingly courageous, and I salute you.

Q: P'taah, would you speak to us about the Board of Directors?

P'taah: Dear one, it is not necessary. There is only one thing that you really need to know and that is that humanity is loved and cherished on every dimension. The numbers and the names of the dimensions do not matter. They do not mean anything to you. The names of the planets do not mean anything to you. There is only one thing that means something to you and it is your own heart, your own soul, your own consciousness, your own potential, your own beauty. That is why the Board of Directors sends messages to you, to remind you of what you already really know, and that is that you are God.

There is nothing else. There are many people who want various information about technology and methodology, but what does it mean to you? It is a form of entertainment because the only thing of importance is that you know who you are. That is all. When you know who you are, you will know everything else.

(The young aboriginal woman addresses P'taah once more.)

Q: Beloved P'taah, I spoke before about the fear about finding the right man. I have had the knowing inside me that I should have an aboriginal husband and have aboriginal children. I am asking if that is the right choice.

P'taah: Well, that is a very good question. The major love affair in your life will be the one that you have with yourself. It is very important that you do.

It seems very important for humanity to rush off and find a mate, and that is all right, but it is not the ultimate love affair because really what you are searching for is unity. There is only one place where there is unity, beloved woman. And when you find it there, we assure you, it will not be a worry to find a lover.

As for your choice, there is no such thing as a wrong choice. There is only the heart's desire. Do not mistake the heart's desire for duty. What is the heart's desire today may well change tomorrow, and that is perfectly all right, okay?

Q: *(Chuckling)* Yes, thank you.

P'taah: Dear ones, sufficient unto the time. Same time, same place. It will be the same channel, so tune in.

Walk free and sovereign, beloved people, and let your path be lit with your own God-light, and know indeed, nothing can harm you. I love you all. Good evening.

▼ Twelfth Session March 25

P'taah: (*Very dramatically*) Good evening. How are you, dear ones?

(*P'taah walks among the audience, looking at each person and occasionally addressing a person on a personal matter.*)

P'taah: One of the most common questions humanity asks from the heart is why? Sometimes it is, "Why me God?" But even when it is not a cry of anguish from the heart, there is certainly the curiosity of humanity to know why and why now. And 'why now' is indeed the choice to come forth to experience the change.

Now with every lifetime it is choice. Every lifetime you choose your situation and you choose your familial engagement according to what it is that you are desiring to bring forth in your life. Let there be no mistake about it, dear ones, it is choice and everything that choice implies, mainly responsibility.

There are people at this time upon your planet who have chosen to come forth, to be birthed, in an area of great unrest. Areas of war, famine, and enslavement by governments, etc.

Now, in these last 50 years of your time, humanity has seen great changes. Great changes in technology and a great shift in consciousness. Dear ones, it is not going to stop. It will become more and more. Not only will you notice this on a global scale, but within your personal life as well. There is no escape.

We have talked to you during these weeks, indeed during these months, about your personal trauma. On a broad spectrum, it is the trauma of all of humanity. We have said to you that humanity is dying of a broken heart.

Now, there are those of you, certainly those of you present here and those of humanity all over this planet who are searching with curiosity, who are aware of the change, who want to be part of it. And humanity is part of it, whether they want it or not, but we are speaking specifically of those who are willing to knowingly step into the fear of the unknown to embrace that which is to come, and it is already appearing in your life.

We can speak of this broadly, to say that there are bottom line fears and nobody is exempt. In these months we have addressed some of you privately and some of you within the context of these groupings to address the personal trauma in your life. We have given you a very specific recipe for the change. We will say this to you, as you come more and more into the knowing, so there is no escape from what you shall bring forth day after day, week after week, of that which you have not resolved thus far.

It is the time where nothing will be hidden. This concerns not only your government, your scientific bodies, and scandals involving your social and economic structure. We are speaking specifically at this moment of your own lives. Nothing will be hidden.

It is at this time that you will bring forth that which is to be observed outside of who you are. To know that whatever is outside is merely a reflection of that which is within. There is nothing outside of you. Nobody ever did it to you. You are not victims. You are sovereign beings.

We cannot emphasize this enough. When you take responsibility for each creation, day-by-day—no matter how horrific it may appear—know it is only a story and you have created it that you may know who you are. That you may embrace who you are. That you may know you are the God/Goddess, that you are indeed sovereign, powerful beings.

If you do not face each situation with responsibility, it will merely represent itself again and again and again, until you finally recognize that there is no escape. You will know there is no hiding. This is the time. You are stepping forth into a wondrous time. There is nothing you can do to stop it and there is nothing you can do to hurry it up either.

It is all simplicity, in truth. We know that your intellect loves to make it very complicated. Part of this complication is called the hiding. And so you will do it. There is nothing else you may rely on, beloved ones. You will merely keep creating it until you get it. So you may relinquish the fear of not getting it, of being the only one on the block who failed the test. You may relinquish that one.

Questions?

Q: Can you please tell me how I can recognize in a situation the purpose for which I created it?

P'taah: Look at the emotion that it engenders.

Q: So I just embrace the emotion?

P'taah: Indeed. What is the recipe, beloved? What is the recipe for transmutation? Take responsibility that it is your creation. Nobody has done it to you. You have co-created whatever it is to find the pearl of wisdom within. Step one. What is step two?

Q: I forgot.

P'taah: Align the judgment. I would be very happy if all of you would write it down. We have tried to engrave it but we have found we were writing with invisible ink. Align the judgment. How do you do that, when really you want to put a knife in the heart?

Q: It is to make the judgment all right, to make it okay. Is that the alignment?

P'taah: Well, it is trying to talk yourself into it. Very well. To align the judgment is truly to understand that the people involved have been part of the co-creation with you first for their own reasons, their own lessons.

But in your life specifically you have created it for your reasons. It is only a story. You have created it and so it is to know that the self has created this that you may come into the knowing of the pearl within. It is to bless those people involved in your drama. To bless yourself. To give thanks for creating it. To give thanks for the whole situation.

Then it is to look at the judgment, the curse of the New Age because you know you are not supposed to judge, and then you judge the judgment and so you find yourselves in a double bind. It is to know, beloved, that every aspect of who you are is a valid, Divine facet of the All-That-Is, even in judgment.

So it is to bless the judgment. It is to pull all to you, to truly embrace it into the God-light of who you are and in this way the judgment which creates the pain—there is no other cause of pain but judgment—is aligned. The iron claws of resistance, which you call pain, are dissolved into your own light. Then you are left with what is a neutral energy within the solar plexus which is then free to move from the solar plexus to the heart and thusly to the crown.

It is to remember you cannot *do* it.

Q: Just allow it.

P'taah: Indeed, and that is most hard for the 'human doings', hmm? You are to be human *beings* in the moment, all right?

Q: Would you speak to me about whales, please?

P'taah: I would be delighted. Let us ask you what it is you understand about this wondrous being, whale.

Q: I don't know what it is I understand. It is what I see.

P'taah: And what is that, dear one?

Q: That they are beautiful.

P'taah: *(Very softly)* They are indeed. They are a reflection
of your own beauty, you know.

Now, that which are called whales are grand and wondrous masters—not only masters of this planet, you know.
Whales are also called oversouls of dolphins, and whales
and dolphins are called in your language, cetaceans.

They are exactly the same soul energy as humanity.
Dolphins reflect to you the joy and spontaneity, the love
and play of children, and so much more also of children
that you do not actually attribute to children.

The whale is also the historian of your planet. The
whales have communication with the star people, and
always have had. There has never been a time when they
have not consciously been in communication with the
star people.

Cetaceans also have a grand love affair with humanity
and you are just beginning to know it. They are reflecting
grand and wondrous lessons to you all in their allowance,
in their surrender to who they are, and in the unconditional love. That is who they are, dear one.

Q: Would it be easy to communicate with them by just
thinking of them and asking them to communicate?

P'taah: Absolutely. It is very simple. If you are in allowance, cetaceans would be delighted to communicate with
you. It is a joyous occasion.

Q: Can I ask you a similar question about birds? I have
responsibility for a couple of these creatures. *(The man
refers to a parrot sitting on his shoulder.)* My conscience
wonders sometimes about who they are and whether the
relationship I have with them is a proper one.

P'taah: What is your definition of a proper relationship, beloved man?

Q: My definition of a proper relationship is whether they are as happy as if they were in the wild, or whether I am doing them a disservice by keeping them as pets.

P'taah: How does it feel to you?

Q: Oh, I love them.

P'taah: Indeed you do. How does it feel to you having a species who are normally in the forest and now with you?

Q: I worry. I really would like them to fly, but there are certain dangers when they are domesticated to which I do not want to expose them, so I hold them back a bit.

P'taah: Indeed. Now, it is such with domestic creatures that they have also chosen their reality. They are not really so helpless. Also the creatures of second density are here as a lesson for you. You know, when your pets love you, it is really unconditional.

And so during a time with a pet, they will teach you many lessons. It is also that you may love them without fear of being hurt. Then there is the trauma of when you lose them. But all of it, all of your life, is of one expression or another. One is called love and the other is called fear. There is nothing else. So when it is that you are loving and in love, it is the creatures that show you how it truly may be.

You see, dear one, when you are with your beloved creatures, you do not have to hold back anything. You can love them absolutely. You are safe.

Q: Could I ask you, P'taah, in a similar way to your response to the dolphin question, who these parrots are in their intelligence and highness of spirit?

P'taah: Well, dear one, they are not of the same vibrational frequency as humans. Now, we would also say from a point of view of the oversoul that you may choose to experience what would be a fragment of soul energy as a creature. But what you regard to be your birds and animals in general, it is not that they are of the same vibrational frequency as human or cetaceans. It is different. It is not less. Nothing is less, merely different.

Q: I perceive them to be very high, like light.

P'taah: Indeed. It is that birds have been a symbol for humanity—the freedom to fly, and the grand phoenix rising again from the fire. So what you have on your shoulder, beloved, is indeed a grand symbology.

Q: I worry about my relationship with the bird that in withholding him from his flight as I do—and I perceive it to be for his well-being—that in some way I am also withholding myself from this thing. A sort of reflection that there is something about this relationship which is not allowing me to be free, but I cannot let them go free because they have been born in captivity.

P'taah: It is a bit of a bind, hmm? However, beloved, we will say this to you. That was a very deep understanding for you and that is very good, being in the knowing and being in the understanding. Knowing it is kinder to hold to you that which has been domesticated that would otherwise die. It is also valid, but it is excellent that you realize what restriction you do put upon yourself, and in this understanding you may change it.

Q: I understand that the Native Americans always gave thanks to the spirit of the animals they killed. That there was a very close relationship between them and animals and they did not ever just kill them for the fun of it.

P'taah: Exactly. It was the same in this country. Animals and trees—they know who you are. There is no separation. The structure of each of you is exactly the same. We have said to you, dear one, the real communication is God-light to God-light, that is from the sub-atomic particles to the very large organ you hold within you called your heart, and we are speaking of the heart-light, hmm?

You all communicate in this fashion with everything. Animals are very sensitive, but even your trees and plants and flowers know who you are. It is a different knowing, but it is certainly a recognition. So as you are moving about in your garden, you are a familiar presence.

Q: One thing more: About 15 years ago I was going through what is referred to as the dark night of the soul. I had always had a good garden and things grew very well for me, but when I was down there in the pits of hell, nothing was growing. Can you explain why the things that grew so well for me before just stopped growing?

P'taah: Dear one, do you really need me to explain it to you? You have already explained it yourself. When you are in such a state of non-loving of self, it turns everything from you. It is an absolute reflection of how you are with yourself. There is nothing outside of who you are which is not a reflection to you.

Q: Good evening. I would like to ask two broad questions. The first one has to do with our spiritual life and the second is to do with what you call the scandal of our socioeconomic and political life.

What do you consider to be the goal of our spiritual life? In particular you mentioned raising the neutral energy from the solar plexus to the crown. Could you elucidate that process?

The second question. What do you think would be the fundamental principles that should be adopted in the future on this planet as the basis of a new socioeconomic and political structure?

P'taah: Ah, I would be very happy to speak to you about this. So this is what you call a mouthful.

The ultimate spiritual goal of humanity—it is to be God/Goddess realized, to be all you can possibly be. It is to fulfill the potential which has always been there. That is the ultimate goal, to be God realized. How does that strike you?

Q: It sounds wonderful.

P'taah: Indeed it is wonderful, and this is, in fact, what is occurring. It has been a long cycle and that cycle is almost at an end.

Now, that which we spoke forth about moving the energy. It is called transmutation and it is a recipe, like an old alchemist's recipe to change lead into gold, to change agony to ecstasy.

The anguish and pain is resistance to feeling. The ecstasy is the oneness with the All-That-Is. We have thusly given forth a very simple recipe of how that may occur for you every time you are in a situation which is bringing forth a further breaking of your heart.

That which is feeling is judged to be good or bad, is judged to be positive/negative, but in truth, feeling is merely energy and it is neutral without judgment. When a situation is judged to be joyful, there is no impediment to the moving of energy. When you are laughing from the belly, the energy moves from the solar plexus to the heart and so you have great joy. When you are judging the situation to be such that you may die from it, that you will be hurt, then immediately there is resistance to the energy and that you call pain.

Now, your socioeconomic structures. We do not have a direct recipe for this, but we will tell you that in the time to come, it will all change because when humanity is in a state of non-separation, a state of unity, it is called a win-win situation. Everybody wins. There are no losers, very unusual at this time, and so the structures as you know them will be no longer. You can already see what is occurring globally. It is called big trouble for the power brokers and politicians.

It is merely a polarity of what you may judge to be the positive things to occur. We have said before. Your planet becomes involved deeper and deeper in crisis, and not only with the structures of bureaucracy and governments and military organizations which will have a hard time trying to hold things together with the changes to occur to the Earth herself.

It has already started, and will increase. It will be like trying to plug up the holes, trying to plaster over the cracks as they become greater and greater.

But we have said many times, it is not to be regarded as the end of the Earth. It is not in truth a great calamity. It is not holocaust. It may certainly be so, if that is your desire, but it is to know that as the changes are brought forth and as it appears that the baddies are winning, it is merely showing the opposite polarity.

As the consciousness expands and as the Christus arises—the crystalline energy arising in the broadening consciousness of humanity—the negative is also arising. It will be thus, positive and negative arising in tandem, until all is embraced into the light because that which is the darkness is merely the absence of light. In this fashion it will truly become a win-win situation for humanity. All right, dear one?

It is time we call for a break. You may refresh your bodies and rest your computer which lies between your ears. Very well, dear ones, we call for stillness at this time.

(After the break)

P'taah: So, dear ones, let us continue.

Q: Good evening, P'taah. Last week you touched upon our fears. Could you expand upon this, and how to work through them?

P'taah: Indeed, what particular fear, dear one, did you have in mind?

Q: Does one look for a particular aspect? You said we attract our fears to us. I am certainly not doing that...

P'taah: We did not say you attract fear, beloved. We said you will attract situations to you to reflect fear. There is a difference.

Q: I see the difference.

P'taah: You may say the fear is the reflection of how you feel about who you are. Now, a core issue for humanity is that you do not feel worthy.

This feeling of unworthiness will manifest in various ways. It may be seen as a need for validation. It may be seen as possessiveness, as jealousy, self-aggrandizement, the need to be right because you see, dear one, if there is need to be right, it is because you fear to be wrong. If you are wrong, you are not worthy. If you are jealous, it is because you fear that you are not enough. If you are possessive, it is because you fear loss.

And so, however it manifests, it comes down to a core issue. You may trace the issue and go deeper and deeper. As our woman would say, it is like peeling an infinite onion.

Now, it is also that humanity has a fear that everybody else on the block is getting it. That your deep dark secrets are worse than everybody else's. That those facets of your personality self are far worse. Nobody else could be so mean, such a liar, such a thief, such a cheat, such a whatever, even, "I am a murderer and nobody else is," or, God forbid, "I am not caring." Do you understand?

So comes the conspiracy of the ego to protect you from pain. There is nothing wrong with the ego, as we have said many times before. It is what you might call a servant who has taken advantage of you, who is in desire of becoming the master. Indeed it is, most often. That is all right. It is only a dysfunction which has commenced out of fear of annihilation.

It is not to push it away, not to subdue or invalidate, not to suppress or repress the ego. It is to embrace it. You may deal with it as you would deal with fear, and that is to give the ego, or the fear, your own face as a child and then to embrace the child, to know that nothing may harm it. Is this of assistance, dear one?

Q: Yes it is. Thank you, P'taah.

P'taah: Would you like us to discuss it more?

Q: Yes, I would.

P'taah: Now, we have found that when you are using your pencil and paper, you may use the logical mind to be the detective. You may know when a situation occurs and there is an emotional reaction of anger, defense, etc., that behind it there is a fear. It may merely be the anger and frustration that you are not able to do that which is your will. That somebody is stopping you from doing what you desire to do. That certainly creates a feeling of anger and frustration.

Then it is to look at what you have created, the manner of it. Write down what it is in the situation that is stopping you from doing what you want to do. Write down what it is that the situation is forcing you to do. Write down the first time you ever remember feeling this way before. You will understand that it is only a re-creation, something you have created time and time again in your life. It is not new.

Unfortunately, beloved ones, there is very little new in your lives. It is the same old soap opera, hmm? When you have come to the place where you have first felt the feeling before, then you are really getting to the nitty-gritty. It is then that you may identify the core issue and then you may indeed transmute it.

Q: So all the experiences are like the onion.

P'taah: There are many core issues. It is theoretically possible for you to do the whole lot in one shot.

Q: I would like to do that.

P'taah: Indeed. So would you all. Bingo! Done! Instant ascension!

So it is that we take these practical exercises which are common practice. There is nothing we are telling you which is not already in existence, and as we pick them up, we deliver them to you for you to utilize.

We have found in these last years that for you to work with your logical mind, with your pencil and paper, may be very beneficial to you. It is not always essential, dear one, but when you have difficulty, so it may be of assistance.

Q: To get back to the whales and dolphins and birds, we have methods of navigation by the stars, and I want to ask you if the whales and dolphins and birds use a form of celestial navigation?

P'taah: Dear one, what you call celestial navigation is very different from the technology of the star people, but the whale consciously understands what you might call the electromagnetic system of the planet, what is called the grid system, in a way. So, for them it is different because they are using different apparatus. Also, they have a conscious knowing, far beyond the conscious knowing of humanity at this time.

It is not the same with other species of creatures, for instance birds, particularly migratory birds. It is that their patterning is within the morphogenetic resonance. The route of their travels, taken by countless generations of birds in these great migrations over many thousands of miles, sets up a patterning, not within their physical brain, but within the morphogenetic resonance of that particular breed of bird. Do you understand?

We have talked to you about the morphogenetic resonance, the collective consciousness. It does not reside within the physical DNA. The physical DNA of all creatures is a physical representation of the light body.

Q: I want to talk about these birds a bit more. I used to fly these birds across Bass Strait and they would let them go when the weather was so foul we could not even find Tasmania.

P'taah: Indeed, and magically they would find their way home.

Q: Right back to their little box. The mutton birds are the same. They actually find their way back to their same little hole in the ground each year.

P'taah: Indeed. They home in on electromagnetic energy. It has nothing to do with celestial navigation, as you have said yourself, when the weather is so bad they cannot see the stars, certainly. Whales, for example, travel for many miles in terms of distance where they see no stars, and yet magically they find their way.

Now, the easiest way to explain that is to say that when the bird leaves its home, it already sets up a homing device of energy, of electromagnetic energy, and in this fashion it finds its way.

With the shift of electromagnetic energy, there is some distortion and often it will become confusing for the animals and they become lost. We are not speaking so much of birds, but what may be termed the physical anomaly of beachings, etc.

That is also a simplistic answer because with cetaceans, the beachings and strandings have another dimension which is to do with the relationship between cetacean and humanity.

Q: I thought it must be something like that, because whereas a pigeon is only gone for twenty-four hours, the mutton bird comes back to the same hole twelve months later. He cannot mark the spot like a dog does.

P'taah: But he already has marked it, but in a different way which is not physically apparent.

Q: In James Michener's book, Hawaii, he talks of the Polynesians who could travel in a canoe and know the direction of land and how far away it was just by the feel of it and by ripples of the waves and patterns in the water. Could you speak a little bit about that because I think we may have had something we have lost.

P'taah: Oh, dear one, you may count on it. (*Delighted laughter*) How is it do you think that your small people of Africa and the People, the grand and wondrous masters of this continent, have survived and how they know every nuance of their country?

Those who are called the great sailors of your bygone age of this Pacific Ocean did not have what is called a very busy intellect. They knew that who they were was an expression of Divinity. They knew that in truth there was no separation between them and their

Earth, between them and their sea, between them and their creatures, between them and their trees and flowers and birds. There was the knowing that they were part of everything.

In this knowing was open allowance so that when a breeze would pass by the cheek, it would bring a message. When a ripple would come under their craft it would be a message. And when a hunter would look at a stalk of grass and smell the wind, he would know and call forth the food for the pot. He would ask, beloved, and in the allowance, so the creature for the pot would come forth and in the consumption there would be gratitude on both parts and, indeed, a dance of celebration and joy and thanks.

So it is when the navigators and sailors in their craft left one land and came to another, they would give thanks to the grand entity called Ocean, give thanks to the grand Goddess called Earth. Each living within each other...within. All right?

Q: Good evening, P'taah. I would like to get back to the socioeconomic side of things, if it is all right. I would like to ask you how that works on your planet, and will we be working toward a similar structure?

P'taah: Everybody here is smiling because we really do not talk about what is occurring elsewhere. It is enough for you to understand what is occurring here.

But the answer, short term, is that it is very different and it works in a win-win situation for all people. There is nobody disregarded. There is not what you would call a lower strata of socioeconomics, in fact one cannot even call it socioeconomic. It is very different.

To give specifics of how it will be for you is not accurate because we are speaking of probable realities, and how it will be, will depend on you. We are not a soothsayer.

However, we would ask you to think of this. That which you call law of your governments is in a place of fear of lawlessness. Economic sanction, and you may call your income tax an economic sanction, stems from the fear of having no money.

You see, beloved, it is that humanity does not truly understand that money is only consciousness. It is only a symbol of energy. In itself, it is worthless, your pieces of paper. So it is a symbol, and indeed, you may say it is an entity because it is an idea-construct.

When the people of your planet understand this truly, there will never be poverty. Where there is abundance for all people, then we would ask you to describe how your socioeconomic structures would be, hmm?

Q: P'taah, what would be fitting words to put on my daughter's headstone, knowing what I know and feeling what I feel about there being no such thing as death? I would like to put something on it which everybody else can read and get a message from.

P'taah: Make them think a bit, hmm? Beloved, we think this would be a wondrous exercise for you, but we would ask that you would come and speak with us about it very briefly. Speak to our woman. Tell her I have invited you to come and speak with me when you have created a message. All right?

Q: Definitely. Invitation accepted.

P'taah: Indeed.

Q: P'taah, in connection with this socioeconomic issue which seems to stir us all, would it be appropriate for you to comment on the baddies that you mentioned?

P'taah: Ah—you know that which we call the baddies. Your power brokers.

Q: The hidden ones.

P'taah: Ah, they are not hidden for much longer, dear one. We will tell you that. The lust for power is what, dear one?

Q: The fear of lack of power?

P'taah: It is indeed the fear of being power-less. Now, it is a grand fight, a struggle, hmm? There are those who are desperate for the power to control the people of the planet, to have all the money, to have everybody enslaved.

Well, that is all right. They may desire it, but it will not occur because it is not in line with universal truth. It is not harmonious. In the meantime, certainly, there will be topplings of the economic structure, a lot of upheaval socially. You have seen it occurring already in your eastern Europe and middle eastern countries.

Q: Are you speaking of Russia or the Arab world?

P'taah: All of that, dear one. Even in Europe there is much social upheaval to come. But we will also say that this will pale into insignificance as your Goddess stretches and moves herself to re-align her energy. Then your power brokers will wonder what it is they are to have power over.

So it is not really dire circumstances, dear one. It is not to be in fear and trepidation of it at all. You live in a safe universe, in truth. Does it seem dichotomy when we say it is all going to fall down about your ears and yet you live in a safe universe?

Well, you know, what can possibly harm you? What is the worst thing that can happen to you?

Q: Death? Unfulfillment?

P'taah: Let us go with death. Well, you will die anyway.

Q: My body will, one day.

P'taah: Is that not a cheerful thought for you? That is how you will think. The minute you are born, you start to die. Wonderful. But you know it is an illusion, this death. It is a grand illusion.

And why is it, do you think, that everybody wants to incarnate right now? Everybody wants to get in on the act. Everybody wants the excitement of the change.

Somebody was asking us the other day, "Where do all the new souls come from?" We have said, there are none. The oversoul of each and every one of you does not just have one shot at a time.

Q: I do not know about that.

P'taah: Well, then, you will soon. What is it that you do not know?

Q: I do not know if my soul lives forever. I just don't know it.

P'taah: That is why humanity is afraid of death.

Q: If I were to lose my daughter, I think I would be very devastated. *(The lady refers to the man who lost his five-year old daughter the week before.)*

P'taah: You may speak to this man. He has lost his daughter. It was very devastating, but you know, it was a wondrous co-creation and in this he has come into a wondrous knowing. We are not speaking of an intellectual exercise, beloved. We are speaking of the knowing within the heart, absolutely.

Q: I have fear of experiencing something like that.

P'taah: But of course you do, dear one. Do you think you are alone? That is the fear of humanity. Annihilation. That there is nothing more, that there is nothing else, that all of this is a pipe dream, that all of this is a fairy story.

Q: I do not know how I can tell myself it is all an illusion. I just don't know.

P'taah: Well, every day you are showing yourself how it is you manifest. Indeed, you have spoken of it very often. Every day you are looking at reflections.

Q: Those little things do not really count.

P'taah: Oh, do they not, beloved? We have said to you that what you are is a macro-molecule of the multiverses. That which is contained within you is a pattern of your whole universe. If you will truly look at how it is in your day-to-day life, moment-by-moment, you will see in the reflection of that how it is in *your* universes, how *you* are.

Now we would also say this. No other lifetimes, no other people out there? No star people, no light beings? It is simply not logical. It is simply not scientific. It is not within your probabilities mathematically, provable with your magical numbers by your physicists.

When science told you, "There is nothing," and when they said, "Spirituality is a myth. There is only science," those who were advanced European people bowed down to the god science and said, "Ah, it is so. It is so. Religion is nonsense, and so it is and the only thing that exists is that which is scientifically provable." Humanity said, "Yeah for science."

Well, now your scientists and your quantum physicists, with a little help from their friends, are proving to you that it is not possible for you to be the only species. It is not possible for you to have only one life. It is not possible that there are not star people.

But you see, dear ones, you have been so effectively programmed, brainwashed, so filled with fear that now you are terrified to allow the possibilities. That is why we sometimes say to you it is a wondrous leap of faith—it is called quantum leap—and the expansion of your con-

sciousness may only occur in the allowance of the possibilities and in the total allowance of the fear. By the
allowance of the fear, you may embrace it, you may
transmute it. You may change what is the molecular
structure. Very exciting, hmm?

And so, beloved ones, sufficient unto the time this
evening. Our thanks. Our joy, indeed, and honor to share
with you in this fashion.

Dear ones, go forth in your fears and embrace them
with joy. Know in truth there is no future. There is only
now. So, be in the fullness of every now moment and let
tomorrow look after itself.

I love you. Good evening.

▼ Thirteenth Session
April 1

P'taah: Good evening, dear ones. What a beautiful gathering. How beautiful you all are. Now, let us speak about your now. (*Addressing a woman*) How is your now?

Q: If I would be in it, I would know, but I am very seldom in my now.

P'taah: Very wise words, indeed. Would it not be wondrous if you could all be in your now? The past would indeed be past and your future could unfold out of the fullness of the now.

If you took an anchor attached to a long chain and tied it around your neck, you would drown if you jumped into the ocean. Well, that is what you are all doing. You are all anchored to your past, drowning in the emotion of what has been long gone in your life.

So you live in re-action every moment, shackled. From the shackles of your past, you strive to your future and your future is just past nows recreated day after day, month after month, year after year.

It does not have to be so. We say to you that you do not have a future. There is no future. There is only Now. What you regard to be the future is limitless possibilities. You are limitless beings.

We say it to you all the time, but you do not really believe us that you are limitless and the probabilities and possibilities of the future are decided in the now so there is no point in worrying about your future.

The past—unresolved pain, unresolved problems, trauma—you will recreate again and again until you can embrace, accept, align who you are now. And it need not be great drama and trauma for you to learn the lessons of alignment. It may be gentle.

There is truly no escape. Whatever it is that is not aligned, you will bring forth. Whatever ideas you have about your reality, you will recreate. Whatever beliefs you have about your world and about yourselves, you will re-create to reinforce that belief structure. So in every now you have an opportunity for alignment.

As you align, as you accept who you are and how it is that you have created a mirror outside of yourself to reflect those belief structures, you will change your future. As you come to accept who you are, so you will come into your ultimate power.

You will know what it is to be a sovereign being, powerful, creative. You will come to understand that there is no separation. That every atom and molecule which makes up your being are the same atoms and molecules which make up every other thing that you observe in your world.

It is very simple, my dear ones. You delight in making it very complex. Well, it is not complex. It is simple.

Who you are indeed is the God/Goddess. That is the bottom line. Who you are is limitless potential called humanity. Who you are is wildly creative. We hear you say, "But we do not know how to express that creativity."

Dear ones, look at your bodies. Is that not the most wondrous creativity? And it is occurring *now*. You are a powerhouse *now*. Everything that has been in your past is who you are *now*. It is all right. You are all right. You are everything you can possibly be at this moment. You are glorious, and when you can truly accept that you are, what do you think are the tomorrows you will create?

Very well, questions.

Q: You spoke once about the fantasy childhood where it has been so painful that we cover it with the childhood we wished we had had. Where the reality is too painful to contemplate.

I heard what you said, that the imagined childhood has its own validity, and I heard you say its own reality.

A few people have said to me, "What about affirmations?" You go back and remember your parents screaming at each other and the pain it created, and you picture the parents being loving to each other and that changes the reality.

It seems that people are thinking that is the way to change, rather than people being willing to actually go to the pain of the parents screaming at one another, and transmuting that pain. Could you just talk about that?

P'taah: Indeed, we did say that where the pain has been too much to bear, a shield comes down so the conscious mind does not remember any more. So there has been a wondrous creation in imagination of the desire in the heart of all children, even now, dear ones, in the heart of the children you all really are.

It is valid. It does have its own reality because there is nothing that you can think or imagine which is not valid and does not have its own reality.

That is all right, however we have said that the only way you may change the past, in truth, is to transmute the pain into ecstasy. In this fashion, it truly *does* change. Why is that, beloved, that it truly does change through transmutation?

Q: In my experience, it is that it frees that energy which is locked to become the vital energy for our lives.

P'taah: Indeed it is so. Now, we have spoken so often about why transmutation creates the changes and the changes that occur in the molecular structure of the body.

That, to many of you, may seem what you may call a tall claim, however we would ask you to consider this. As you have come into some understanding that there is no physical dis-easement which is not created by an emotional dis-easement, so you understand that as you change the emotion, you change the physicality.

When you change a tumor into healthy cells, it is a molecular change. It also releases hormones into the body to create youth and vitality. That is what joy is. That is what occurs within you when you are in joy. When you want to dance with joy, what is it, beloved ones, that vitality? What makes the heart sing, hmm?

Joy changes everything. It creates physical change. We say it changes the past and changes the future. It changes what you term to be past lives and future lives in exactly the same way because nothing is separate. Nothing.

It is only separate in your own consciousness. But many of you are coming to know an altered state of consciousness wherein you are tapping more into your dreamtime and you are getting glimpses of other probable realities, other lifetimes.

It is all occurring simultaneously. Without the separation, what is occurring to your focus and consciousness now is affecting the soul energy of you, which in turn reflects on every aspect of you.

Love is the thread, and indeed the glue, which holds your universes and your lives together. The energy which keeps your body flowing, alive, growing, is love, the divine thread.

In this fashion, we find it quite extraordinary that you do not really understand that you are expressions of Divinity. Without the Divinity, you would not exist. If you did not exist, the universe would not exist.

You are it, hmm? You are the central sun of your universe, beloved ones, and if you are the central sun of your universe, you can see that it is impossible that you are not all right.

You do not look at the sun and say, "There is something wrong with it. It is a swine of a thing because it does not shine today." You do not say to the moon, "We do not like you because you are not full this evening."

You see, dear ones, you can see perfectly well the Divinity of everything else but yourselves. Is it not silly? Well, that is all right and soon you will understand that the judgments you have about yourselves, which in turn you reflect outside because it is too painful to look inside, is nursery knowing—kindergarten.

It is time now for the flowering into the adulthood of humanity. This is your life, beloved people. You create it moment-by-moment, every part of it. It is your wondrous creation and it is indeed entirely up to you how you create it every now moment.

You have an opportunity every moment to live in the fullness of it, in the joy of it. Even when you are judging yourselves and judging the situation, you may say, "This is my opportunity that I, in my wisdom, have created that I may pluck the jewel from within."

We would ask that you remember this when next you are having a fight with your bureaucracies, officials, your neighbors who are not doing as you would wish it, your children, etc. It is you who create it all.

That was a very long answer to your question, beloved, It is clear now?

Q: Beloved P'taah, concerning the now you were talking of, could you please comment on the, "your needs will be met," which would take the strain out of the future.

P'taah: Is that like 'you live in a safe universe,' dear one?

Q: Of course.

P'taah: Well, if it is that you create your own reality absolutely, and if it is that your beliefs which create the reality tell you that there is not abundance and tell you that life is a struggle, and the bureaucrats are all bastards and are only out to get you, and that you have to work very hard to be supported, then indeed that is exactly how it will be for you.

Now, we speak so often about it, we are surprised you do not get bored with it. Your universe is your creation. Why would you create a universe which would not support you? If you desire to do so, then that is all right. However, if you desire abundance, then that is also all right. And so it shall be.

You know, you really do not need anything because you have everything. What does that tell you, dear one?

Q: That I am safe.

P'taah: Indeed. It also tells you what you do not believe. If you are in need, you do not know that you have everything. It is the knowing that creates it. Do you know it, dear one?

Q: Yes I do.

P'taah: Very good. That is why you have such trouble manifesting, dear ones, because you desire it and in the desiring you do not understand that you have it already. As is the thought, so is the manifestation.

Q: I have a fear about creating thought-forms. When I am riding along on my motorcycle, I sometimes get a picture of me falling off and getting hurt. It is not something I desire. I do not want to manifest this. The more I think about it, the more I think that the thought will be followed by the action, so then I think of a way out to protect myself.

P'taah: Now it is also that you do not have to experience it physically. Hands up any woman in the room who has not at some stage feared rape and violence. Three. You see, as you fear something, you will certainly draw it to you. Fear is not an idle thought. Fear lives in the gut.

When you are making pictures of yourself falling off your cycle or lying mutilated in a ditch, when the feeling is like a kick in the stomach, then there will be something to align. When it is an idle thought without the emotion, it is not called a power pack. Do you understand?

Q: I think so. Could you say it might serve me to simply accept the thought as being a polarity and just let it go?

P'taah: Absolutely, you may indeed. All of you have quite lurid thoughts in imagination. Well, you do. I know that you do. That is all right.

Truly, when you are living in fear, it would be beneficial for you to align the fear. Then you need not experience it in physicality. Does anybody not understand what we are saying? And how do you align fear, dear one?

Q: Accept it. Totally surrender yourself to it.

P'taah: Indeed, and in this fashion the block of the energy is dissolved. The energy is then free to move from the belly to the heart, and thus creates the change. Very simple.

Q: So could we say that the things that may prevent one from accepting one's fear may be the beliefs?

P'taah: Very often. Then you may say, "If I have no fear of having an accident, does this mean that I will not have an accident?"

Well, there is no such thing as an 'accident'. If you create an 'accident', then it is to look at the why of it.

Q: Good evening, P'taah. If one is confident in one's ability, if one trusts oneself and loves oneself, one would not have an accident?

P'taah: If you are driving your car or your cycle or your aeroplane and you are confident of your capability, then indeed that which is called accident is not on your mind.

But you are not alone on the road. It is possible that somebody else is there to show you a grand lesson which has nothing to do with your confidence or ability as a driver. You would be merely pulling forth a situation to contemplate.

To be confident is wonderful. If you were not confident, you would not drive a vehicle. If you were less
confident, you would not walk on the streets of the cities
of your planet at nighttime, nor would you swim in your
oceans, etc. Humanity, innately, is confident. All we are
saying to you is that there are various reasons for an
accident.

Q: Greetings, P'taah. How can we understand sexual
guilt? A lot of people seem to have it.

P'taah: The whole of your culture has this problem, dear
one. Do I really need to explain where it comes from?

Q: Basically, yes.

P'taah: It is part of your culture. Sexuality is not nice. It is
downright sinful, hmm?

Q: That is the only explanation?

P'taah: We have spoken to you about the morphogenic
resonance of your culture, the collective consciousness.
We have spoken to you of the sexuality of humanity. We
have given forth much in this area.
  The Christian church would prefer that humanity would
not have genitals. If it were possible for you to regenerate
in any other fashion, they would prefer it. So the children
are taught very early that it is not quite nice to have
genitals and there are certain things you must not do with
them, or to each other, with them.
  So after your birthing, you are tapping into the collective consciousness of your culture. Even when you have
become adults—well, certainly grown up—and understand intellectually that it is perfectly okay to do whatever you want with your genitals, the belief structure is
already there.

Then there is the structure of your marriage wherein sexuality is used as a weapon of power, of revenge. There is the judgment of sexuality. Look at the greatest epidemic of your time. Once upon a time it was called the bubonic plague which had nothing to do with genitals.

The plague of this time has everything to do with genitals in the minds of people. Of course, it has nothing to do with genitals at all, your AIDS.

Now, guilt is a lesson which has not been learned.

Q: Yes, we know that.

P'taah: Guilt about anything, genitals notwithstanding, if you will excuse the expression. We are becoming very clever, are we not? (*Laughter.*)

Any lesson only requires acceptance, alignment, to be learned. When you are taking ultimate responsibility for what you have done in your life that you feel guilty about, you say, "I did it because I wanted the experience."

Q: Sometimes one does not know what one is feeling guilty about. There is just a guilt feeling within. What does one do about that?

P'taah: I suggest you find out.

Q: Oh-oh.

P'taah: Come, come. If you have a re-action, then ask why.

Q: It would probably have something to do with what one feels right now.

P'taah: Oh no. You don't think so, do you? There *is* only now, beloved. When you are in re-action now you say, "Why? Why am I angry? Why am I guilty?"

If you are angry, it is because you are afraid. There is pain underneath the anger. When you are guilty you are saying, "I should not have done it."

Q: I understand. It is so simple.

P'taah: Indeed.

Q: P'taah, for the last 13 years I have been living in a perpetual state of nausea. I have tried everything in the book. I am aware it has nothing to do with diet, but with emotion. I have been trying to work out whether the root emotion is fear, anger, or confusion.

P'taah: Beloved, there is only one root emotion and that is fear. You may go to the time when you did not have the nausea. We would speak with you another time, but we would say to you. When was it that you did not feel it, and what was it when you felt it the first time?

We would ask you to go to these times that you have conscious memory of how it is for you. It is not only to go to the physical occurrences, but to the feeling, because indeed it is the feeling that will give you your signpost to the knowing of yourself.

It is fear of your universe, beloved, of not being in control. The fear of doing, the fear of being wrong if you do. But it is truly for you to come to the feeling because you have already given yourself a signpost. All right?

Q: As far as I am aware I have felt the things you have mentioned my whole life.

P'taah: Indeed you have.

Q: So where is the signpost?

P'taah: We have said to you to think of the times when you have not felt the nausea.

Q: I know there have been times when I have been happy. It is basically unhappiness.

P'taah: But of course it is, beloved.

Q: I have gone back to the times when I have been happy and the nausea lifts for a while, but then it descends again. I do not know how to remove it permanently from my life.

P'taah: *(Softly)* Well, the first thing is to make it all right because you see, all of you have a heavy judgment about ill-health, diseasement. Do you understand?

When you make it wrong and when you are in a struggle to alter it, you are then not able to align the fear that created it in the first place. We would ask you to look at your fear of doing, your fear of your universe, that you have no place in it. When you are on the roller coaster for enlightenment, it is because who you are now is not enough.

Very well, dear ones. We shall take a break. We would ask that you be still for just two minutes.

(After the break)

Q: P'taah, you spoke last week about two topics which I wonder if you could expand on. One is about the phoenix rising from the ashes, and the other is the whale beachings.

P'taah: And what was it we were saying about the phoenix rising from the ashes, beloved woman?

Q: I feel personally that I am approaching some transition to do with that sort of energy, but I am not sure what it is. It kept coming back to me all week, that I needed to ask you about it.

P'taah: The transition is personal for you, but it is also the transition of the whole of humanity. You may think of humanity and the consciousness of humanity in a cyclic form.

There have been already grand and wondrous civilizations, a grand and wondrous knowing where there has been communication with the star people—indeed the star people and that which you regard to be humanity knew no separation—where there was no separation between the people of your Earth and every creature and every plant and tree, every blade of grass. All in total honor of each other's Divinity. This has not only been once upon your planet.

So it is that humanity has been through the long dark night of the soul, and the wheel has turned. Within the breast of all humanity is the fervent yearning for that which you have had, that which you have lost.

It is not just because of the cyclic changes which are to occur, not only on a physical level, but that you are creating it also and you may say it is a multi-dimensional change. As the changes occur within the breast of humanity, so the changes are reflected in your universe.

You may also say that your Goddess called Earth will be the phoenix arising. Out of what appears to be great cataclysm, great Earth changes, so indeed will be birthed a new Earth. Do you understand?

Q: Yes. I think I do. I have had intimations of that but the logical mind does not comprehend it. Somewhere here *(pointing to her heart)* it does.

P'taah: Indeed it does.

Q: It is like being all part of humanity inside and yet not being able to reach out to be part of humanity.

P'taah: *(Tenderly)* Ah, there is the rub, hmm? It is for all humanity, beloved woman. It is not merely that which be you who feels in separation and isolation. It is called the anguish of humanity. That which is the fervent desire within your breast will cause the change. *(The woman weeps silently.)*

(Softly) And so it is for all of you, isolated in your own grief, in your own anguish, in your own fear, in the terror of what has been your past in this life and other lifetimes, that you indeed will step forth into the light, the God-light of who you are. And we have said to you that your anguish is such that there is no other species which could survive it.

We would remind you that when you look at your terrifying universe which seems to get worse and worse with each passing day, where everywhere you look is the reflection of the agony of humanity, that indeed, beloved people, it is only the polarity of what else is occurring.

What you are creating with your fervent desire is something so wondrous, so extraordinary, something so miraculous that you will cast your glance back to this life, to these times and the times of your own history, and you will be amazed. You will be so surprised that in all of these years, humanity did not know how simple it all truly is, because, dear ones, you will know in truth that you are the God/Goddess.

That which is called whale is a grand mirror for humanity, that which is called dolphin, indeed. They love humanity unconditionally. It is not to judge what appears to be the agony of whale. They have chosen out of love, and they do not judge humanity.

(There is a moment of silence, then a young woman continues)

Q: Good evening, P'taah. I was wondering why there is so much evil and hate in the world today. Where did it come from? Why is it destroying everything?

P'taah: You know, dear one, that which you judge to be evil and that which you judge to be destructive has always been there, but now is the time when nothing may be hidden. So these situations which are not harmonious, which are not in line with universal law, are created upon your planet so you may understand that it is a fight for life.

Now, in your history you understand fight to the death? What is occurring now is a fight for life. Do you see how it changes the whole complexion, merely by the different words?

Everything in your universe is positive/negative. Your universe would not be your universe if there were not positive/negative. So as in electric light when the positive charge embraces the negative charge it creates light, so this is occurring now in your universe.

It is not that the negative and what you judge to be evil is truly greater at this time, but it is certainly reflecting its polarity, which is the light. It is to remember that as the consciousness of humanity is expanding and growing to the light, so it is that the opposite is showing its face more and more. The people are coming to know they cannot hide from who they are. Not any of you.

There is no escape, beloved ones. You are all coming to realize that the only way you will create the change is by knowing who you are. Know thyself and know God.

That is reflected everywhere outside of who you are. All of the years your governments and religious bodies and power brokers have hidden knowledge, they have worked secretly to control humanity. (*Powerfully*) No longer.

No longer will anything be hidden. Your power brokers will only have power if you allow it. The way you disallow it is to take your own sovereignty. You do not have to do anything to them. You will not change anything by fighting it. You will not change anything by suppression or repression. You will change it by changing who you are in your own estimation, in your own knowing. That is your power-sourceness—who you are.

Q: How do I know who I am? How do I find that?

P'taah: Every time you judge anybody or anything outside of who you are, look and know that it is a reflection of you. Thusly, you will know who you are.

It is not to judge who you are, beloved. It is merely to know, to accept who you are. To love who you are, and to know in truth that you are a shining light and nothing can harm you. You are beloved, indeed. (*The young girl is sobbing quietly.*)

You will create the change in your whole universe when you love who you are. Your universe depends upon you, beloved people. You are not separate from anybody or anything. Not a thought is separate. How you are out there is how you are inside. None of it is separate.

Those who you judge to be evil are only a reflection. If it were not part of you, how would you perceive it. But it is also to know that when you look at that which is wondrously beautiful, it is also who you are.

Q: I feel like I am a modern woman, but I fell back into the old mythology about the nice virgin waiting for the knight in shining armor. She waits for 10 or 20 years, or a lifetime. So I made the decision not to manipulate anything, even if it means I remain single for the rest of my life.

P'taah: Beloved woman, *you* are the knight in shining armor. Do you understand that you are? All of you are waiting for the wondrous lover to ride up on the white horse, but it is *you*. That is why we have said to you all along, when you have this wondrous love affair with yourself, how could anybody *not* fall in love with you? Do you understand?

Then it is that the love affairs are not born of need and desperation. They are born in sovereignty and honor, integrity, respect and you know that nothing and no one can harm you because indeed you cannot harm you. When it is thus, there is no fear. Then you may love without possession.

Q: This love I feel for a certain man is free of jealousy and possession. No yearning, no pining. It is just there. For me love has also been connected with lust and passion.

P'taah: It is also connected with pain. For all of you, love equals pain. That is the patterning, not only of this lifetime, but lifetime after lifetime.

Then there is your belief structure about relationships. When you truly love who you are, the whole meaning of love affair will change. You will truly know that you are the central sun of your universe. So be it.

Q: P'taah, everything has energy, so when we live in a place with furnishings and furniture and objects which belong to other people, or which we have brought with us from an unhappy situation in another location, do these objects bring with them these unhappy vibrations? I have things in my house from my childhood and from my former marriage. Would this affect me?

P'taah: It would depend on the emotions of your childhood and marriage. As these emotions are mostly not so joyous, we would say you may indeed align your furniture and your objects with your desire for the now.

Q: I thought that they might be keeping me emotionally in the past instead of in the now.

P'taah: Only if you allow it. You are the powerhouse, beloved woman. You are creating your own reality. Energy is not quite so concrete.

Q: It seems easy.

P'taah: Oh it is. Do you understand how it may influence you?

Q: Can you expand?

P'taah: When you are living with objects of another life-time called your past, and this time of your past was not happy, then indeed you may be giving yourself a constant reminder because memory is also energy, hmm?

So it is that you may create the change in the energy. Acknowledge it. Align it.

Q: Yes, I can do that, P'taah. Also last week you said that you write with invisible ink on our hearts. Why is this?

P'taah: I said to you that I desire to engrave the wisdom so that you would not forget it, that you would hear what I say to you. But, I said, it appears that I write with invisible ink because you do not hear me. We are not saying you do not hear anything, beloved ones.

Q: What is it that stops us from hearing?

P'taah: Your own limitation. Your own belief structures. Your limited understanding of yourselves. Your desire to be right. Your fear of being wrong. Your fear of not getting it.

Q: Thank you, P'taah. I understand.

P'taah: You know, all of the words that have been spoken in all of these times with you, they truly represent the most simple concepts and ideas. You see, you want it to be complicated. If it is not complicated, then how could you have not got it before, hmm?

In all of your teachings, it has been complicated. It has been hidden. So when we speak to you, you say, "No. It cannot be this simple."

How simple is it? There is no judgment in the whole of the universe. That which you term to be God does not judge you. God/Goddess energy simply is, and so are you.

If you love who you are, you will change your uni-verse. You may transmute agony into ecstasy that you may know oneness and non-separation. We have given you the recipe thereof.

There is no separation in the universe. You are not separate from anything or anybody. All knowledge lies within you. Your molecular structure is only a reflection of the universes. We have said you are a micromolecule of the multiverses. All is within you.

Know who you are and know God, because you are. There is no if, but, or maybe. There simply is, and in the is-ness of now you may know it.

Everything we have said forth to you is simple and in that simplicity is the knowledge of the multiverses because you are the multiverses, beloved people. There is no separation.

There is no separation. Who you are is everything. How can you be in non-abundance? You have everything within you. How can you be in dis-easement? You are God!

It is not a fairy story. That which has been hidden will now be made manifest. If it is a fairy story, then your quantum physicists should take up reading science fiction instead of fairy stories.

Now is the time that your scientists will be assisting humanity to come to know who they are in non-separation because in your culture, science has become law. If your scientists tell you that there is no separation, if they tell you all of the things that I tell you, we must be right!

You see dear ones, there will be no escape. Once your scientists and intellectuals would turn away from Spirit and say, "You cannot prove it. It is bullshit."

Well, you see how it occurs? Now the scientists are saying, "There is more to all of this than meets the naked eye, and more to all of this than meets the spectrum." So one way or another we will get you there. Oh, indeed it is good.

Beloved ones, it is not to *do* anything. There is nothing to do. No past, no future, only Now. When the going gets a bit rough for you, think how it is at this moment for you, in the joy and the upliftment.

Very well, dear ones, sufficient unto the time. Our thanks and I love you all very much. Go forth in love, beloved ones.

Good evening.

▼ Fourteenth Session
April 8

P'taah: Good evening, dear ones. It is a joy to see you all again. This evening is a summation, a summary.

For those of you for whom this is a new experience, you will be able to read all those wondrous words of wisdom. As you are reading, you may absorb them into your computer *(points to head)*. More importantly, you may allow the resonance of truth into your heart.

In these times to come, all of you will create wondrous dramas for yourselves and you know it is no big deal. We would ask you to remember, this wondrous and precious life is your very own. You have created it. You have chosen it. So it is for each and every one of you to dive into life wholeheartedly.

You are all chasing that elusive thing called happiness, called joy and tranquility. Well, you may certainly have it if that is your desire. But it is also to know that you create its opposite as well, which is discordancy and pain and anguish. But, beloved people, you create it so that you may find the jewel within.

Now, we are not speaking of some pipe dream. It is not to take your life so seriously. Life is for the joy, for the fun of it. And when you go through these moments and you ask yourself, "Why the hell am I here?" then know that you have created it all.

We urge you to look at balance. That which you judge to be bad, that which you judge to be not desirable in your life, is only a polarity of what you judge to be very desirable. When you can take one step back, when you can see the polarity, then you may embrace both harmony and discordancy.

Know that all things are valid, that all things are of Divine essence, else they would not exist. It is so simple, it is truly so simple. Your life is your creation absolutely.

There is nothing to fix. You may create the changes you desire merely by embracing that which is now, however it is for you.

To run away from the pain, to become invulnerable, to bury your head in the sand, to pretend that you do not live in pain, to pretend that there is nothing in your life that does not create anguish for you, will only continue to draw to you that which creates the pain.

You are so beautiful. You are so powerful. It is our fervent desire that you will know that you are.

Let your life be simple, my beautiful people. Go for the laughter. Go for the joy. But when it is not as you think it should be, make the most of it also. If you are going to be angry, *be* angry. If you are going to be sad, *be* sad but do it with your whole heart. Then when you are tired of that, know that it is all right. All that is required is that you feel the feeling. That is all. Very well, dear ones, we will have some questions.

Q: P'taah, could you tell us something about the crop circles and its keys for us?

P'taah: I will not. (*The audience applauds, knowing P'taah won't be sidetracked.*) You will do so.

Q: We should have expected that. However, there is a new shape appearing, a heart shaped one, and I wonder if you Pleiadians are in the thick of these crypto-grams. Are you leaving it entirely up to us to find it ourselves?

P'taah: Oh, it will not take long. You may regard the cryptograms of your crops at this moment merely as pretty patterns. And as you regard them as such, you will certainly find that they ignite ideas within humanity. We would not spoil your fun, beloved people.

Indeed we will not, but we thank you for your question, dear one.

Q: I might add it seems that these crop circles are starting up in the Tully region

P'taah: It has already started, dear one. It is not new. We have told you before that this area of your continent is what you may call blessed with visitations.

Q: So we are talking then about the indentations of hard craft or about designs made by consciousness?

(*The audience laughs sympathetically, understanding the man's persistence.*)

P'taah: What do you think is a multidimensional answer to that, beloved?

Q: It could easily be the sign of operation from multi-dimensional beings for us to tune in to.

P'taah: Ah, how extraordinary, indeed! Thank you, beloved.

Q: Could you please tell me how the Pleiadians are nourished?

P'taah: You may know we are not here really to speak about the Pleiadians, my sweet one. We are here to speak about humanity. It is much more important. What we would say to you truly is that we are not here for entertainment. We are here that you may know who you are.

Q: Should that not be a reciprocal thing?

P'taah: Dear one, when the timing is right, you will know not only about the people from the Pleiades, but you will know about people from other star systems as well.

You see, beloved, we have said most often before that what people are regarding as the transition from third to fourth density is impossible to describe to you in your consciousness of limitation. So we have taken what is called a boardroom decision that we shall speak to you so you may reflect and know who you are because when you know who you are, you will be able to answer all questions. All right?

Q: Good evening, P'taah. How do I get to know everything that you know?

P'taah: How do you tap into universal wisdom? Know who you are because all wisdom is contained within you, all knowledge.

Q: Last time you said that each time one judges another, the other is a reflection. Is that all, to know myself completely?

P'taah: Is it not amazingly simple?

Q: Yes. I just want to know it all now.

P'taah: You are not alone, beloved. That is the yearning within the breast of all people, to know now. So it is possible that it may occur now. It is possible that you may do it in a blink of an eye, but it is not very probable.

But you see, it is that you are totally in love with your life as it is at this moment because you find it exciting. All of the drama, all of the yearning, all of the pain—it is a wondrous theatre.

When you will acknowledge that, in truth, you have created it all, when you will take true responsibility, you will truly take responsibility for your own life. Then indeed you will have a little change in your drama.

So it is bit by bit. When you evolve from relation-shit into a relation-ship, you will know that it is the ultimate reflection of how you are with yourself.

We remind you that there is nothing outside of who you are but a reflection, nothing! You are the central sun of your universe. That is the beginning and the end of the story.

When you understand that you are the central sun of your universe, as you know that all things are contained within you, that it is your responsibility and your creation, when you acknowledge the judgment you have of those about you to be an absolute reflection of who you are, then you will create wondrous, wondrous change. It is as simple as that.

Q: Beloved P'taah, I have discovered a jewel. Your advice, "Do what makes your heart sing," causes me often to check what I am doing at the moment. So I was trying to figure out what makes my heart sing. Even when I have a temporary pleasure or excitement, it is not really what makes my heart sing. So I discovered that nothing makes my heart sing. My heart sings or it doesn't. If it sings, it sings no matter what, regardless of obstacles. There may be a different tone to the song, but it sings anyway.

P'taah: You see, beloved people, you are becoming heart addicts. Because what is occurring as you are creating the shift and changes within you, as you are on this adventure of discovering who and how you are, as you are beginning to open, to have this wondrous love affair with yourself, nothing else is quite satisfactory.

Why is it, do you think, that at this time there are many people who are not in a so-called relationship, a one-to-one relationship? It is that many of you are fighting for the search for self, to come into a greater awareness. To have the new discoveries in your world is the most exciting thing that ever happened to you.

And I will tell you this. The voyage of discovery does not get less. As we are moving forth into the time of truly great changes, so what you are doing in your moment-by-moment life is preparatory to have a harmonious shift.

You truly are wondrous beings that you have created yourselves at this time and place. You truly are wondrous. We are not a soothsayer. We are not a gypsy with a scarf and crystal ball and rings, and we do not really talk to you about what is considered to be your future, but as you may have gathered by now, you are in for a very fine ride within your carnival called life, most exciting.

It is so that I may say to you with great eveness that I honor you all. You truly do not understand how important you are, each individual, because it has been in your life, in your culture, that you regard yourself in a diminished state. Nobody has ever told you truly how wondrous you are, how powerful you are, and how each and every one of you is so important to your universe.

We understand how it is that you will say, "How can one person make any difference?" It is especially difficult when you are in victim mode, the mode of 'they did it to us.' It is very difficult to understand how important each of you is when you are not taking responsibility for your life.

If it were not for you—we are speaking on many levels here—your universe would not exist as it appears to exist to you now. It simply would not be the same universe.

So as each and every one of you, in what is called your time spans of lifetimes, takes on a physical body, lives your life to the best of your ability, however that is, you do not understand what a wondrous tapestry you are creating—a wondrous tapestry called life.

You know what happens when you have a wondrous tapestry and when the threads are pulled. It is no longer the same picture, and so it is with you all. Each of you is a precious, unique jewel.

Q: I have a problem with everything being a reflection. How do I recognize what I am looking at? Often I see something and say, "Did I create this?" How do I understand what to learn from it? Is it the emotion?

P'taah: There is only the emotion, beloved. How does it feel to you?

As we said to you before, what you are is imagination and feeling. There is nothing else. So when you are looking at a picture outside yourself that you have created, it is to say, "How does it feel?" and "When did I feel it before?"

So it is to learn what the trigger is. You see, we are learning all these wondrous therapeutic words from our woman and her beloved friends.

Q: So many feelings are coming up. Is this a very special time that everything seems to come up at once?

P'taah: Absolutely. It is the time you are in and it will be more and more so. As you become very clever at opening up your heart and become vulnerable and allow the feelings, so the greater part of who you are will say, "Very good, dear one, now try this lot."

So there is really no escape. Once you put your foot on the train, it will not stop until you reach ascension. Now we are teasing you a little—a non-stop shuttle to ascension.

Q: P'taah, you said to me recently that I am now in the flowering of my womanhood and that I could have it all and for as long as I want it. I would like to know more about that.

P'taah: What do you want to know? It is your life. It is your choice. Go for it.

Q: I just did not understand the full implication.

P'taah: Well, dear one, it is you who are writing your own life and you know that you are coming into your own flowering. You are coming to realize your potential, the God-I-Am within you. You are coming to know the God/Goddess. So it is a matter of allowance.

We spoke, too, about embracing the void, the Goddess. It is called allowance, surrender, vulnerability. To say, "This is who I am." To allow your imagination, the feeling. To understand that as you may step into the wellspring of feeling—it is called the void of creativity—there is nothing to fear, nothing to fear.

Q: It seems too good to be true.

P'taah: Now, beloved, we would not fool you. We do not tell fairy stories.

Q: No, of course I know that.

P'taah: And when we speak forth to you, "It is such and such," we are being even with you. If you choose not to believe, that is your right. If you ever feel that what I say forth is not truth, so be it. Then it is not your truth and that is all right.

Q: I did not mean that.

P'taah: Oh, I know that. So, what else is there to know, beloved woman? Go forth in joy. It is your life.

Q: So the only limitations are the ones I put on myself.

P'taah: Dear one, the only limitation for the whole of humanity is the limited box of your belief structures. That is the only thing that stands between you and your powerful God/Goddess. That goes for all of humanity.

We are not speaking in idle jest when we say you are most powerful. There is nothing, no thing that you cannot be. Your potential, the potential of your species, is awesome. Your grandeur is unimagined at this time. You are indeed mighty beings. If it were not such, why would we come?

Q: All this discussion about power, is this power at the expense of someone else?

P'taah: Beloved, have we not spent much time with you discussing what is called a win-win situation? I have discussed this with you at great length, not even in general.

(Strongly) Power has nothing to do with power over people. It has to do with knowing your own power to be God because that is who you are. So let us not speak about this. A win-lose situation is not a situation of Godhood. It is a situation of fear.

Q: A week ago I experienced more power than previously and I believe that it was at another person's expense, but I felt good about it. Is that all right?

P'taah: Why do you ask me if it is all right? If it makes you feel good, then it is fine. All things are valid.

There is no judgment. We have also told you that many times. I am not the God in heaven with a beard judging you right or wrong, good or bad. So why do you ask me? I am not your judge.

Q: I just asked for confirmation.

P'taah: You do not want to be the bastard?

Q: Correct.

P'taah: Well, I will tell you something, beloved. Until you can embrace the fact that you are a bastard, you will never know that you are also the God, because you are all things.

All of you are all things. If you were not, you would not recognize the bastard in someone else. It would not come into your consciousness. You are all things.

If you desire to be the bastard and if you are finding joy in it at this moment, then that is perfectly valid. But you see, what occurs is that when you are having joy and in the joy there is fear, the joy will dissipate. Is that not exactly how you create your lives day-by-day? *(Softly)* Why else are you not living in joy all the time?

We shall take a break. Beloved ones, we would ask that you create stillness for a moment and we shall return soon.

(After the break.)

P'taah: And so, dear ones, questions?

Q: P'taah, you say you are not a soothsayer. Is it because you cannot or you wish not?

P'taah: It is because we do not desire probable realities—that which you regard to be your future—to be set in concrete.

Humanity is in enough limitation with belief structures and what humanity regards to be inevitable. Look at the things in your life that you do believe to be inevitable in regard to your health, in regard to that which is called death, in regard to what you understand to be immutable scientific law, which is not, in truth. Do you understand?

So when we speak about what is called Earth changes, in a way we are certainly speaking about that which is considered to be your future and the future of your planet. However, this future is a cyclic change. How you will experience it is up to you. Do you understand, beloved?

We desire that you would focus on non-limitation. To understand it is truly limitless. That you understand that you may change your future. It is not cast in iron.

And we will not speak to you of your personal future because it is desirable that you understand your own power in creating your own reality and that you would have some understanding about probable realities. That, however it is, it is valid. It is real, including what is called dreams, that which is imagination.

So you may create your future any way you desire. Indeed, you are limitless. All right, dear one?

Q: When one sees a possible problem or learning experience on the horizon, what is the best way to prepare oneself for it, or the best way to bring peace to oneself to handle that situation before it even arises? I am not trying to divert or to suppress the problem because I know that it will only raise its head again and again, but what is the best way to approach...

P'taah: Indeed. Now, what do you think it might be? How do you think it is when you see a situation about to occur and when you are saying to yourself, "Hmm, this is going to be a beauty."

Q: Should I just relax about the whole thing and be as cool as I can in approaching it?

P'taah: Be a cool cucumber.

Q: Just take it as it comes?

P'taah: How about knowing that you have created it, and it is to be in allowance. Allowance, to be open, to be vulnerable.

Q: ...and just admit to myself that this is painful, if it is painful?

P'taah: ...and when you are in trepidation, beloved. When it is that you may see that you have a situation on your hands, it is to say, "Why is it that I have created it and what am I afraid of?"

Q: And if I can explain to myself what I am afraid of?

P'taah: It is to say that is all right, to be in allowance, to be vulnerable. When you are in vulnerability, indeed you are expressing the Goddess.

Q: And accept other people's interpretation of the situation for them?

P'taah: Dear one, that is their story. That is not your responsibility.

Q: And if I feel there is nothing to be done, then do nothing.

P'taah: Absolutely. How anybody else views a situation is their business.

Q: I think I have cornered myself into a position where I wish to be seen as the master of the situation and therefore non-action seems not to be appropriate. But that is my problem isn't it?

P'taah: Indeed, and we are speaking as we have spoken before about being seen to be. That is the fear of not being enough, social consciousness, etc.

Q: That is very strong, I know.

P'taah: Indeed, for all of you. It is to be in allowance. To be able to say, "The bottom line is fear and I am afraid of being seen as not worthy, as being not enough, to appear to be out of control."

Well, that is all right. It is allowable that you would be afraid, but then it is to dive into the fear, to allow it to be.

Then, poof, it is gone and there you are, suddenly in understanding of your own power.

Q: So, in other words, we are just creating every problem only to really feel that particular feeling. That is the only reason for it, and once we have felt it, there is no more need for it.

P'taah: Once you have learned the lesson, beloved, it is not necessary to recreate the situation again. It is also to know that if you create exactly the same story, suddenly it does not mean anything to you. There is no reaction. It is a no thing.

Q: And so, whatever I create is really just to experience fear or to experience love.

P'taah: Indeed.

Q: That alone. There is nothing else to gain, is there?

P'taah: What else is there, beloved? There is only feeling, and you may feel or you may suppress the feeling. You may hide from it, and when you suppress the fear, you experience pain. When you judge the situation, you create the resistance called pain. There is no other cause of pain but judgment.

Q: Social consciousness—this concrete wall of limited thought which we have built around ourselves. On a global scale, from your vista, do you see some cracks in the wall?

P'taah: Indeed. They are very visible. They are very visible globally. You have your newspapers. You see what is occurring in your world, dear one, day by day. We have said before to you, this is the time where nothing may be hidden.

So what is it that you think occurs when nothing can be hidden? It is called cracks in the concrete walls of social consciousness because, if you are exposed, you can bet your boots that you certainly feel it.

That is occurring on a personal level with humanity, as well as globally, with your government. It is not only of this continent, but of all governments of your world, of your institutions, of your religions, and your great financial structures.

Q: P'taah, I find your words powerful for me, particularly tonight. It made me realize that I am still pussyfooting around. I also realize this pussyfooting around is because of remnants of fear, and the fear is fear of my own power.

P'taah: Indeed.

Q: And now my question which I cannot answer myself. Why should I be in fear of my own power?

P'taah: Beloved one, in the history of your time, woman has been enslaved and in chains, because of power. That is why woman is very afraid. In your history, when there were women of knowledge and of power, they have died for that.

You know, when you are birthed, you are tapping automatically into the morphogenic resonance of your gender, of every woman or man that has ever lived upon your planet and more. So you are not separate.

Nothing has ever occurred to one person on this planet that has not affected every other person. What you do to yourselves and what you do to each other creates ripples which go through time barriers. Nothing and nobody is unaffected.

There is no separation, beloved people. Even your physical structure that you feel is a solid mass, that you feel to be separate from the rest of your universe, is not separate.

Your molecular structure changes and exchanges every moment of your time.

How can you be separate? How can you be apart from God/Goddess? How can you be in truth apart from each other?

In these months we have talked about your pain, the pain of humanity, and how it is reflected. We also said that when you look at beauty and joy, that is also who you are. When you look at somebody and think that person is very beautiful and are full of admiration, who do you think you are looking at? It is you!

There is no separation. Every breath you take is a communion. Every breath you draw into your body is Divinity. Every time you exhale a breath you are giving out your own Divinity to your universe. You are not separate.

Q: P'taah, you are saying we are all One. We all heard of the Hundredth Monkey Syndrome. Would it be so then, that if one person becomes enlightened, that we all become enlightened?

P'taah: Absolutely. Humanity taps into what is called morphogenic resonance, the collective consciousness. So when humanity comes into an understanding, more and more people will have this knowledge. It creates an energy and the energy becomes a mass which affects everybody.

Now, it certainly works on an individual level, but when you are speaking of the Hundredth Monkey Syndrome, it is wondrous. In this fashion you may understand that 100 of your years ago, people did not understand the computer and crystal technology.

When your children are at school, they already know how it is. They may learn the mechanics, but it is part of their being.

Humanity drives a car in your culture and so the children really know how to drive a car, all right? And so it is with this coming of knowledge. All of you are building the resonance to change the shape of humanity.

Q: Wonderful!

P'taah: Indeed it is.

Q: P'taah, I and others have asked technical questions and you have not wanted to answer them. Sometimes I have been frustrated and maybe others, too. I found that because you keep putting it back to us, I have been forced to get in touch with myself.

P'taah: Indeed. That is so.

And when you want the entertainment and when you want to have a question answered about the technology and the technology of the star people, there are other energies which will give forth certain information. It is certainly what you may call restricted, and it is, in a way, a sop to your curiosity.

But what we really say, beloved, is that you are the answer. You. If I give you the answer, you have an intellectual understanding of that which is called transition, of the star people, of multidimensional realities. But you do not live in your head.

The only thing of concern is your heart. What are you? You are a vibrational frequency. You are energy powered by Divinity. What creates your reality is your imagination, embraced by emotion. There is nothing else.

So, of course, the answer is you. There is nothing else.

How will you know your own power? How will you know your own sovereignty? How will you know how it is to live in honor of self, in integrity of soul beingness?

You will not know it from your brain. You will not know it from your intellect. You will only know it from your heart. You will only know it when you are vulnerable.

You will only know it when you say, "I did it. This is my life. I have created it. Who I am is God/Goddess, All-That-Is expressing in this dimension of reality. There is no thing and no body from which I am separated."

You are the answer, beloved people. There is nothing else.

Q: Why is it that we are here?

P'taah: You are here because you desired to be so. But you are also a dream of the All-That-Is, a dream of God, if you like.

You see, beloved, there is not one answer, really. There are as many answers as there are people upon your planet and then more and more.

That is how vast you are, you see, because you are grand and multidimensional beings experiencing in every dimension of reality. It is merely that you focused in on this one at this time and that is wondrous. However, your consciousness may expand to include more than merely this little reality. That is your potential.

Q: P'taah, with respect to making decisions for the future, I know you have always said live in the moment, but it seems to be that we get caught up with having to plan for the future.

P'taah: That is all right. As long as you understand that when you make a decision in the now moment, you may change it again any time you want. A plan is not concrete.

Q: No, I realize that. But there seems to be a conflict between doing what makes the heart sing in this moment and doing what would make the heart sing later. Like maybe a little sacrifice now would make my heart sing more later so I am willing to sacrifice now.

P'taah: Very well, beloved, I will tell you this. If you are waiting to be happy tomorrow, it will always be tomorrow.

It is all very fine to make plans. We understand that that is the way it operates. You have a financial plan, and a plan for education, a plan for marriage, a plan for when you have your babies, etc., etc.

Well, that is all right. It is just to know that if you are living in expectation of how something may be, it may be that you will be very disappointed. If you are living in expectation of how it may be, you are also limiting all of the myriad possibilities.

We are not saying do not plan. We are saying live in the moment. If in this moment you say, "Now I will make a plan," that is all right. Then when you say tomorrow, "Now I have changed it all," that is also all right. That is called living in the moment. That is called, plans are not concrete. They are not of iron bars, all right?

But if you are waiting to be happy, you will always be waiting to be happy. I will be happy when I am married. I will be happy when I have a wondrous lover. I will be happy when I have one million dollars in the bank. Well, you will still be saying it when you are ready to translate from this physical life. Do you understand?

Q: Yes, basically I do. Putting it into a day-to-day thing, today I feel like dancing all day. Tomorrow I feel like dancing all day, and the next, and the next.

P'taah: Dancing is very good.

Q: Am I scared of judging myself as being lazy not to dance every day?

P'taah: Are you?

Q: I probably would judge myself to be.

P'taah: And? Does that also have something to do with your belief structure which says, "I must work very hard to make my money?" And "People will think that I am a bum if I do not work?"

All of that is all right. Just be aware of it. That is called social consciousness which we have discussed with you at great length. It is all valid.

If your belief structures do not work for you, if they do not bring you joy, then you may change them.

Q: What if going against that would make your heart sing?

P'taah: Then you better look at what it is. Are you playing life as a safe game? Be a good boy today so that you do not have to suffer tomorrow?

What is this called? Divine retribution? If you are not happy tomorrow because of a choice that you have made today, it is only another little creation so that you may come to embrace the fear.

Q: So if one is doing something in order not to feel guilty, that is the wrong attitude to do it with?

P'taah: Dear one, it is not wrong. There is no wrong. It is simply that which does not serve you so well.

If you do not feel good about yourself, look at why. That is all. If you do not feel good and you desire to create change, go to the feeling. It is so simple. Be who you are now. There is no judgment, not anywhere, except within you.

All right? Dear ones, it is all very simple.

(*P'taah approaches the host and tenderly kisses his forehead.*)

Beloved man, our thanks for what you have created in this time. We have not finished, all right? There is more to come. Not in this moment, but certainly again. (*To the hostess:*) Beloved woman, our thanks, indeed. It has been an honor to be with you.

Q: P'taah, just a simple heartfelt thank you to you and the Board of Directors.

P'taah: Dear one, the Board of Directors is in greater joy. It is you who makes my heart sing and the exchange of energy in this fashion is wondrous beyond compare. It has been a joyous privilege and this is not goodbye. I love you.

(*Addressing the audience.*) You are worth loving. You are worthy of all wondrousness. You are quite spectacular. I give forth thanks to you all. Beloved ones, go forth in the light of who you are. Be in joy. Good night.